A MANAGER'S GUIDE TO STRATEGIC RETIREMENT PLAN MANAGEMENT

Daniel Cassidy

WILEY

John Wiley & Sons, Inc.

Published by John Wiley & Sons, Inc., Hoboken, New Jersey.
Published simultaneously in Canada.

Throughout this book, we have included short case studies about the issues facing our clients and how they resolved them. Due to our confidentiality agreements, we cannot disclose their names. In some cases, we made minor changes to the case study to maintain confidentiality.

For general information on our other products and services or for technical support, please contact our Customer Care Department within the United States at (800) 762-2974, outside the United States at (317) 572-3993, or fax (317) 572-4002.

Wiley also publishes its books in a variety of electronic formats. Some content that appears in print may not be available in electronic books. For more information about Wiley products, visit our web site at www.wiley.com.

Library of Congress Cataloging-in-Publication Data:

Cassidy, Daniel, 1966–
   A manager's guide to strategic retirement plan management / Daniel Cassidy.
      p.   cm.
   Includes index.
   ISBN-13: 978-0-471-77173-9 (cloth)
   ISBN-10: 0-471-77173-2 (cloth)
      1. Retirement income—United States.   2. Retirement—United States—
Planning.   I. Title.
   HB181.C394   2006
   658.3'25—dc22 2005036107

Printed in the United States of America.

10 9 8 7 6 5 4 3 2 1

To James B. Cassidy
1924–2004
Father, Husband, Brother, Soldier

CONTENTS

ACKNOWLEDGMENTS

This book would not have even begun without the pushing and prodding of Ron Lang, who serves on my firm's board of advisers. It all started with Ron suggesting (but with Ron it sounding more like "ordering") that I call his daughter Beth Lang Golub at Wiley. My virginal journey into book publishing began after a short conversation with Beth the following day. Thank you to both Ron and Beth for your faith and support during the entire process.

In addition to Ron, the other members of my firm's board of advisers have been invaluable to me over the years. Thanks to Ben Bailey of Massachusetts Capital Resource Company, Barry Hinckley of Bullhorn, and Tim Conway of Newstar Financial for helping me grow and expand my horizons.

Thanks are due to my editor at Wiley, Deb Englander, and her assistant, Greg Friedman, who have helped shepherd the book through publication. Deb always believed in the book and that gave me great confidence as I pounded away at the keyboard. Also, I would like to thank Lesley Cook from my firm who helped pull together the final manuscript. Thanks Lesley for getting the ball over the line. Thanks also to Ken Lizotte from emerson consulting group, inc. who has started me down the path of publishing first with articles and now with this book.

I would not have been able to write this book without the support of my clients. For over eight years, my clients have invited me and my firm into their world to help them. I am forever grateful for their trust and friendship. In particular, I would like to thank Janet Fayle of Plan, who was our first client back in 1997, as well as Ed Sindoni from Kadant, who was the first client to ever give me a bear hug during a business meeting. Ed, you have now redefined a close business relationship for me.

Any professional relies on his colleagues for growth and assistance and stands on the shoulders of previous generations. I have been blessed by

viii ACKNOWLEDGMENTS

working with many actuaries and professionals throughout my career. I
would like to thank them for helping me develop as an actuary and consultant: Steve Gould, Ben Haas, Sue Velleman, Dick Grenier, Tom McCord,
Marcus Robertson, Ian Duncan, Bill Gooden, Judy Anderson, Marcus
Rafiee, and Peter Hayes.

And finally, to my wife Audrey, who continues to amaze me in managing our household while I run a business (and in the last months, write a
book). My everlasting love.

Daniel P. Cassidy
www.arguscl.com

Introduction

Managing retirement plans is an ongoing process. Regardless of the type of plan you manage—from profit sharing to traditional defined benefit program—you have to familiarize yourself with the rules of the plans as well other issues including investment risk and legal requirements (see Figure 1.1).

Managing retirement plans can be a difficult and daunting task for a number of reasons. Not only are the number and variety of plans ever increasing, but the day-to-day management itself is complex. This book will help you navigate the process, whether you are self-managing within your organization, outsourcing the total retirement plan management to outside vendors, or a combination of the two.

Overview of Retirement Plans

A retirement plan, in the employer model, is multifaceted:

- *Employee relations.* First and foremost, the employer is holding an asset of the employee—whether it is a 401(k) account balance or the accrued benefit in a defined benefit plan.
- *Asset management.* Employers must invest these assets in a productive manner. Specific rules regulate.
- *Retiree relations.* If your retirees and other inactive employees still participate in your plan, you must continue to take their needs into consideration as you manage the plan. These people no longer have a

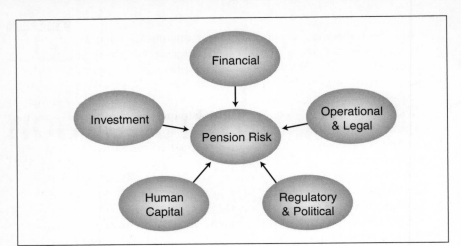

FIGURE 1.1 Strategy map

Source: Argus Consulting Ltd.

HISTORY OF RETIREMENT PLANS

Retirement plans are a by-product of the Industrial Age. Kaiser Wilhelm was the first to enact a social insurance plan that would cover workers in turn-of-the-century Germany. Railroads were the first industry in the United States to embrace retirement plans. In both cases, the initial goals were identified as providing retirement income for workers after they have completed a useful working life.

Before the industrial age, there was no need for this "continued income" after retirement for the following reasons:

1. *Agrarian culture.* With the vast majority of the workers engaged in producing "food" for our society in a very wide distributed system, there was no central control/depository system to facilitate a savings vehicle.
2. *Mortality.* People did not live very long lives and however long they lived, they worked until they died. Medical science was not such that people lived past their useful working lifetime.
3. *Social structure.* Monarchy-based systems did not encourage personal asset accumulation; in fact, monarchies encouraged social welfare through noblesse oblige.

After the industrial revolution, larger businesses such as railroad companies or steel mills and others that encouraged the development of the middle class had the means to provide long-term security plans. Price controls during World War II also contributed to the increased use of retirement plans as a part of the overall compensation package as companies who were unable to increase direct pay looked to other means to attract qualified workers. Further social changes, including the increased power of unions, pushed retirement plans into the mainstream.

Many people point to the failure of the automobile manufacturer Studebaker's pension plan in the mid-1960s as a pivotal moment in pension plan history. Directly out of this highly visible pension failure came federal action to regulate pension plans. In 1974, the watershed legislation called the Employee Retirement Income Security Act (ERISA) was passed and signed by President Gerald Ford in one of his first acts as president. From that point on, pension plans have been regulated on the federal level. Briefly, ERISA added significant provisions to protect workers and beneficiaries such as minimum vesting schedules, minimum funding standards, stringent fiduciary standards, and limitations on prohibited transactions. It also increased reporting requirements and established an insurance program for defined benefit plans (Pension Benefit Guaranty Corporation).

At the time of ERISA, defined benefit plans were the predominant retirement plan at larger employers; in fact, for most people, the term *pension plan* is synonymous with a traditional defined benefit pension plan. The number of defined benefit plans peaked in the mid-1980s with over 170,000 plans. However, due to many factors, including changes in legislation, the number of defined benefit plans has dropped to under 30,000. Now the vast majority of plans are defined contribution plans where the participants bear the investment risk.

Many critics point to two reasons for this sudden decline:

1. Pension plans were used in legislation to balance the federal budgets (increasing complexity with no real added value).
2. By limiting benefits to highly paid managers, this reduced the business owners' incentive to continue sponsoring plans for their rank and file employees.

Finally, in the last several years with significant volatility in the equity markets and prolonged period of economic uncertainty/recession, we may be witnessing the last rites of the traditional pension plan.

direct tie with the employer, but an indirect one through the retirement plan.

- *Systems integration.* Payroll and plan management systems must communicate with each other in an effective manner. As employers make changes to one, the impact on others needs to be considered.
- *Legal and tax issues.* Our government encourages creation of retirement plans by providing substantial tax benefits both to the employer and employee. However, to continue to get these benefits, the employer must maintain the plan in compliance with an enormous amount of tax and legal requirements.

Whether the chief financial officer or vice president of human resources is managing the plan, he or she needs to keep all of these facets in mind.

As with any management task, there are several levers that a manager can use to apply pressure to get a desired result (see Figure 1.2).

In this book, we will examine the specifics of the plan in which managers can strategically affect the outcome of the retirement plans. You won't become an expert in ERISA legislation, but as one of my clients said, the book will "give you the questions you need to ask." Going further, our goal is to empower you by providing an explanation of the levers you can use to impact the real outcome of your plan. Only you know the right answers for you, your employer, and your employees. But first, you have to know what questions to ask.

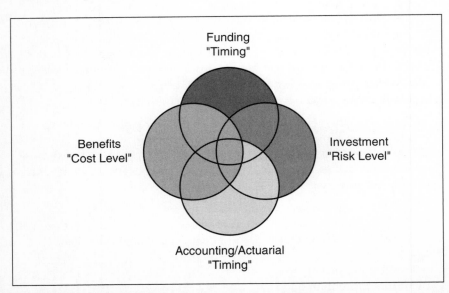

FIGURE 1.2   Retirement plan corporate governance tools

Source: Argus Consulting Ltd.

The Basics of Retirement Plans

Before digging deeper into the strategic management of retirement plans, it is worth taking a step back to review the fundamentals. As with most industries, the retirement plan community uses both technical language and nontechnical jargon. This can be very confusing to many managers as they work to understand their organization's plans. Managers who have recently taken charge of their company's retirement plans may feel like they are caught in the Talking Heads song "Once in a Lifetime" singing "And you may ask yourself—well . . . how did I get here?" The answer to this question is usually found in how previous managers evaluated the pros and cons of the various options available to them, which we will now discuss.

Why Have Retirement Plans in the First Place?

You may wonder why an organization goes through all the trouble of having a retirement plan. Boiled down to its core, the answer is that it is in the best interest of our society to promote private wealth accumulation in order to ensure that our citizens can avoid living in poverty after their useful working lifetime.

Before the United States set up the Social Security program in the 1930s, the overwhelming majority of our population over age 65 was dependent on either public/private assistance or had no income at all (see Table 2.1). Only a little more than one third were able to take care of their needs independently.

Table 2.1 Dependency of Senior Citizens in the U.S. in 1932

Dependency status of population over age 65 in 1937	% of Population
Self-dependent	35.1%
Dependent with public/private assistance	18.5%
Dependent with no income	47.5%

Source: Social Security Administration, "Historical Development," 3.

> The U.S. social welfare structure has been shaped both by long-standing traditions and by changing economic and social conditions. In its early history, the United States was an expanding country with a vast frontier and a predominantly agricultural economy. Up to 1870, more than half of the country's adult workers were farmers. In the years that followed, however, industry developed rapidly and the economy tended to be increasingly characterized by industrialization, specialization, and urbanization. The result was a nation of employees who were dependent on a continuing flow of income to provide for themselves and their families.
>
> The first form of social insurance in the United States was workers' compensation. Workers' compensation made employers responsible for the costs of compensating workers and their families if the worker was killed or injured on the job. Later, the first retirement programs were developed in the late nineteenth century for government workers, including teachers, firefighters, and police officers. During the economic crisis of the Great Depression of the 1930s, the United States recognized the extreme poverty that many elderly citizens were living in, and created the Social Security system in 1935. Using current workers' payroll taxes to finance the retirement of current retirees, over 70 years after the programs' inception, the United States Social Security system is still providing income and reducing poverty for retirees.

With this goal of reducing poverty in old age, our government did two things:

1. Raised taxes to fund the new social security program (see boxed material).

2. Promoted the establishment of company-sponsored retirement plans by reducing taxes—or in the language of Washington, provided tax expenditures—thereby allowing companies to take tax deductions for contributions to pension plans. Pension plans that meet the requirements to receive the tax deduction are called "qualified plans."

Thus, from the employer's standpoint, the first solution has no choice element involved—you must pay taxes—and in the case of social security taxes, these are shared equally between employee and employer. However, the second solution of promoting new retirement plans is completely voluntary; a company can choose to sponsor a plan or not—it is up to them. However, to answer the question posed in the Talking Heads song, we got here by jumping over the various hurdles required to get the government-approved tax deductions.

Tax Overview

To understand the full value of the government's tax policy to promote company pensions, you need to understand some general tax policy issues. As you will see below, the tax advantages of a qualified retirement plan go far beyond just the initial company tax deduction.

First, the general rule for taxation for wages (and retirement plans are considered wages from a tax perspective) is the general tax rule: Timing of income to the employee is coordinated with the deduction to the employer. This general tax rule has a fancy name that is sometimes used in IRS and other publications: the Constructive Receipt Doctrine (CRD). Simply put, the company gets a tax deduction at the same time that the employee pays tax on the wage income. You can extend this general rule to the following corollary: If an employee is not taxed on the wage income, then the employer cannot take a tax deduction on the wages paid. However, the government, in order to promote qualified plans, has suspended the CRD in several areas.

Suspension of the Constructive Receipt Doctrine

There are three major areas in retirement plans where the CRD is suspended.

1. *Employer contributions.* Not many employers would find sponsor plans if the CRD were not suspended for qualified plans. If our government did not suspend the CRD for employer contributions, employers would be making contributions that would not be deductible immediately since the employees do not receive their benefits until years later in their retirement. So, clearly, it is in the government's interest to allow employers to immediately deduct their contributions. Since the government does not want this tax deduction abused, it has placed limits on the amount of the deduction.

2. *Tax-deferred income.* Assets within a retirement plan trust are invested in the hope of earning future interest, dividends, and capital gains.

Normally, the CRD would call for the immediate taxation on interest and dividends paid as well as on any realized capital gains at the sale of the asset. However, retirement plan trusts do not pay any taxes on their income. Income taxes are only paid by participants when they ultimately receive their benefits. Again, this suspension of the CRD encourages employers to make contributions to retirement plans; in fact, it encourages them to make larger contributions earlier in an employee's career in order to take full advantage of the trust's tax-exempt status.

3. *Distributions favorably taxed.* This last area where the CRD is suspended is sometimes overlooked by participants and employers alike but it applies both when participants make a distribution choice and then when they receive payment of their benefits.

   - *Choice.* Applying normal tax policy with the CRD, if a person has a choice between two payment options, the IRS would tax the person on the most advantageous basis to the IRS. For example, in a retirement plan context and if the normal CRD were applied, if you had the choice between a single lump sum of say $1,000,000 or an annual annuity of $100,000, you would have to pay tax on the full $1,000,000 regardless of which option you chose. If you in fact did choose the annuity, you could get a tax bill from the IRS for $300,000, but only have a $100,000 annuity payment—so you would be in the hole $200,000 immediately. However, after year one, you would receive all $100,000 tax free, since you paid all the tax in year one. The IRS knew that this would not work for the vast majority of the plan participants, so they suspended the CRD for pension plans when there is choice involved.

   - *Timing.* In addition to suspending the CRD when choice is involved, the IRS went further and said that participants and beneficiaries will have to pay taxes once they receive their benefits. So, participants will only pay taxes on benefits received. This goes beyond the choice issue above and includes spouses. For example, if a participant selects an optional benefit form that continues to the spouse after the participant's death, the spouse will only be taxed as he or she receives the benefit.

Overview of Qualification Rules

In order to take advantage of these rules, an employer must follow the specific regulations set out by the government. In the United States, two agencies have oversight responsibilities for retirement plans—the IRS as well as the Department of Labor (DOL). The IRS is clearly interested in making sure the tax regulations are followed since retirement plans represent significant tax expenditures employee benefits; in fact, they represent the largest tax expenditure of the U.S. government in fiscal year 2006. Employer pension plans alone represent $99 billion in tax expenditure, according to the Office of Management and Budget.

The DOL, on the other hand, is focused on safeguarding employees' rights. Issues such as vesting, spousal rights, and fiduciary duty are clearly in the purview of the DOL.

The following is a brief summary of the major qualification issues that any manager should be familiar with.

I.   Plan Document
     A. Plan must be written.
     B. Trust created and maintained in the United States.
II. Exclusive Benefit Rule
     A. Plan must be used for the exclusive benefit of employees and their beneficiaries.
     B. In general, trust assets must never revert back to the employer. In fact, if assets do revert back, the employer would pay income tax as well as an excise tax that can put the total tax rate at 90%—so it is very rare for employers to take a reversion since they only net about 10 cents on the dollar.
III. Minimum Age and Service Conditions
     A. Employers can limit who is eligible to enter the plan based on age and service. The predominant condition is age 21 and X years of service; however, other limits can be used for certain employers such as educational institutions.
IV. Minimum Vesting Standards
     A. Employee contributions, such as 401(k) salary deferrals, are always 100% vested.
     B. For employer contributions and benefits, a plan can specify a service-based schedule of vesting. Common vesting schedules include:
         1. 5-year cliff vesting—Participants have no vested benefit until they reach 5 years of service. After 5 years of service, they are 100% vested.
         2. Graded vested schedule—Participants vest in a portion of their benefit over a series of years (see Table 2.2).
V.   Age Discrimination
     A. Not allowed to stop benefit accruals simply on the attainment of an age (for example age 65). Can stop accruals based on service.
VI. Alienation of Benefits
     A. In general, benefits may not be assigned or alienated such as a

Table 2.2 Sample Graded Vesting Schedule

Years	Vested
3	20%
4	40%
5	60%
6	80%
7	100%

wage garnishment. This is why you may hear that if someone files for personal bankruptcy, the debtors cannot force distribution from a qualified plan. However, there are several significant exceptions, including divorce and federal tax liens. In divorce, the parties can enter into an agreement to split the benefit in two. This is done through what is called a qualified domestic relations order.

VII. Benefit and Contributions Limits

A. The IRS imposes limitation on either the amount of benefits paid out of a defined benefit (DB) plan or the amount of contribution that goes into a defined contribution (DC) plan. These limits are indexed and can change annually. More information on this is included in the more specific discussion of each plan type.

VIII. Nondiscrimination of Benefits and Integration with Social Security

A. In general, the government would like all retirement plans to provide comparable benefits to all employees, regardless of their pay level. However, the government recognized that Social Security—financed through payroll taxes shared by employees and employers—is significantly skewed in the level of benefits provided to lower-paid employees. That is, lower-paid employees will contribute fewer dollars to the Social Security program, but receive about the same in benefits as higher-paid employees. This skewing of benefits to lower-paid employees was intentional and one of the major goals of Social Security. In order to encourage employers to sponsor private pension plans, the government allowed them to take into account this skewing. In fact, the government allows employers to "integrate" their plans with Social Security by providing higher benefits to higher-paid employees. There are limits to this and rules that employers must follow. In general, most private plans do take advantage of this integration. One small note: 401(k) plans (described later) cannot integrate matching benefits.

B. Related to this issue is an area called "top-heavy" plans. These are plans that are typically due to employee turnover of non-vested benefit amounts result in the highly paid employees/owners receiving the vast majority (over 60%) of the benefits of the plan. This is typically an issue for small, closely held organizations. In these cases, the qualification rules call for minimum benefits as well as shorter vesting periods.

IX. Prohibited Transactions

A. Plans are not allowed to enter into prohibited transactions—basically self-dealing—with retirement plan assets. Prohibited transactions could include owners of a company using plan assets to buy a property from the cousin of the owners. There are some significant exemptions from these rules—including profit sharing plans investing in company stock, financial services firms using their own proprietary investment funds, etc.—but in general, plan sponsors should keep all transactions involving retirement plans at an arm's length distance.

Overview of Plan Design Types

Even though there are hundreds of thousands of retirement plans in the United States, they basically come in two flavors: defined benefit or defined contribution. In simplest terms, the plan defines either one of two things:

1. Benefits that are actually paid out to participants after they leave employment—hence the name *defined benefit*.

2. Contributions into the plan while a participant is employed—hence the name *defined contribution.*

The plan defines either what goes into the plan or what comes out. Now we will describe each of these broad types in more detail and highlight why an employer would select one type versus another.

Defined Benefit Plan

Basic Structure

The focus of DB plans is on the benefits payable out of the retirement trust. These benefits are typically defined as an annuity—an annual payment of $X paid over the lifetime of the participant. The plan document (the legal document that spells out all the plan provisions) will include an operative sentence such as "The participant will receive an amount equal to . . ."

Funding

The key difference between DB and DC plans, beyond the difference of benefits paid versus contributions made, is who bears the investment risk. In the case of DB plans, the employer bears the investment risk. The employer must make all contributions and investment decisions for a DB plan. (Note that a few DB plans require employees to contribute to the plan, but these types of plans are not very common in the United States since the contributions are not tax deductible.) If there is a shortfall in assets, the company is wholly responsible for making up the difference. In practice, an actuary (see boxed material) is employed to calculate the value of the benefits promised by the DB plan. This liability value is then compared with the current asset value. If there is a shortfall, company contributions will be required and the actuary determines these in compliance with IRS rules. If there is a surplus, that is, assets are greater than liabilities, no employer contribution will be due at this time.

Pension Benefit Guaranty Corporation Insurance

Since DB plans can become underfunded, that is, where assets are less than liabilities, Congress recognized the need for an insurance program to cover this contingency—similar to the Federal Deposit Insurance Corporation (FDIC) for banks. It set up the Pension Benefit Guaranty Corporation (PBGC) to insure most DB plans. DB plans pay an annual premium into a fund that is based both on the number of participants as well as the level of funding in the plan. Plans in poor financial condition, that is, underfunded, pay a higher premium, and vice versa. The recent bankruptcies in the airline, automotive, and steel industries have put the PBGC system under tremendous strain. Currently, the PBGC itself has a deficit of over $20 billion. Serious concerns about this deficit has prompted Congress to consider raising premiums. However, the entire system itself may be in jeopardy as more and more DB plans terminate, reducing premium income and leaving the poorly funded plans all alone.

Sample Formulas

DB plans define the benefits paid using a formula, typically in one of three ways:

1. Formula based on compensation and service (most common). Example: Annual benefit paid will be equal to 1% of annual pay times years of service up to a maximum of 30 years.

2. Formulas based on service only (common with hourly/union workforce). Example: Annual benefit paid will be equal to $200 per year of service up to a maximum of 30 years.

ROLE OF THE ACTUARY

Many managers, once they become involved with a DB plan, immediately become aware of a business professional whom they had never encountered before—an actuary. Compared with other professions (over 400,000 attorneys, 300,000 CPAs), only 13,000 actuaries practice in the United States. With so few actuaries, misperceptions arise about what exactly is an actuary. This is highlighted in a funny joke about the definition of an actuary—that's where they bury dead actors. All kidding aside, let's describe what an actuary is and how he or she can help you manage your retirement plan.

What is an actuary? In general, an actuary is a business professional who analyzes the financial consequences of risk. Actuaries use mathematics, statistics, and financial theory to study uncertain future events, like those in pension programs. They evaluate the likelihood of those events, design creative ways to reduce the likelihood and decrease the impact of adverse events that actually do occur. Their work requires a combination of strong analytical skills, business knowledge, and understanding of human behavior to design and manage programs that control risk. This combination of skills—which is an amalgamation of legal, management, and statistical training—produces a professional with whom you should develop a close relationship to help you navigate through the complexity of running your plan.

Traditionally, actuaries have tended to focus solely on DB plans—helping to calculate the annual contribution requirements and annual pension expense, including the financials of the company, and so forth. However, as the marketplace has changed with the increase in DC plans, actuaries have retooled and broadened their scope of services to include all types and areas of retirement plans. Many clients now look to their actuaries for independent, professional advice on all issues surrounding their retirement plans.

3.   Formula based on neither service nor compensation (rare). Example: Annual benefit will be equal to $10,000.

Since formula type number one is the most common, we will spend some more time describing the two major types of this formula. These types differ in what pay is used in the formula:

■ Final average pay formula
  • Pay used—Pay during the last several years of a person's career
  • Averaging period—Typically three or five year average
  • Example—1% of five-year average final pay times years of service

- Career average pay formula
  - Pay used—Pay during the entire career of a person, from hire to termination
  - Averaging period—Entire career
  - Example—1% of career average final pay times years of service

How Does a Plan Sponsor Choose Between a Career Average Pay Formula versus a Final Average Pay?

In simplest terms and ignoring any difference in administration (keeping track of an entire career of earnings compared to just the last five years), the two interconnected issues that plan sponsors need to deal with are inflation and "fast-track" employees.

Regarding inflation, if the goal of a retirement plan is to provide a certain level of retirement income—possibly enough to maintain an employee's standard of living—then it could be difficult to design a career average pay plan to accomplish this. For example, during an extended high inflationary period, a person's pay will be increasing significantly, but the retirement benefit will be calculated using significantly lower pay levels prior to the inflationary period.

Similarly, a fast-track employee who is hired and is promoted through the ranks to a higher pay level is difficult to adequately handle in a career pay environment. As with the inflation issue, fast-track employees will still have some of their benefits based on significantly lower pay levels and employers could have problems providing a comparable level of benefit to a person who was promoted at a more moderate pace throughout his or her career.

If these are your concerns, then a final average pay plan may be the right answer for your company. However, note that the final average pay plan, while doing a better job of meeting retirement goals during an inflationary period, will have significantly higher cost, since it is providing larger benefits.

Form of Payment

Most DB plans express the benefits paid as an annual annuity. That is a payment received periodically while a participant and/or beneficiary is alive. Also, participants can choose from a variety of options forms. These optional forms are "actuarial equivalents," meaning that they have the same financial value to the participant and spouse, assuming their future life expectancies.

- *Single life annuity.* Payment is made while the participant is alive (no payments made after his or her death).

- *Joint and survivor annuity.* Payment is made while the participant is alive, and then continues after his or her death. The amount continuing to the beneficiary can vary typically between 50% and 100%. For example, with a joint and 50% survivor annuity, the participant would receive $100 while alive and then the beneficiary would receive $50 after the participant's death.

- *Lump sum payment.* A single payment of the entire accrued benefit is made.

Hybrid Plans

It is worthwhile now to mention hybrid plans. Examples of hybrid plans include cash balance, defined lump sum, and pension equity. These are DB plans that communicate the benefit in terms of a lump sum in order to facilitate employees' understanding. As you can see in Figure 2.1, hybrid plans have become very popular, especially in the larger plan marketplace.

Instead of expressing the benefit as an annuity at normal retirement, hybrid plans describe the benefit as a lump sum—employees can then easily compare this value to, say, the account balance in their 401(k) plan. Even though these plans express the benefit as a lump sum and look and feel like a 401(k) plan, they are in fact DB plans, subject to all the same rules and regulations. In the vast majority of hybrid plan designs, the participants can in fact receive the entire lump sum value immediately. This

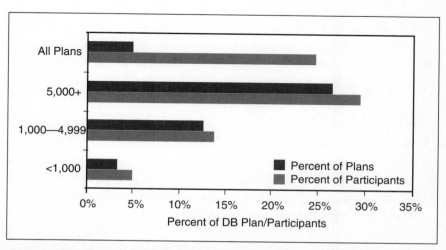

FIGURE 2.1   Prevalence of hybrid plans in 2003 by plan size

Source: Pension Benefit Guaranty Corporation. *Pension Insurance Data Book 2004* (2005), 60.

portability is greatly appreciated by employees who can then decide exactly what they want to do with the money, for example roll it over to an individual retirement account (IRA).

Most hybrid plans were not started up from scratch, but instead are just your typical DB plans that were amended to include the hybrid features. Most of these transitions took place during the 1980s and 1990s. Several high-profile hybrid transitions, for example, IBM's change from a traditional final average pay plan to a cash balance plan, have been challenged in court on age discrimination charges. The courts have provided conflicting judgments, and the federal government has yet to publish definitive regulations and standards. So, due to this uncertainty, employers have recently shied away from transitioning to hybrid designs.

Timing of Payment

In addition to the form of payment, participants can also typically elect to commence their benefits before age 65. The plan will spell out how much the benefit will be reduced since the participant will be receiving it earlier than expected. Some employers use these early retirement provisions to achieve other human resources goals like reducing head counts. By providing enhanced early retirement benefits, this may just be the right incentive that allows people in their fifties and sixties to elect to retire.

IRS Limitations

With DB plans, the two operative limits are those on pay and benefits:

- *Pay.* Pay in excess of $220,000 (2006) cannot be used in the calculation of benefits.
- *Benefits.* The plan cannot pay out more than $175,000 (2006) per year to any participants or beneficiaries.

Defined Contribution Plan
Basic Structure

The focus of DC plans is on the contributions made into the retirement trust. These contributions are typically defined as a percentage of pay—an annual contribution of X% of pay will be made into the trust. The plan document will include an operative sentence such as "Each year the employer shall contribute to trust . . ." Contributions are made to the plan on behalf of employees. Individual accounts are set up and assets are invested on behalf of employees.

Funding

As mentioned earlier, the key difference between DB and DC plans, beyond the difference of benefits paid versus contributions made, is who bears the investment risk. In the case of DC plans, the employee bears the investment risk. The employer's responsibility for funding stops after it makes the required contributions. The investment responsibility is now typically handed over to the participant; however, the employer is still responsible for selecting appropriate funds for the employees to chose from. There is a broader discussion later in the book.

Since the participant's benefit is ultimately the account balance, a shortfall can never exist. If the assets have negative performance, then the participant's balance will go down. The employer does not have to make up this shortfall. On the other hand, if the assets perform well, the participant's balance will go up.

PBGC Insurance

Since the account balances are always 100% funded, there is no need for any PBGC insurance coverage.

Sample Formulas

DC plans define the contributions made to the plan and have a predetermined formula for allocating the dollars to participants. The employer contribution amount need not be based on any formula, such as X% of profits; however, the allocation method must be written down. Just like DB plans, there are a variety of DC plans to choose from. However, unlike DB plans, many DC plans contain more than one type and many times include an element of employee contributions. In a quirk of the U.S. tax code, employee contributions to DC plans can be made on a tax-deductible basis. Probably the most common is a 401(k) plan that includes employee salary deferral, company match, and a discretionary company profit sharing contribution.

- 401(k) plan
  - Description—Employees can elect to contribute a percentage of the pay on a pretax basis. This is typically matched by the employer.
  - Example—Employees can elect to deduct up to 10% of pay. The employer will match the first 6% of employee pay.
- Profit sharing plan
  - Description—Employer will make a discretionary contribution to

the plan. Many times the level of contribution will be tied to profits, but there is no requirement to have it strictly based on profits.

- Example—The company will make a discretionary profit sharing contribution to the plan. Or, the company will contribute 10% of its pretax profits to the plan.

■ Employee stock ownership plan (ESOP)

- Description—A special type of profit sharing plan that invests primarily in employer stock. These plans have significant differences in operation, fiduciary, deductibility, and funding from profit sharing plans. In general, ESOPs are used to increase employee ownership in a company as well as to facilitate ownership changes in closely held firms.
- Example—The company will contribute X% of pay to the ESOP and invest in company stock.

Allocation Methodologies

For profit sharing plans, the allocation methodology can vary based on the employer's goals and objectives. The simplest is to allocate equally based on pay. However, companies may choose to allocate based on age, or on age and service. Generally, if the company chooses one of these alternative allocations, the plan will need to be tested in order to prove that it does not discriminate in favor of highly paid employees (see nondiscrimination discussion above).

Form of Payment

Most DC plans pay the benefits as a single lump sum. Some plans allow other forms of payment, like level payment over 10 years or a single life annuity. However, these alternative payment forms are becoming rarer, with most participants selecting the lump sum and either taking the cash or rolling the account over to an IRA.

Timing of Payment

Since DC plans pay lump sums and the annual contributions to DC plans are limited, there is no ability to integrate an early retirement program like DB plans. This one disadvantage of DC plans is not viewed by plan sponsors as a problem. It is more of an advantage of a DB plan than a disadvantage of a DC plan.

IRS Limitations

For DC plans, the IRS imposes limits on pay and contributions.

- *Pay.* Like DB plans, contributions cannot recognize pay in excess of $220,000 (2006).

- *Contributions.* No more than $44,000 (2006) can be contributed on behalf of an employee in any one year (an additional $5,000 [2006] employee contribution is allowed for participants over age 50).

Advantages and Disadvantages of Defined Benefit Plans and Defined Contribution Plans

How to decide to sponsor one plan versus the other is an exercise in decision making and goal setting. It is hard to say one is better than the other. We have put together Table 2.3 to compare side by side how each type achieves certain objectives.

Nonqualified Plans

Our discussion so far has focused on qualified plans—those plans that seek to meet the qualifications rules in order to provide the tax benefits to both employees and employer. However, in many instances, the employer would like to provide benefits that specifically do not meet these qualification standards. For example, many employers want to provide benefits in excess of arbitrary limits set by the IRS capping pay at $220,000 (2006), contributions at $44,000 (2006), and benefits at $175,000 (2006).

In order to do so, an employer typically adopts a nonqualified plan, which is simply a contract between individual employees and the employer promising certain contributions and/or benefits. By moving beyond the qualification rules, the employer is then at liberty to adopt whatever plan provisions it wants. However, by not following the qualification rules, the employer and employee will not enjoy the significant tax advantages of being qualified.

Table 2.3   Comparison of Typical Plan Features

	Defined Benefit Plan	Defined Contribution Plans
Participation	Automatic	Voluntary
Contributions	Employer	Employer and employee
Investment risk	Employer	Employee
Disability coverage	Yes	No
Loans	N/A	Allowed
Distribution form	Annuity	Lump sum
Benefit guaranty	PBGC	N/A

Source: PBGC, Pension Benefit Guaranty Corporation.

Basic Structure

Even more so than DB and DC plans, nonqualified plans can be designed in a variety of ways to achieve specific and sometimes individual goals and objectives. Many nonqualified plans simply work as restoration plans that duplicate the features of the qualified plans but without the IRS limits. For example, if a DB plan only counts pay up to $220,000, a common nonqualified DB plan would be to calculate the benefit on total pay and then subtract out the piece that is paid in the qualified plan. The following example may help illustrate this point:

Qualified plan formula: 50% of final average five-year pay (but no more than $220,000)

Sample executive: average pay $300,000

Qualified plan benefit: 50% of final average pay (the lesser of $300,000 or $220,000) = $110,000

Nonqualified plan benefit: 50% of final average pay (without limits) minus qualified plan benefit—50% of $300,000 = $150,000 minus $110,000

Net nonqualified plan benefit = $40,000

Funding

In general, these plans are not funded since the employer has very little incentive due to the lack of tax deduction. The issue of funding a nonqualified plan brings the employee and employer into significant conflict due to their competing objectives.

- Employee
  - Avoid current taxation
  - Secure benefit as much as possible
- Employer
  - Get current tax deduction
  - Use funds in its business, i.e., business use of capital better than an investment securing a promise to pay

From the employee's perspective, the security issue can be further broken down into two pieces:

1. *Unwillingness to pay benefits.* With no funding, the employee is at the mercy of the management to pay the benefits when they become due. With changes in management, merger and acquisitions, and so forth, this concern is very real in today's corporate environment.

2. *Inability to pay benefits.* Since the payment of benefits comes out of the general assets of the company, the executive is at risk if the company goes bankrupt. If the company does goes bankrupt, the executive would typically lose out. Some say that this result actually is not a bad one since if the executive did his or her job better while employed, the company would not have gone bankrupt. However, you cannot simply dismiss this concern.

A variety of tools are available that can attempt to solve some of these concerns, such as rabbi trust and indemnity insurance among others. However, there are no magic bullets that can solve all the issues; if there were, there would be immediate taxation on the employee.

Administration

Retirement plans, at their core, are simply vehicles used to accumulate wealth while employees are working. Employers must keep track of the value of this wealth through systems and procedures. All of this is generally called administration. This is a good place to start our discussion about strategically managing retirement plans since it is the most concrete area with identifiable people and steps.

Roles and Responsibilities

Many people play a part in managing a retirement plan—from the payroll clerk to attorneys who specialize in Employee Retirement Income Security Act (ERISA) plans. Also, depending on a multiple of variables (e.g., size of the plan and whether union employees are covered), you may be faced with managing a small or large set of professionals. Regardless of how many different people/firms you decide to use, the actual roles and responsibilities do not change—you may simply decide to use one source for multiple roles.

Key Roles

Below is a brief overview of the roles and responsibilities of people managing a retirement plan. From the employer's perspective, these roles can either be performed in house or outsourced.

EMPLOYER

- Key role
  - Overall responsibility for plan
- Responsibilities
  - Whether to sponsor a plan at all? What the formula will be?
  - When should the plan be terminated?
  - Who should manage the plan on a day-to-day basis?
- Example
  - Company ABC with role fulfilled by the board of directors or delegated to a senior executive group

FIDUCIARIES

- Key role
  - Safeguarding assets of the plan for plan beneficiaries
- Responsibilities
  - How best to invest plan assets
  - Make key decisions regarding plan administration such as interpretation of plan document language
- Example
  - Pension committee of Company ABC

PLAN ADMINISTRATOR

- Key Role
  - Maintaining plan records and accounts to determine benefits
- Responsibilities
  - Methods and procedures to ensure plan is operated in accordance with plan documents and all legal parameters
- Example
  - Human resources department of Company ABC

TRUSTEE

- Key role
  - Holds assets of the plan
- Responsibilities
  - Are the appropriate controls and procedures in place to ensure that all moneys following through the plan are proper?
  - Ensuring that the participants get the correct benefit payments, taxes are withheld appropriately, assets are invested appropriately

according to fiduciaries instructions, and new contributions are invested as soon as feasible

- Example
  - Trust department of financial institution (bank, insurance company, mutual fund company, etc.)

RECORD KEEPER

- Key role
  - Maintain detailed participant information in order to determine benefits
- Responsibilities
  - Determine to the penny what benefits are payable to each participant
  - Maintain any and all information necessary to calculate benefit, communicate with trustee to pay benefits, and assist in any government reporting
- Example
  - Third-party administrator who works directly with payroll provider to receive contributions

INVESTMENT MANAGER

- Key role
  - Invest assets in accordance with fiduciaries'/trustees' instructions
- Responsibilities
  - Provide prudent investment management, including diversifying assets in order to reduce risk of substantial loss
- Example
  - Investment management arm of financial institution (e.g., mutual fund)

Other Outside Professionals

The following roles, given their specific requirements, are typically always outsourced to the appropriate professional. It is extremely rare for any of these roles to be performed in house. These professionals must comply with their own industry professional standards.

ACTUARY

- Key role
  - Determining the liabilities of a defined benefit plan (not applicable to defined contribution plans)

- Responsibilities
  - Calculate cash contribution and accounting expense requirements according to regulations
  - Assist plan sponsor in administration issues
- Sample professional designation
  - Enrolled actuary
  - Fellow of the Society of Actuaries

LEGAL COUNSEL

- Key role
  - Assist other parties (employer, fiduciaries, plan administrator, etc.) with complying with legal requirements
- Responsibilities
  - Draft plan documents
  - Assist in interpreting plan language
- Sample professional designation
  - State bar admittance, membership in American Bar Association

ACCOUNTANT

- Key role
  - Audit the trust
- Responsibilities
  - Provide assurance that financial statement of plan's trust is accurate
- Sample professional designation
  - Certified public accountant

INVESTMENT CONSULTANT

- Key role
  - Assist fiduciaries with investment-related decisions
- Responsibilities
  - Selection and monitoring of investment managers
- Sample professional designation
  - Chartered financial analyst, registered investment adviser

Examples

As mentioned above, each employer will decide exactly how to fulfill each role with some companies using a completely outsourced model, while others are using more internal resources. Currently the trend in the retirement industry is for more outsourcing and bundling of services together with one firm. Table 3.1 shows typical examples of administrative structures.

Vendor Management

With so many vendors listed above, managing all these relationships can be a difficult chore. This difficulty has been one of the major contributing factors in the move to bundling providers.

Vendor Selection

BASICS

From an employer's point of view, probably the best thing that can be said about the retirement plan marketplace is that it is very competitive, with

Table 3.1   Administration Model Examples

	Small Employer	Mid-Sized Employer	Large Employer
Definition	Family-owned business with 100 employees	Small publicly-traded firm with 1,000 employees	Multinational corporation with 15,000 employees
Fiduciaries	Owner	Senior management group	Two committees—one focused on administrative/human resources issues and one focused on investments only
Plan administrator	Company	Human resources	Outsourced third-party administrator
Trustee	Local bank's trust department	Trust company of mutual fund company	Separate trust company
Record keeper	Company	Retirement services group of mutual fund company	Separate outsourced third-party administrator
Investment manager	Investment broker using retail mutual funds	Institutional priced mutual funds selected by advisors within mutual fund company	Separately managed accounts by multiple managers

multiple providers competing for your business. However, the flip side of this coin is that it can be difficult for an employer to choose the right vendor for its particular plan and participants. We have outlined the process we use with our clients in Table 3.2.

The first step that we recommend to clients is to take time to benchmark where they are as well as what their goals are. Time spent at this initial stage will go a long way to helping you make a better decision later on in the process.

The next step is drafting a request for proposal (RFP). A sample RFP based on this process is provided in Appendix A. As you can see, our RFP is very streamlined and focuses on the critical needs of our clients. We view an RFP as the start of a conversation between the vendor and our clients. It is us trying to communicate how our client is unique and different from others, and what their key drivers are. We look to promote honest open dialogue with the vendors. Our only goal is to help our clients make the best decision that fits their needs.

Table 3.2 Vendor Selection: Process Overview

Step	Description
Benchmark current investment performance and fiduciary review	Benchmark current plans including: Competitive performance analysis of the investment funds Analysis of the participant elections among investment funds Summary profile of investment funds, including administrative fees and expenses
Plan design review	While you have decision makers in a room to review vendor selection, it is often worthwhile to confirm any outside plan design issues.
Provider search	**Initial search** Identify and prioritize selection criteria for potential 401(k) service providers. Then, using these criteria, contact providers that could meet your needs. Contact these providers for preliminary information requests regarding their services. Prepare a written summary for management's review and selection of finalists. **Finalists' Interviews** After selecting finalists, schedule face-to-face meetings to choose the provider that best meets the needs of the participants.
Trustees/board approval	Prepare reports for trustees and/or board meetings as necessary to review the selection process and receive approval of management's decision.

This is in contrast to many other RFPs that you may have seen with over 250 questions and getting into the minutiae like whether the administrative system is owned or leased or asking the same question multiple times since the person who put the RFP together just cut and pasted from various sources. In general, we recommend that you ask as many questions as you want, but with each question, you ask yourself, "What will I do with this information and will it help me make a better decision?" If your answer is, "Not sure and not really," then do not ask the question. What we are saying is that we find managers make better decisions when they focus on the few critical items that are really important to them, rather than getting bogged down by too much meaningless information.

Face-to-face interviews are critical to making your final decision. As we tell our clients, there are three very competitive providers who you would be happy with. What is important now is for you to meet, converse with, and understand the actual people who will be running your plan. At the end of the day, even with Web technology and telephone automation, when there is a problem—and inevitably there will be one—you need to feel comfortable with the people at the other end of the telephone. Each firm has a style, a feel, an ethos—and you cannot get this just from reviewing an RFP response. In these interviews, our roles as outsider are mostly to listen, but more importantly, to keep the conversation on track and help our client differentiate between the providers. We might only ask one question during a 90-minute presentation or we may ask several.

Why Use Outside Consultants?

Many plan sponsors use outside consultants to help them navigate the search process. There are several reasons for this strategy :

- *Expertise.* Hiring a retirement plan provider is a complex purchase. By hiring experts, you get access to their knowledge and methods. Most useful is that the outside expert can help you prioritize your goals, and facilitate discussion about what is really important for your firm such as the need for an open investment platform or online benefit statements. Furthermore, many staff people are generalists. For example, the human resources staff may be responsible for the retirement plans, but also payroll, medical benefits, and facilities. With the liability of making the wrong choice a very big mistake, many plan sponsors make the choice to hire experts to help them through a very visible, critical decision that will affect their employees' retirement savings.

- *Marketplace awareness.* Understanding your goals and then applying them to the marketplace is critical to maximizing your efforts. With so many provider options, you would be swamped if you went to the entire marketplace to solicit bids. An outside firm will help you winnow the list down to a manageable size from the most competitive providers given your individual goals and objectives. This initial step will save you time and money in the long run. The ability to communicate critical information and help you make better informed decisions is the primary reason to hire an outside firm.

- *Negotiation ability.* Outside firms work on multiple searches throughout the year. Vendors know that they must maintain good working relationships with search firms in order to be included in the next search performed by this firm. If you decide to go it alone, vendors have a significant advantage since you will only be doing a search once.

- *Process management.* Keeping a search committee on track through a complex purchasing decision is often difficult. With an outside firm helping to spearhead your search, you maximize your staff's time by having them focus on key tasks such as final decision making.

Ongoing Vendor Management

Since the decision to select a retirement plan vendor should be considered a medium-term decision, it is imperative that you manage this relationship assuming at least a five-year tenure. The key step is establishing clear communication channels between your organization and the vendor. That is why we consider it imperative that you meet with the vendor's service team (in addition to any salesperson) personally during the evaluation phase. You need to get a feeling for this group who will be responsible for taking care of you and your plan once the sales process is complete.

Many times we are hired by a client when a vendor relationship has gone south. The reasons that vendor relationships sour include:

- *New personnel on the vendor side.* This is the number one reason why we are called in by clients. We hear things like, "XYZ just reassigned us to a new group because . . . and we don't like the new person." Those are the easy ones to fix. Sometimes we hear, "Karen at XYZ just left. She's the fourth service rep to leave in two years. We always have to train new ones." This one goes to the core of the vendor's business management—retaining their own employees. In our practice, if you are experiencing this type of vendor service, you may be best served by moving your business.

- *Poor communication between vendor and client.* Many times we hear clients say things like, "Whenever Mike from ABC responds to a question, we don't understand his answer—so we call you." Or, consider another case that just happened to a client of ours. The chief financial officer received a form letter from their bundled service vendor— signed by someone they did not know, saying, "Due to quarterly contribution requirements, you must make a $2 million contribution by next week or else. . . ." No call from the main client service representative, no other communication, just "do this or else." My message to clients is that if you are getting this type of service, you should look around. My message to vendors is, you can always improve client communication, and if any of the things above sound familiar, you have serious problems and will be faced with one of two scenarios: your clients are already searching around and you do not know it, or your clients are too busy to do a search right now, but when they free up, they will do it and be gone.

- *Lack of follow-through by vendor.* This is probably the next biggest issue we find. An example of this would be a client asking for a report of some participant elections. The client service person says that it will take two days. The client does not get it for two weeks, or worse, never gets it and has to call the vendor again. Clients and vendors are all businesspeople and understand schedules, timing, and staff management, and that some things take time. What clients do not like is to be told to expect things by a certain date and not get it.

- *Mistakes.* We list mistakes last, because in fact, this is the least common issue that clients call us about. Some typical mistakes we see include payroll for the preceding month not being entered into the system for nine days due to a programming error, a benefit calculation done incorrectly, a participant communication letter with typos, and so forth. Clients understand that mistakes happen, but in the vast majority of cases mistakes can be fixed. What clients need is the trust that when mistakes happen, vendors will fix them and work to prevent them in the future. This trust is the key. I could have also written *respect*. When mistakes happen, vendors should take responsibility for them, treat their clients with respect and dignity, and work to fix them. In fact, in many cases when we have been called in to help a client through a vendor situation due to errors, the client/vendor relationship is improved. Vendors dig in, fix the problem, work to communicate the solution, and move on. That's the way it should be.

Overall, we see ongoing vendor management as an extension of the search process. First, we recommend that you have an annual service review in which you review successes and failures during the previous year. At this meeting, we recommend that you focus on the goals and objectives identified during the search process—basically what is important to you the client, what makes your organization different from all the rest. For example, if you identified improving employee participation as a goal, I would have this as a key benchmark during annual service reviews. If you identified employee communication meetings as critical, focus on the success of your vendor to run, manage, and educate employees.

During the search process, we also highlight the entire fee and cost structure of your vendor relationship. Many vendors are compensated indirectly through asset-based fees. By having the total fee explicitly stated in the search process, this provides the groundwork for open, honest business discussions about ongoing service levels.

At this meeting, we recommend that you spend time to identify goals for the coming year. This provides focus to your vendors and increases the likelihood of success. Without this focus, your vendors are basically in the dark about what you want to achieve. They then have to guess on issues like, "Does client XYZ want to have employee meetings in their regional offices?" As the client, you should feel empowered to dial in the service level and requirements that you want—understanding that some of the requests can be easily handled, while others may require some investment on your part. However, it is best to have this discussion rather than blindly accepting what your vendor "recommends" for clients like you (see Appendix B).

Fiduciary Duty

Fiduciary issues surrounding pension plans have been in the news lately—and not for positive coverage. Trustees of pension plans are being sued by participants (e.g., Enron). This is not a welcome trend. Once being a fiduciary of a company plan was something that senior finance and human resource (HR) managers accepted routinely, without a second thought. Now, these very same managers are often asking themselves what have they gotten into.

Fiduciary Basics

The issue of fiduciary liability boils down to a single sentence: When you are holding money for other people, you must consider their needs exclusively. Let's start at the beginning

Who Is a Fiduciary?

A person becomes a fiduciary by doing one of the following things:

1. Exercising discretionary control over management of the plan (for example, hiring investment managers, etc.), or
2. Giving investment advice for a fee, or
3. Exercising discretionary control over administration of the plan.

Typical fiduciaries include boards of directors, members of retirement plan committees, and individual executives such as chief financial officers or investment managers. People who are not fiduciaries include legal counsel, accountants, actuaries, or third-party administrators. These service professionals usually limit their work to providing advice and counsel to plan sponsors, and do not have any discretion to make decisions.

Notice that I wrote "doing one of the following things" to introduce the criteria for a fiduciary. This is critical. The Employee Retirement Income Security Act (ERISA) addresses the actual facts of the situation to determine if that action was a fiduciary act. Then, whoever made that decision is a de facto fiduciary.

For example, a third-party administrator is not typically considered a fiduciary since he is only following the plan rules. However, if in the course of administering the plan the third-party administrator interpreted a particular section of the plan document, then this interpretation would be considered a fiduciary decision; hence, the third-party administrator would be considered a fiduciary for this act. As you can imagine, third-party administrators work very hard to have this not happen. That is why they will contact plan sponsors to sign off on any plan document interpretations that they make in taking care of the plan.

What Must Fiduciaries Do?

ERISA places several restrictions on fiduciaries of pension plans. These restrictions have been called the "highest known to law" and are put into place to insure the retirement assets of beneficiaries. It is worthwhile to consider the specific language in ERISA spelling out standards of fiduciary conduct. In general, fiduciaries should:

- "Act solely in the interest of the participants and beneficiaries." This priority should be in the front of every fiduciary's mind when he or she makes plan decisions that could affect participants.

- "Act with the care, skill, prudence, and diligence under the circumstances then prevailing that a prudent man acting in a like capacity and familiar with such matters would use in the conduct of an enterprise of a like character and with like aims." This section is often cited as the part of the definition that elevates a fiduciary's conduct from the typical "prudent man" to "prudent expert." You do not need to be an expert in retirement plans to act as a fiduciary, but this section clearly expects you to engage qualified professionals if you are in fact not qualified.

- "Diversify the investments of the plan so as to minimize the risk of large losses (unless under the circumstances it is clearly prudent not to do so)." Again, fiduciaries are responsible for holding money that "belongs" to others, so fiduciary standards take a very conservative viewpoint. The goal identified here can be summarized as follows: It is better to avoid a large loss than to achieve a large gain.

Table 4.1 is a simple method that we use with our clients to assess their fiduciary compliance.

Table 4.1   ARGUS Fiduciary Assessment Tool

Argus Consulting has developed methodology to help plan sponsors gauge their fiduciary effectiveness. Our mnemonic for the tool is ARGUS. Each letter represents a critical factor that can be scored. The total score indicates the state of the plan's performance.

Initial	Factor	Description	Scale	Your Score
A	Assets	How does overall asset performance compare with that of peers, a benchmark index, or expense ratios?	0 = if you don't know 1 = if you haven't been checking within last 12 months 2 = if you have reviewed within last 12 months	
R	Regulations	Are plan documents, tax filings, etc., up to date? Is a system in place to manage ongoing compliance?	0 = if you don't know 1 = if your plans are up to date, but no system in place for ongoing compliance 2 = if you have a system in place for ongoing compliance	
G	Governance	How well do fiduciaries understand and carry out their governance role?	0 = if you don't know who is a fiduciary and/or don't have regular meetings 1 = if you know who is fiduciary and have ad hoc meetings as needed 2 = you have scheduled fiduciary meetings at least twice a year	
U	Understanding	Do participants understand their pension plan benefits? How is the communication program?	0 = if participants ask "What pension plan?" 1 = if participants know about it but may not appreciate its full value 2 = if participants understand the plan's value and effective channels of communication exist between human resources, participants, and providers	
S	Staff	How effective are both the outsourced and insourced staff who support the pension plan?	0 = if they don't know who does what, when, or for how much 1 = if they know who does what, but may not know for how much 2 = if within last 3 years they have performed an administrative audit and/or competitive bid process	
Total ARGUS Score			Maximum Score = 10	

(continues)

Table 4.1 (*continued*)

ARGUS Score and Evaluation
0 to 3 Plan is in danger of disqualification. Plan sponsor needs to take corrective actions immediately. Possible courses of action include compliance audit, IRS/DOL voluntary corrective programs, fiduciary review, provider search, etc.
4 to 7 Plan is operationally effective, but plan sponsor and participants may not be receiving full value from pension plan. Possible courses of action include investment performance monitoring, communication review, and provider search, etc.
8 to 10 Plan is performing well with plan sponsor, and participants are receiving benefits from pension plan. Overall performance of plan is excellent. Continue current program with a view toward providing incremental improvement in weaker areas that have been identified.

When you begin to discuss the legal status of any pension plan, it is important to remember that all activities of the pension plan should be written down. Two documents that fiduciaries should review are the trust and plan documents (sometimes these are combined into one).

TRUST BASICS

By law, this trust owns the assets of the pension plan. It is a legal entity. Money goes into it and gets paid out of it. There's no need for you to be an expert trust attorney, but some familiarity with basics of trust is a great starting point to discuss these issues.

Trusts are established by one entity (a company) for the purpose of another (perhaps its employees). All actions of the trust must be written down in a trust document. What actually constitutes a trust document can vary. However, most trust documents will include:

- Defining all parties involved and who appoints them.
- Defining what actions can and/or must be taken.
- Who can trustees hire as investment managers?
- Whether the trust can pay plan expenses and any other issues surrounding prohibited transactions (self-dealing).
- Limitations on their duties—some trustees will limit their responsibilities in the hope of reducing their liability.
- Termination—how the trust can be amended and/or terminated.

Fiduciary Setup—Case Study

For a typical mid-sized employer, the following is an example of the people who are fiduciaries. You can use the analogy of a family tree—with fiduciary status originating at the board of directors, and then quickly multiplying farther down the tree (see Figure 4.1).

Many of our clients appoint nonexecutive employees to positions on the retirement plan committee for the practical intent of making sure the needs of rank and file employees are heard. We believe this policy is worthwhile because these employee fiduciaries become de facto ambassadors back at the office and around the water cooler. One client of ours takes it a step further, and perhaps, further than we would recommend. This client runs an election to select these representatives to sit on the investment review committee. This particular client happens to have a culture that values collaboration over "command and control," which is apparent in how the client runs the entire business. We have concerns about an election and the impact on their fiduciary duty and other practical concerns, but overall, this shows how far an employer will go to involve participants in the operation of their plans.

A recent survey by Diversified Investment Advisors shows that multiple areas within an organization participate in investment committees (see Table 4.2).

As you can see, there could easily be a dozen fiduciaries within an organization. Again, it is important to remember that it is the act itself that makes one a fiduciary. When you consider that your HR staff may be communicating with participants on a daily basis about issues related to plan administration, and that each of these conversations could be interpreted as a fiduciary act, then it is critical that your company take these issues seriously.

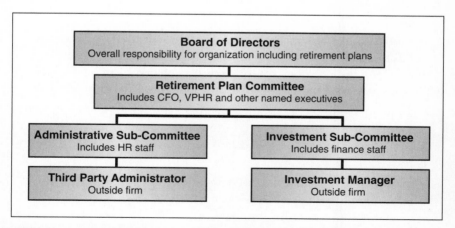

FIGURE 4.1   A sample hierarchy of individuals that often act as fiduciaries at a midsized employer

Table 4.2   Primary Responsibility for Selecting and Monitoring Investment Managers

	All Employers Offering a DC Plan %	Stand-alone DC Plan %	Both DC and DB Plans %
Dedicated investment review committee	36	29	39
Pension committee	27	20	31
Finance department employee	10	11	10
Human resources department employee	14	24	9
Other company employee/committee	7	8	6
No-one inside company	6	8	6
Total	100	100	101

Note: Numbers may not add up to 100% due to rounding.
DB, defined benefit; DC, defined contribution.
Source: Diversified Investment Advisors, *Report on Retirement Plans 2005*, (New York: Diversified Investment Advisors, 2005), 10.

Fiduciary Best Practices

In our work with clients, we spend a lot of time helping plan sponsors in their role as fiduciaries. Here is a sample of some of their best (and not so good) practices:

- Preschedule meetings with regular agenda items. This is probably the number one best practice that we recommend clients adopt to manage their fiduciary duty. An example of this would be:
  - Two meetings per year scheduled five to six weeks after the end of a quarter.
  - Standard agenda items such as "Administration," "Investment," "Participant Communication," and "Compliance."
  - One person is responsible for collection of agenda items that will be discussed, and these are sent around previous to the meeting.

- Clients often ask us how many meetings should they have during a year to comply with ERISA requirements? There is no right answer here, but we typically respond that it depends on several factors including:
  - How experienced are the fiduciaries?
  - How long have they been fiduciaries?
  - Are there any pressing problems (poor investment performance) that need to be addressed?
  - Do fiduciaries change very often?
  - Have any significant plan changes/mergers taken place recently?

- Our firm is usually hired initially because of a particular concern or issue. This usually leads us to hold more frequent meetings for a period of time to manage this situation as well as to conduct basic fiduciary training. However, after this initial period of activity, we usually see fiduciaries reduce their meeting frequency to either quarterly or semi-annually. At a bare minimum, we would suggest fiduciaries meet at least once per year. However, we are more comfortable recommending that they meet two to four times annually.

- *Communicating to participants about the activities of the fiduciaries.* Piggy-backing on top of other required communication, such as the Summary Annual Report, some of our clients include a short communication piece about the fiduciaries and their activities. This could be a simple statement saying who is on the committee and an overview of their responsibilities and activities during the year. We believe this gives participants comfort that someone is looking out for their interests and puts a face to the fiduciary issues. If you decide to provide more communication, we recommend that you specify who participants should contact with questions about fiduciary issues. It is best to have a point person/department who responds to all inquiries from participants.

- *Requiring all fiduciaries to confirm their status in writing.* This exercise is worthwhile because it forces you to go through all your processes, to document who makes decisions, and to get their signature to confirm their status. We do not think the fact that someone did or did not sign a fiduciary consent form would change much in court. We feel that the process of going through this exercise is key. Simply talking with all your service providers about this puts fiduciary issues at the forefront of all future interactions—and this is where it should be.

- Beware of asking independent consultants (e.g., actuaries) to sign on as fiduciaries. This request is really a double-edged sword. On one hand, independent consultants provide significant advice to the retirement committee, and in many cases this advice is the primary source of information that is used in making a decision about the pension plan, even though the independent consultant does not have any discretion to make the final decision. So, a retirement committee might assume that it would be advantageous to have this consultant "sign on" as a fiduciary. On the other hand, if an independent consultant signs on as a fiduciary, he or she then has a significant role in the operation of the plan. Problems could arise if he or she disagreed with a decision of the employer, forcing more frequent meetings of the retirement committee to monitor the plan, increasing professional fees due to increased responsibility, and so forth.

■ *Affirmative election to limit investment choice under a 401(k) plan.* During the 1990s, the trend in 401(k) plans was to offer increasingly more and more investment options for participants to select (see Table 4.3).

Recently, many fiduciaries have wondered "how many are enough?" In fact, surveys show the number of investment options tailing off as revealed in Hewitt's 2005 "Trends and Experience in 401(k) Plans," a survey of 450 large companies.

Other surveys confirm the same finding, including Fidelity Investment's *Building Futures* report on corporate defined contribution plans, which found that 11 percent of companies reduced their number of investment options during the previous year. These reports suggest that, in general, plan sponsors are offering the same or fewer funds (see Figure 4.2 for survey results from Diversified Investment Advisors).

In the past, many fiduciaries felt that adding funds decreased their fiduciary responsibilities since participants could pick and choose from

Table 4.3   Number of Investment Options Offered

Number of Options	Percent of Plans			
	1999	2001	2003	2005
1–5	7%	2%	1%	1%
6	7%	7%	2%	2%
7	12%	7%	3%	3%
8	18%	12%	6%	4%
9	12%	12%	9%	9%
10	10%	14%	10%	10%
11	8%	10%	10%	10%
12	6%	10%	8%	11%
13	4%	5%	7%	7%
14	3%	4%	9%	8%
15	1%	5%	8%	7%
16	3%	3%	5%	4%
17	—	3%	5%	4%
More than 17	7%	7%	17%	20%
Average	**11**	**12**	**14**	**14**
Median	**9**	**10**	**12**	**13**

Note: 427 plans reporting in 1999; 422 plans reporting in 2001; 486 plans reporting in 2003; 448 plans reporting in 2005; percents do not total 100% due to rounding.
Source: Hewitt Associates LLC, *Surveys Findings: Trends and Experiences in 401(k) Plans 2005* (Illlinois: Hewitt Associates LLC, 2005), 37.

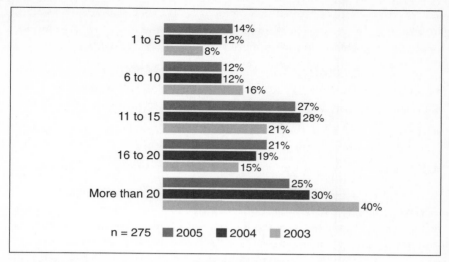

FIGURE 4.2   Number of investment options—trend

Source: Diversified Investment Advisors, *Retirement Plan Trends in Today's Healthcare Market 2005* (New York: Diversified Investment Advisors, 2005), 13.

a wide variety of funds. Fiduciaries also thought that if they had 20 funds in their investment line-up, then if one fund "tanked," it would not be so bad.

However, recent notices from the Department of Labor have changed people's opinion. The Department of Labor's view is that more funds equals more oversight. As a result, many fiduciaries are looking at cutting back the number of fund choices. Combine the Department of Labor's view with the complexity of communicating 20-plus funds and you can see this as a reasonable course of action.

Another argument that we bring up with our clients when we are talking about how many funds is the right number is to go back in time. Before the mutual fund industry successfully marketed daily valuation for 401(k) plans, most, if not all, 401(k) profit sharing plans had one single investment vehicle that was selected by the trustees. Allowing participants investment elections is a relatively new phenomenon that came about predominantly by the mutual fund companies. These companies had invested large sums of money in their technology to daily value mutual funds for individual investors, so it was only natural for them to look at alternative distribution channels. What better distribution channel than a

401(k) plan where contributions come in with every pay period. Adding investment choice was considered cutting edge and empowering employees to participate in their retirement savings. After 15 years of living with daily valued 401(k) plans, we now have learned:

- Employees struggle to successfully manage their investment.
- Some make very poor choices.
- Some never change their investments (which raises the question why we need daily valuation of funds).
- Some do not even understand the basic differences between equities and bonds.

Given these problems, an entire industry of providers of investment advice (e.g., Financial Engines) has grown up to assist participants with managing their plans. Companies spend a lot of time educating employees, having seminars, and sending educational material to help employees. Many companies do not fully realize that giving investment choices does not guarantee a positive outcome for participants. These companies are moving to limit options, adding lifestyle funds—basically balance funds with risk-tolerant specific asset allocation, providing better default options—since many employees never even make a single investment election. Overall, we group all these activities into the category of fiduciaries stepping up to their responsibilities and taking a realistic look at their participants and making informed choices that are best for them and not letting the newest marketplace feature drive their retirement plan management.

Probably the only "losers" in this new movement are those participants who use their 401(k) plans to aggressively trade and utilize very risky investments. When our clients ask about limiting choice, we typically respond that this is a retirement plan, not someone's individual brokerage account, and that your first duty is to safeguard the assets. If a participant wants more choice, we recommend our clients respond with something like, "Feel free to call Schwab and open up a brokerage account with them—you'll have all the choice in the world. But this retirement plan is just that—a retirement plan—and the trustees have made their decision to offer these funds to all participants."

As an aside, clients ask us what does Argus Consulting Ltd have in its 401(k) plan? Answer—no choice. We have only one investment option—a balanced fund. We prefer to have our consultants focused on our clients' issues rather than making their own elections. On top of that, it is a whole lot easier to review the performance of one fund.

SARBANES-OXLEY—IMPACT ON PENSION PLANS

For most HR staff at public companies, the passage of the Sarbanes-Oxley Act of 2002 (SOX) was met with benign awareness. It was a "finance and reporting" problem. You were not the chief executive officer (CEO) or the chief financial officer (CFO) (and did not aspire to be) and you were not going to be signing any attestation certifying the financial statements. You had good processes in place to handle your administrative tasks and you supplied budgets as requested.

However, your internal auditing staff kept badgering you about "controls." Then your external auditors got into the game and started asking for the same thing—"Show us your controls." Besides feeling like you were suddenly in some bad sci-fi movie facing down aliens who keep telling you to "Show us your leader," you may have come to the realization that you need to familiarize yourself with those parts of SOX that are going to substantially impact your pension plans.

Background

When Senator Paul Sarbanes and Representative Michael Oxley worked together to draft new legislation, they were responding to recent corporate scandals (e.g., Enron) as well as to failing confidence in the markets overall. Their solution, in simplistic terms, was to increase the disclosure of information as well as the rigor of financial reporting. It only took them about 100 pages, broken down into 11 sections (called titles). Although I will not go over every detail of the Act here, I would certainly encourage anyone working at a public company to read through SOX (okay, I am an actuary and really enjoy reading such legalese!), or to visit the Public Company Accounting Oversight Board's web site (www.pcaob.org).

In fact, the titles of SOX alone give a very good sense of the general focus, so that alone is a good start. Table 4.4 will provide you with a quick overview with commentary on titles that impact pension plans directly.

Immediate Impact on 401(k) Plans

This first impact of SOX was on 401(k) plans. The two major areas were in response to abuses at Enron and a third was a general change to all ERISA plans. This has been written about in many publications so I will simply summarize the results:

1. *Blackout period.* SOX does not change overall fiduciary duty during blackout periods when the participant's ability to direct investments

(continues)

(continued)

Table 4.4   SOX Titles and Their Impacts on Pension Plans

Number	Title	Comments: Pension Plan Impact
I	Public company accounting oversight board	Creation of new agency funded by companies with public securities
II	Auditor independence	This is why your auditors are saying things like, "We can't do that work any more, you need to find another firm to do it, then we'll audit it."
III	Corporate responsibility	CEO and CFO personal responsibility is in here as well as 401(k) blackout periods.
IV	Enhanced financial disclosures	Covers all new disclosures including "controls," loans to executives.
IX	White collar crime penalty	Increased ERISA penalties.

is limited. SOX adds two rules: the first is increased advance notice requirements; the second puts limits on personal trading by executives.

2. *Loans to executives.* A main goal of SOX was to address the abuse of corporate assets by executives, particularly the use of loans. The focus of this provision was not on 401(k) plans, however. 401(k) plan loan provisions became, in the words of our military officials, "collateral damage." Many public companies now, with the blessing of the Department of Labor, have eliminated loans to executives within the 401(k) plan in order to comply with SOX.

3. *ERISA penalties.* In an attempt to make plan fiduciaries wake up and take their responsibilities seriously, SOX increased the penalties for both individuals and corporations who violate ERISA. Maximum fines for individuals were increased to $100,000 from $5,000 and the maximum prison time increased to 10 years from 1 year. Fines for corporations who violate ERISA increased to $500,000 from $100,000.

The above changes had immediate and visible impact on pension plans. However, the additional requirements of SOX focus more on business issues and have far-reaching impact on the management of pension plans.

Controls

More important to the ongoing management of your company are the requirements contained in Sections 302 and 404 of SOX. These sections cover both the attestation of the CEO and CFO on the overall financial statements as well as an assessment of the internal controls. This is where the ongoing impact of SOX will be felt by pension plan management. I'll briefly describe what is covered under these sections and then explain internal controls.

Requirements of Sections 302 and 404

Section 302 requires that the CEO and CFO certify that the financial statements do not contain any material errors and that they provide a fair representation of the financial condition of the company. Also, this attestation must certify the internal controls of the company. This begs the question, "What are internal controls?"

Internal Controls

For nonauditors who do not deal with accounting issues, the definition of an internal control is sometimes difficult to understand. In brief, controls focus on *how* the numbers are generated, not *what* the numbers are. A corporate audit focuses on *what* the numbers are, while a control audit focuses on *how* the numbers are put together and how are you going to detect an error (now or in the future).

Here's the Securities and Exchange Commission definition (selectively edited down for you nonaccountants):

> A process . . . to provide reasonable assurance regarding the reliability of financial reporting . . . in accordance with generally accepted accounting principles . . . that pertain to the maintenance of records . . . that receipts and expenditures . . . are made only in accordance with authorizations . . . that provide reasonable assurance regarding prevention of or timely detection of unauthorized acquisition, use or disposition of . . . assets that could have a material effect on the financial statements.

A control focuses on:

- Reduction of the possibility of financial restatement.
- Security of assets.

(continues)

(continued)

- Approval of transactions.
- Maintenance of records.

In addition, the mere fact that your company has never had any error in its financial statements (i.e., it has never had to restate earnings, etc.) does not mean that your controls are strong.

Designing a control necessary to comply with SOX is beyond the scope of this book. In summary, the process is similar to other business process maximization (think six sigma). One starts off with a risk assessment, identification of inputs, constituencies (staff, vendors, etc.), flow charts of process, who owns the process, who will control the process, what one does if there are exceptions, testing the process, and so forth. The output of a formal control will be answers to the following:

- What is the activity?
- Who performs it?
- How often?
- What is the evidence of the control?
- How are exceptions monitored?

IMPACT ON HUMAN RESOURCES

Where does HR come into play in SOX compliance? Thankfully, many of the internal controls and processes in HR are not in the scope of the CEO/CFO attestation. For example, controls over complying with HR policies are typically not included.

The major role HR will play will be in three areas:

1. *Culture.* SOX changes the culture of public companies and how they prepare financial statements and run their companies. Formalization of the controls has changed the environment at public companies. Also, if your company operates internationally, SOX will stress the relationship across borders. Consulting firm Deloitte and Touchelle provides an appropriate metaphor for SOX and a company's culture: "Good governance must be stitched into the fabric of the company. Strong internal control should become part of the corporate DNA."[*]
2. *Communication.* SOX compliance requires that HR, legal, finance, and treasury operate together in an effective manner. HR, with expertise in communication, should play a key role going forward.

---

[*]Deloitte Development LLC,"Under Control Sustaining Compliance with Sarbanes-Oxley in Year Two and Beyond" (Deloitte Development LLC, 2005), 3.

3. *Oversight.* For those processes that HR owns and are deemed material (e.g., pension plan), HR will play a lead role in complying with SOX internal control requirements. Critical to this is the oversight of third parties and experts (actuaries, investment managers, plan administrators, etc.) who all play a part in the operation of benefit programs.

OVERSIGHT

Expanding further on this third role, HR typically plays a critical role in the management of outside vendors who perform critical processes that impact a company's financial statement. For example, if the pension plan is determined to be material, controls must be put in place to comply with SOX. This will mean coordinating with outside vendors to satisfy your auditors that work performed is also controlled. For third-party administrators, like 401(k) vendors, they will typically provide you with a Statement on Auditing Standards (SAS) 70 audit.

What Is an SAS 70 Audit?

An SAS 70 audit is a single audit report, performed on the service organization's operation that can then be used by its clients' auditors. For example, if T. Rowe Price administers your 401(k) plan, they can hire a firm to audit their internal procedures. Then your auditors can ask to see T. Rowe Price's SAS 70 audit. The main benefit of an SAS 70 audit is that your auditors do not have to go on site at T. Rowe Price to examine their controls. They can rely on the SAS 70 audit.

In addition to administrators, HR also spearheads other outside providers like actuaries. These types of professionals are considered specialists and are not covered by SAS 70 requirements. A specialist is a professional who provides expertise and a specialized service (e.g., actuarial valuations). In these cases, companies are required to do a specialist assessment that will include documenting each specialist. This will include looking at:

- Reputation
- Certification
- User controls

In providing our actuarial services to clients, we have had to comply with additional requests including:

- *Credentials.* What professional bodies (e.g., American Academy of Actuaries) are we a member of?

(continues)

(continued)

- *Assumption setting.* Document the objective criteria used to set critical assumptions (discount rate, return on asset assumptions, etc.).
- *Data handling.* Document the data-handling process, including resolution of issues (i.e., informal telephone conversations may no longer be sufficient).
- *Valuation process.* Providing additional documentation about changes, reasonability of results, peer review process, etc.

Results So Far

Wrapping up this first year of SOX compliance, companies can now get over the deadline mindset. SOX is not going away and controls need to be integrated into all business processes. Problems identified by audit firms include a "project mindset," overextension of internal audit teams, and ignoring risks.

Also, not everyone has received passing grades on their work so far. *Compliance Weekly*, for example, prepared a report in conjunction with Raisch Financial Information Services with some interesting findings:

- 7.7 percent of the internal control assessments filed this proxy season have been given "failing grades" by the companies' external auditors.
- Industries with the highest "adverse opinions" provided by auditors include computer hardware and software (18.2 percent), metals and mining (17.2 percent), and consumer services (16.7 percent).
- Auditing firms delivered varying "failure" rates during their internal control audits; for example, PricewaterhouseCoopers failed 9.3 percent of its 398 SOX 404 audits while KPMG failed 5.5 percent of its 348 audits.

PRIVATE COMPANIES

In addition to public companies, many private firms have also responded to the business climate changed by SOX. A recent survey by Foley & Lardner LLP, titled "The Impact of Sarbanes-Oxley on Private Companies," reported that SOX has impacted more than 75 percent of private organizations. Also, many organizations plan to adopt several measures of SOX, including CEO/CFO attestation. While currently not required to adopt any of SOX, these private organizations have voluntarily moved in the direction of SOX compliance.

In summary, while SOX focuses in on increased disclosure and reliability of financial statements, HR will also play a current role in compliance, as well as a more lasting role as SOX changes the environment and culture.

Financial

Much of the focus of today's retirement plan management now surrounds financial matters. This is true in general, but with administrative issues sorted out, managers can now move beyond wondering whether the pension checks are being mailed to crucial issues such as the funding of the plans, who should bear the investment risks, and so forth.

You will recall the graphic we introduced back in the first chapter (see Figure 1.1).

Three of the four governance tools can be broadly categorized under finance. These are:

- Timing tools
  - Funding
  - Accounting/actuarial
- Risk level tool
  - Investment

The fourth tool—plan design—will be examined in Chapter 6.

Defined Benefit Concerns

Refer back to Figure 1.1 to refresh your memory of the governance tools available to you in managing a retirement plan. The three financial tools (funding, accounting/actuarial, and investment) are all available to the defined benefit (DB) plan sponsor. We will discuss each one in detail but in reality, all three are interwoven.

Funding

BACKGROUND

This governance tool is focused on a corporation's decision to put cash into the retirement plan. Ideally, a company would have a formal funding policy, and in fact, many do at a most basic level. The typical funding policy would say something like

> The company will fund the plan from time to time as required to meet any minimum required funding amounts and, at its discretion, may contribute more than the minimum required funding amount.

It is hard to call this statement a policy—it basically says that the company will pay at least what it is legally required to do, and may do more, but gives no parameters surrounding this decision. This ambiguous, but typical, funding policy was driven by the actual language contained in the Employee Retirement Income Security Act (ERISA) which rather than clarifies the issues actually makes it more confusing. In the applicable ERISA section 402(b), it states

> Every employee benefit plan shall—
>
> (1) provide a procedure for establishing and carrying out a funding policy and method consistent with the objectives of the plan and the requirements of this subchapter.

However, ERISA is using the words *funding policy* here to mean the plan's fiduciary policy on deploying the assets, what is normally called an " investment policy." (We will discuss this later when we examine the investment governance tools.) The decision to fund, actually make cash contributions into a plan or not, is truly an employer decision, and not a fiduciary decision. This poor word choice has confused the topic in the minds of many employers and fiduciaries. This confusion has led to the very simplistic funding policies of most employers.

FACTORS TO CONSIDER WHEN ESTABLISHING A FUNDING POLICY

If you want to move beyond the bare bones funding policy of the past, an employer should examine the following factors.

Funded Status. The first, and primary, consideration should be the funded status of the plan. Briefly, the funded status of the plan compares the current assets versus the current liabilities. Your actuary uses several different asset and liability measures for multiple purposes—some for budgeting cash contributions, some for expense for accounting statements, some for the trust reporting.

- *What liability to use?* The liability measure we recommend you consider is the current market value of accrued benefits. There are two very similar liabilities that approximate this: either the current liability contained in the ERISA valuation report, or the accumulated benefit obligation (ABO) contained in the Financial Accounting Standards Board (FASB) accounting report. The differences between these two measures are beyond the scope of this book, but you should be able to easily capture either of these two measures.

- *What asset value to use?* As with liabilities, the actuaries may be using several different measures of liability. For funding policy purposes, the only useful measure is the actual market value of assets—the spot number without any actuarial smoothing applied. This would be called the market value of assets or fair value of assets.

- *What should the target funding status be?* Ideally, all plans would be maintained at over 100 percent funded status. That is, assets are greater than the value of the benefits currently accrued today. Table 5.1 describes these calculations.

Being at least 100 percent funded achieves several goals:

- *Prudence.* The employer has promised participants a benefit. These benefits are deferred wages to which the participants are legally entitled. The employer should have assets set aside to cover the current value of these promises. If these assets are not set aside, the participant could be exposed to possible cutbacks in benefits if the company goes bankrupt, such as happened with several airline companies in recent years.

Table 5.1   Sample Plan Funded Status

Value	Underfunded Plan	100% Funded Plan	Overfunded Plan
1. Assets[a]	$90	$100	$120
2. Liability[b]	$100	$100	$100
3. Funded status % [1. / 2.]	90%	100%	120%
4. Surplus/(Deficit) [2. − 1.]	($10)	$0	$20

[a]Assets = market value of assets.
[b]Liability = either the current liability or accumulated benefit obligation.

- *Societal good.* Maintaining the funded status of pension plans at over 100 percent helps the entire society. When an employer does not maintain well-funded plans, everyone pays the price if the plans go into bankruptcy and the Pension Benefit Guaranty Corporation (PBGC) must take over the plan. Society's interest is that all companies honor their debts—to suppliers, to landlords and, yes, to employees.

Funding a pension plan above 100 percent is a decision that moves into the other factors to consider.

Competing Uses for Corporate Capital—Overall Capital Structure. Companies face decisions about how to use their capital on a daily basis. Should they invest in a new factory, should they refinance their existing debt, should they sell a division and use the proceeds to retire some debt? All of these decisions relate to the overall capital structure (debt versus equity) of the corporation. Thousands of Wall Street professionals, including investment bankers, spend all day working on finding the optimal capital structure—that structure that will maximize the value of the shareholders. In general, as a company takes on debt, it can expand capacity and grow faster. However, with the increased debt comes increased risk for bankruptcy. There is a point at which a company has added so much debt that the risk/reward trade-off goes negative and shareholder value is reduced.

Pension plans on one level are like any other debt of the organization. If a company had an underfunded plan, it could simply issue more debt, use the proceeds to pay off the fund's shortfall, and have the plan be perfectly funded. But on one level, all this accomplishes is replacing one form of debt (pension liability) with another (publicly traded debt).

Ultimately all of these decisions impact the risk borne by shareholders, since a company is only an artificial legal structure to represent the interests of the owners/shareholders. Refer to the box on Boots later in this chapter for further discussion on the overall shareholder risk issue.

Impact on Financial Statement. Well-funded plans, those over 100 percent funded, are in a good position to manage the impact of the pension plan on their financial statements. At the simplest level, if you have put away enough money to cover the current promised benefits, all you are left with is paying for the benefit accruing this year. Accountants call this value of benefits accruing this year "service cost." Since employers can control the service cost by making changes to the plan, they are entirely in control of the ultimate cost that shows up in their income statement.

However, if a pension plan is less than 100 percent funded, that is, underfunded, the accountants require companies to "pay off" this short-fall, much like you have to pay off the mortgage on your home. In the pension plan world, this "mortgage" is also comparable with an adjustable rate mortgage, one that changes every year. However, unlike adjustable rate mortgages where homeowners "win" when the interest rates go down, companies "lose" when the interest rates go down. And that is exactly what has happened since mid-2000 through the end of 2005.

Impact on Investment Risk Tolerance. It is worth mentioning that the funded status of the plan will most likely have an impact on how much risk you take in the plan's investments. Most investment advisers would recommend that plans that are less than 100 percent funded invest in a lower-risk portfolio since the downside of negative returns could drastically affect the employer and participants. A lower-risk portfolio would be one with a high percentage of assets in stable, fixed-income vehicles that are highly liquid.

Conversely, if the plan is overfunded, many investment advisers would recommend a more aggressive portfolio since the employer and employees will not be negatively impacted. A more aggressive portfolio would include more equity exposure, global and developing market exposure, as well as possibly less liquid investments like private equity.

Ultimately, these decisions should be based on a consideration of all the stakeholders—shareholders, participants, and management.

SAMPLE FUNDING POLICIES

The following are alternative funding policies that move beyond the typical "minimum funding" policy. We would encourage plan sponsors to consider these alternatives. Whether or not a change is actually made, discussing, debating, and weighing the pros/cons of the various policies would shed light on how the employer will respond to future funding needs.

Maximum Policy. Example—Each year, the company will contribute the maximum tax deductible contribution allowable.

- Advantages
  - Takes full advantage of government's tax allowance
  - Provides security to pension participants
  - Reduces PBGC premium to minimum level
  - Allows plan sponsors to maintain some control over determination of maximum deductible contribution level using actuarial assumptions

■ Disadvantages

- Large cash contributions until pension plan becomes fully funded
- After reaching full funded status, future contributions may not be tax deductible, so participants miss out on future deductions
- No explicit factor included in policy that focuses on employer's ability to make contributions

100 Percent Funded on Accrued Benefits Basis. Example—Each year, the company will contribute the amount necessary to maintain the pension fund at 100 percent funded on an accrued benefits basis. For the accrued benefit measure, we will use the ABO listed in our financial statements (alternative—use the current liability as disclosed in our actuarial valuation report).

Alternatives—Target 125 percent (or any higher number) accrued benefits basis.

■ Advantages

- Avoids adverse impact of being underfunded, such as balance sheet hit (other comprehensive income), PBGC notification to participants, etc.
- Provides security to pension participants if target is set appropriately
- Reduces PBGC premium to low level and possibly to minimum level

■ Disadvantages

- Large fluctuations in contributions required since target is based on assumptions out of control of plan sponsor—if ABO based, market rates; if current liability based, 30-year treasury rates
- If target is set too low, could still expose participants to adverse market impact
- No explicit factor included in policy that focuses on employer's ability to make contributions

"Rainy Day" Policy. Example—The plan's minimum funded status is 100 percent of ABO. The company will make the necessary contributions to maintain this funded status. In years when the company's pretax profits are above $X, the company will make additional, tax-deductible contributions in order to attain 150 percent ABO funded status.

Alternatives—Vary the hurdle $X, use profitability (profit margin greater than X percent), use different profitable target (175 percent ABO)

- Advantages
  - Explicit recognition of company's profitability and ability to make contributions above minimum level
  - Builds cushion for unprofitable years—"rainy day" fund—when expectation is little, if any contribution would be made
  - Avoids adverse impact of being underfunded, such as balance sheet hit (other comprehensive income), PBGC notification to participants, etc.
  - Provides security to pension participants
  - Reduces PBGC premium to low level and possibly to minimum level
- Disadvantages
  - Large fluctuations in contributions required since target is based on assumptions out of control of plan sponsor—if ABO based, market rates; if current liability based, 30-year treasury rates
  - Builds expectation that company will in fact follow contribution pattern in profitable years. However, competing capital demands may be more appealing to shareholders

Accounting/Actuarial

Accounting/actuarial is a governance tool that focuses specifically on the timing of contributions and expense. At best, accounting and actuarial methods provide an employer with a good estimate of liabilities and assets as well as a reasonable budget for future contributions and expenses. At worst, these methods are used to distort the true value of assets and liabilities, thereby manipulating the balance sheet and income statement of employers. Our goal here is not to make you an actuary, but to assist you in understanding the actuarial process. With this information, you will be better able to manage the relationship with your actuary, get better information from him or her, and then make better decisions yourself on behalf of your company.

BACKGROUND—ACTUARIAL PROCESS

DB plans, at their basic level, are just vehicles used to hold assets that are invested in order to pay promised benefits in the future. Forgetting the asset side for a moment, the first question any plan sponsor asks is "What is the value of the promise we've made to participants?" Since these payments are made in the future, several unknowns exist:

- When will the participant take the benefit?

- How long will the participant live? The spouse?
- If the benefit is pay related, what will the future pay level be?
- What will inflation be between now and the time the person begins payment?

Actuaries use a fancy word to describe all these unknowns: *contingencies*. For any contingency, the actuary makes an assumption that is used then to value the size of the promise. In a simplified case, an actuary may assume that everyone begins their benefit at age 65 and will live for 15 years. As you can imagine, with the complexity in DB plans, the actuaries make multiple decisions on all the various contingencies in order to come up with a best estimate of the value of the liability.

After this stage, the actuary goes through a budgeting process where the liability is assigned to either the past (accrued benefits), present (this year's benefit accruals), or future (future years) (see Figure 5.1).

After this budgeting assignment, the actuary goes through the mechanical process to comply with either accounting or the ERISA contribution rules in order to determine the ultimate numbers the client needs.

Since no one can predict the future perfectly, the actuary's assumptions will not match up with reality. However, the actuary monitors these errors, makes adjustments and repeats the process. When it works properly, the actuarial process is self-correcting.

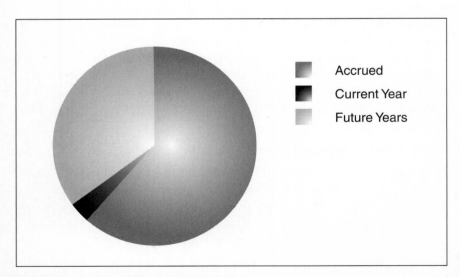

Accrued

Current Year

Future Years

FIGURE 5.1   Actuarial budgeting

WHERE CAN MANAGERS IMPACT THE ACTUARIAL PROCESS?

Many managers responsible for DB plans will admit that they do not really understand what their actuary does. Traditionally, actuarial valuations were a black box—information went in and then numbers came out. It was if the plan sponsor was caught in *The Wizard of Oz*—with the Wizard behind the curtain. Recently, however, with the advent of sophisticated modeling software, actuaries are now able to peel back the curtain and give their clients better information (especially graphically), which allows the plan sponsor to make better informed decisions (see the forecasting box).

In general, plan sponsors can impact the actuarial process with regard to timing of expense, like the old adage, "You can pay me now, or you can pay me later." Decisions are made during the actuarial process in areas like assumption setting and methods selected, which can impact when the company will recognize the expense. For simplicity sake, let's discuss two extremes:

- *Conservative.* Setting assumptions and methods that will produce higher contribution and expense amounts. This will enable the trust assets to grow faster, and increase the funded status of the plan and security of participants. If continued for an extended period of time, conservative methods and assumptions will produce a plan that is "fully funded" from a tax standpoint and unable to make tax-deductible contributions. Examples:
  - Assumptions—Low discount rate (time value of money produces higher liability), lower mortality rate (people live longer), lower termination rates (people work longer and earn larger benefits), etc.
  - Methods—No asset smoothing (subject the plan to market fluctuations), no smoothing of actuarial errors (no smoothing of errors in future).

- *Aggressive.* Just the converse of conservative—setting assumptions and methods that will produce lower contribution and expense amounts. By setting aggressive assumptions, the plan sponsor is hoping that investment returns and other assumptions will help them meet future cash contribution requirements. If continued for an extended period of time, aggressive methods and assumptions may produce a plan that is continually underfunded. Examples:
  - Assumptions—High discount rate (time value of money produces lower liability), higher mortality rate (people live shorter lives), higher termination rates (people work less and earn less benefits), etc.

- Methods—Five-year asset smoothing (push gains/losses into future years).

We would encourage you to have an in-depth discussion with your actuary and push back on any and all assumptions contained in the valuation report. The key assumptions for your plan will vary, but in general, the following list provides a starting point for your focus.

The top five actuarial assumptions are:

1. Discount and return on asset assumption
2. Salary scale—pay-related plans only
3. Mortality table
4. Optional benefit form—especially if lump sums available
5. Retirement rates

At a minimum, we recommend that you ask for an assumption review every five years. This will provide you with a realistic comparison between what you assume and what actually happened.

HOW TO KNOW WHERE YOU'RE HEADING: FORECASTING DONE RIGHT

It's that time of year again. You're in charge of your company's DB plan. You have just finished with your auditors to finalize the year-end financials. Now, all the chief financial officer (CFO) wants to know is—how do we look for the rest of this year? And the next?

So you need a forecast. But before you get your plan's actuary on the telephone, step back to review our forecasting checklist. It will save you both time and money.

Purpose

The first step is to think about the purpose of your forecast. With today's computer systems, it is not a lack of information that is the constraint, but having the time and focus for analysis and decisions. Giving your actuary a focus will serve you by focusing his or her efforts and energy. Also, it will serve you when speaking with your CFO—better to explain one graph and have her make a decision than explain 10 graphs, leaving her more confused than at the start.

For public companies, pension expense (or what actually shows up in the financial statements) is of primary concern. Actual cash contributions are typically of less importance. Private companies, on the other hand, regard cash contributions as much more important and relevant than pension expense. For companies that are thinking about terminating or freezing their plan, knowing the funded status of the plan is critical. Or maybe your investment manager is evaluating a change in asset allocation by shifting more money to fixed-income securities.

CASE STUDY

A $20 million pension plan of a public company was very well funded. However, the recent downturn threatened to erase the surplus and possibly require cash contributions for the first time in over a decade. By doing a forecast, the controller was able to quantify the date and level of the expected first cash contribution to help the CFO do a capital spending budget.

Time Horizon

Probably the next important thing to consider is time horizon. This will relate directly back to your purpose, but in general, we would recommend a 10-year time horizon for a forecast of an ongoing DB plan for a healthy company. This is recommended for several reasons including:

- Five years or less would be too short and highlight only tactical, short-term solutions rather than strategic.
- Longer than 10 years is too long since the compound effect of all assumptions over time reduces the confidence level of any decision.
- Between 5 and 10 years, you can readily see how decisions made today will affect results while at the same time being able to evaluate longer-term effects on a strategic basis.

CASE STUDY

Here's an example of when a short time horizon is appropriate. This company has a frozen plan that is currently underfunded and wanted to come up with an asset allocation strategy that would protect its downside risk while waiting for economic conditions to change and enable them to terminate the plan. Forecasting the plan over a five-year period provided sufficient time to evaluate different asset allocations as well as different contribution patterns.

(continues)

(continued)

Investment Portfolio

Make sure your actuary knows exactly how your DB plan portfolio is currently invested. Many investment managers will have made significant changes in the preceding, year so your actuary's information may be old. Also, future investment expectations have changed a lot lately, so be sure your actuary gets in touch with your investment manager to confirm any investment-related assumptions.

CASE STUDY

An investment manager was recommending adding hedge funds to a DB plan portfolio. Uncertain as to how this nontraditional investment would interact with others within the portfolio, the plan sponsor looked at the results of a 10-year forecast. It showed the impact both in terms of projected returns and volatility as well as on funded status and expected pension expense. With this information, the plan sponsor could make a more informed decision as to whether to add hedge funds or not.

Contribution Level

If you know how much your company has budgeted for cash contributions in the next year, by all means tell your actuary. This will be useful information that he or she can put into a forecast. But don't worry if you don't actually have a figure: your actuary will make a reasonable assumption.

CASE STUDY

A DB plan was recently hit by a large increase in cash contributions. The company was in a cash surplus position, so it wanted to model the effects of making an additional contribution over and above that required by law. Performing a 10-year forecast provided the needed analysis to make an informed decision.*

---

*From Daniel Cassidy, "How to Know Where You're Heading: Forecasting Done Right," *Employee Benefit Plan Review* (November 2004), 16.

Investment

We spent some time talking about the fiduciary issues—especially investments—in Chapter 4. Here we want to focus on the financial impact of the investment decisions made in the context of a DB plan. Clearly, the investment decisions made by the fiduciaries of a DB plan will impact the overall cost of the plan, since the plan sponsor bears all the investment risk. If a shortfall develops, the employer must make it up, and vice versa, if a surplus develops, the employer can reduce their contributions.

INVESTMENT PROCESS

It would be impossible to describe all the various ways that plan sponsors have deployed the assets in DB plans. However, it is possible to discuss the steps that all plan sponsors should take as they make investment decisions. Making investment decisions is just like other management decisions: planning, execution, and feedback.

PLANNING

Step 1. Analyze Objectives and Constraints. During this phase, you should collect information about your plan. Anything that will have an impact on the plan's ability to satisfy benefit payments needs to be examined. Information collected should include funded status, liquidity requirements, cash flow needs, forecasted contribution amounts, and average age of active and retiree participants.

All of these data will have impact on the overall objectives and constraints placed on the plan's investments. For example:

- *Time horizon.* Is there any indication that the plan will be terminated in the near future? Medium-term future? If not, most plans invest for the long haul.

- *Return goals.* Many plan sponsors look at various return goals, such as
  - Absolute—Tied to assumptions using in liability measurement and actuarial valuations.
  - Relative—Tied to an index such as inflation, indices such as a balanced 50 percent equity and 50 percent fixed-income index. Some new trends are looking at using liability-weighted trends.
  - Funded status—Maintaining or improving the funded status of the plan.

- *Risk tolerance.* The other side of the return equation is the risk the plan is willing to bear. As more risk is introduced, the expected return rises. As some point, the trade-off of more return is offset by an unacceptable level of risk. Now plan sponsors are taking a broader view of risk and looking beyond the plan itself to the entire corporation (see Boots' box). However, this expansive viewpoint, while gaining adherents, is not currently being applied throughout the pension world.

- *Constraints.* Anything that will limit the universe of investable assets should be discussed and agreed to. These typically include

- Liquidity—Where the plan must keep a certain percentage of assets in cash to pay benefits.
- Marketability—Some plans only want to invest in assets that are highly marketable. Less transferable, long-term assets such as some private equity issues would not meet this marketability test since sale of the asset would have a dramatic effect on its value.
- Allowable securities—Some plans want to limit investment to a select list of securities. This type of constraint has its roots in historic trust law when states would issue approved lists of securities. Typically constraints here would include derivatives, uncovered calls, private placements, and sin stocks (tobacco, alcohol, firearms). For some larger DB plans, use of derivatives has increased dramatically as has the use of nontraditional assets like private placements. Since derivatives are critical to most risk-based investment solutions and reduce risk as opposed to increase risk, we believe that they will become "allowable securities" in many more DB plans.

Step 2. Select Appropriate Asset Allocation. Coming out of step 1, you will have a better picture of where you want to go with the plan's assets. The first, and most important, step is to decide on an appropriate asset allocation given your situation. Most DB plans have recently invested in 60 percent equity and 40 percent fixed income. Mercer's recent survey of Standard & Poor's 500 companies ("How Does Your Retirement Program Stack Up?—2005") confirmed this average asset allocation; in fact, equity exposure was slightly higher at 65 percent equity, 30 percent fixed income, and 5 percent other (including real estate).

Most plan sponsors typically work with their investment consultant and/or actuary to decide on the appropriate asset allocation. In practice, as you can see in the sample investment policy, the plan sponsor typically agrees to a target allocation for each major asset class. In addition, the plan sponsor also provides an upper and lower limit for each asset class. This allows the investment adviser room to make tactical changes in asset allocation without going to the plan sponsor for further permission. We typically assist our clients in forecasting the impact of their asset allocation decisions, and show the impact on funded status, pension expense, and any other variable critical to our client.

Step 3. Develop an Investment Policy Statement (IPS). After all the hard work in the first two steps, now it is time to document the decisions in an IPS. See Appendix C for a sample IPS for a DB plan. As discussed in the previous chapter, ERISA calls for a "funding" policy, but in fact, this "funding" policy is what is normally called an investment policy statement. Besides documenting your decisions in steps 1 and 2, we suggest that you also:

- Identify all parties involved.
- Specify delegation of duty.
- Specify performance criteria including when you would terminate an investment manager.
- Require the investment manager's signature that he or she has read, understands, and agrees to follow the IPS.

EXECUTION

The plan sponsor has done the hard work now and needs to execute its plan. In practice, how plan sponsors do this is very individualistic—no two sponsors are exactly alike—and the choices are overwhelming. We would like to spend time on two major trends: one that is here right now (total retirement outsourcing) and one that we see significant client interest in (reducing interest rate risk).

Total Retirement Outsourcing (TRO) with Manager-of-Manager Model. This trend, focused primarily on mid-sized employers with DB plans in the $10 million to $100 million range, is propelled by financial services firms' technology investments. After 20 years of investing in their technology to manage 401(k) plans, the financial services firms then shifted over to manage all aspects of DB plans—administration, investment, and actuarial. In the past five years, several providers such as NY Life, Diversified Investment Advisors, MassMutual, Fidelity, T. Rowe Price, and others have aggressively expanded into this space. The advantages to a plan sponsor are tremendous, especially if the provider also manages your company's 401(k) plan.

But like a lot of "new" trends, this is actually an old idea. Before ERISA, insurance companies dominated the DB plan marketplace. They provided everything for the plan sponsor, from actuarial, administrative, and legal services. The investments were typically very conservative fixed-income investments geared toward securing the annuities of the retirees.

This new TRO trend comes at a time when the investment choices underlying the offering are more open and provide the plan sponsor with substantial choice. Many of these TRO providers offer a "manager-of-manager" model that many mid-market clients find appealing. In this model, the plan sponsor hires a single financial services firm—let's call it the quarterback firm. This quarterback firm has preselected a host of other fund managers that it offers to clients. The quarterback firms' offering to the client is that it provides a best-in-class offering in each major asset class. So, instead of going out to hire eight different managers, you hire the single quarterback firm who has already done the work in hiring the best managers. Hence, the term *manager-of-manager*. The quarterback firm hires and fires the underlying managers without the plan sponsor's intervention. Several advantages are offered by these models:

- Quarterback firm serves as a fiduciary on your committee.

- By combining assets of all their clients, the quarterback firm gets access to money managers that the normal mid-sized plan sponsor would not be able to do or have the time to invest in.

- Cost sharing. By leveraging the assets of the DB plan, the quarterback firm provides other services like administration, Web access, and actuarial services, so the total cost of administration typically goes down.

- One contact person. Instead of working with separate firms—actuaries, administrators, investment manager, and trust—you have one contact person for all questions. Very appealing.

Disadvantages of the manager-of-manager model include:

- *Cost.* Depending on how efficient you currently are, you may not realize substantial cost savings. In fact, you may see cost increases because the manager-of-manager model basically adds another layer of investment fees on top of the underlying investment manager's expenses.

- *Difficulty in performance measurement.* When analyzing the performance of a manager-of-manager provider, plan sponsors need to take an additional step when compared to evaluating say a single manager, like a small cap equity manager. This additional step is trying to analyze the effectiveness of the quarterback—how successful are they in hiring and firing managers? On one hand, when you see a quarterback firing a manager, that is bad—that means that the manager did not perform well. On the other hand, the firing may be for reasons unrelated to performance, like staff turnover or style drift or capacity issues. During your due diligence, you need to try to separate the effectiveness of the quarterback from the effectiveness of the underlying fund options.

- *Bundling everything together.* All eggs in one basket issue. If you do not have good investment performance, but like the administration services, plan fiduciaries may be presented with a very difficult decision.

- *Sophistication.* Many of the investment products offered in the manager-of-manager model are not the cutting edge products that would be available à la carte.

- *Conflict of interest.* Some clients appreciate the independence of actuaries and investment managers and hesitate to bundle these services. In recognition of this, many manager-of-manager models allow plan sponsors to maintain their actuary.

Reducing Interest Rate Risk. The 60 percent equity/40 percent fixed-income asset allocation does not show any signs of changing. However, many plan sponsors are looking at the 40 percent fixed-income exposure and wondering if there might be a better way to manage that side alone.

Most of the problems today that you see in the media (airlines going bankrupt with underfunded plans) came about because of a mismatch in the duration of the liabilities and the assets. Duration is a measure used by investment managers to quantify the impact of changes in interest rates on the value of an investment—typically a bond portfolio. Basically, it is a measure of interest rate sensitivity. Bonds with longer duration are more sensitive to swings in interest rates than shorter durations and vice versa. Liabilities, like pension plans, have a duration too. By using the projected benefit payments paid out of the plan, one can calculate an equivalent measure of duration as the one used in fixed-income investing. The vast majority of the fixed-income portfolios of DB plans use the Lehman Brothers Aggregate (LB Agg) Index as a benchmark. LB Agg is a broad market index of fixed-income vehicles issued by government, corporate, asset-backed, and other organizations. Currently, the duration of the LB Agg is around four years.

Compare this with the duration of most mature DB plans (typically 10 to 15 years) and you can see the problem. Over the past several years, as interest rates have declined, the value of the fixed-income portion of the DB plan portfolio has decreased some, but the liabilities with their longer duration have increased substantially more.

Many clients, although hesitant to reduce their equity allocation, are seriously looking at ways to extend the duration of their fixed-income portfolio. Some initial steps like investing in longer-term fixed-income products pegged at the Lehman Brothers Long Government and Long Credit will get plan sponsors in the right direction. However, limitations exist, since these initial steps probably will only get the portfolio to a 10-year duration. For those plans that want to match the duration of your DB plan's liabilities, other options are available and we are seeing more and more plan sponsors exploring them. Some of these options may be more appropriate for larger plans and include using futures, swaps, and zero coupon bonds to extend the duration nearer to the plan's duration.

Even though now may not be the best tactical time to extend the duration of the plan's portfolio given the low interest rate environment, we are seeing clients seriously considering this now for possible implementation.

Feedback. Regardless of how you deploy the plan's assets, you need to perform periodic reviews of performance. The road map for your review should be your IPS. Benchmarks, criteria, and other performance-related items should be identified in the IPS. As mentioned in Chapter 4, plan sponsors can choose their own schedule for review commensurate with their needs. Our recommendation is to review performance no less frequent than annually, with twice a year our recommended standard. More frequent reviews would be called for if problem issues are identified, a new manager is hired, funds have been placed on a watch list, the economy or financial markets are struggling, or your company is experiencing internal issues.

The issue of when to fire an investment manager is difficult, but must be addressed in a professional manner. Typical criteria for firing investment managers include significant underperformance over a market cycle (typically thought of as no less than three years), change in investment personnel, nonadherence to investment policy such as investing in nonapproved asset classes among others. We recommend a system of putting a manager on watch when any of these issues come up, and then more diligent review to determine the next course of action. Sometimes, after a manager is on watch, the issue resolves on its own. Other times, it does not, and then the plan sponsor should terminate the investment manager.

IS THE 60 PERCENT/40 PERCENT ASSET ALLOCATION DEAD?

News flash! During 2000 and 2001, Boots, a U.K. pharmaceutical company, sold all of the equities within its pension plan and invested in bonds. This was hailed as the beginning of a new trend that would affect pension plans in both the United Kingdom and the United States. Many experts thought that pension plans would change their asset allocation from the traditional mix of 60 percent equities and 40 percent fixed income, but guess what happened next?

Nothing. Even Boots, in its most recent annual report (2005), showed a 10 percent allocation to equities.

Boots' drastic change in investment strategy was a fantastic exercise in application of enterprise risk management (ERM). In fact, Harvard Business School is drafting a case study for its students. Now, with four years passed, let's examine Boots' decision within the current environment, including why companies should review their asset allocation from a risk management perspective and offer insights on why companies—even given the strong evidence—are still not prepared to go all the way to bonds.

Background

Boots cited three advantages to moving 100 percent into bonds in its Boots Pension Scheme Trustees Review 2001:

1. *Increases security for participants.* Matching pension assets and liabilities increases security since any change in value of the liabilities is matched by an approximately equal change in assets.
2. *Reduces investment management fees.* Boots used active management for its equities at a cost of 50 basis points. By moving to 100 percent bonds with a "buy-and-hold" strategy, it reduced its investment management fees by over 95 percent.
3. *Reduces Boots' financial risk.* Again, matching the assets and liabilities reduces the risk to Boots' shareholders of having to make up any future deficit.

Other issues that put the Boots decision into context include (1) pension plan benefits in the United Kingdom are typically linked to inflation (as opposed to U.S. DB plans, where the benefits are fixed once you retire); (2) Equitable, a very large insurance company, was failing in the United Kingdom; and (3) the stock market had just passed its peak and had dropped 25 percent when Boots began its shift to bonds.

Enterprise Risk Management Lessons in the Boots Case

Regardless of whether you agree with Boots' decision or not, from an ERM standpoint we can only applaud its process. That is because the firm followed the classic steps of ERM:

1. *Identify risk.* What are the risks present in a DB plan?
2. *Quantify risk.* How big are the risks? Always focus on the largest risk first.
3. *Separate risk.* What risks do we want to bear? What risks can we transfer to the marketplace?
4. *Manage risk.* After implementation, continue to monitor the situation and make changes as needed.

(continues)

(continued)

General Risk Management Framework for Pensions

Moving away from the specifics of the Boots example, let's now focus on the general framework that pension plan sponsors need to follow when deciding on an appropriate asset allocation for their plan.

Identify the Stakeholders

Pension plans have many stakeholders, such as participants, management, and shareholders, among others. The risks associated with a plan affect each party differently. A simplified example will highlight how different stakeholders have different risk profiles. Assuming a $1,000 benefit to be available 10 years from now, notice these differences in Table 5.2.

In addition to participants and shareholders, other stakeholders include:

- *Government/society.* Our society, through our elected officials and government agencies, has as its goal the commitment to see that pension plans are fully funded while also providing appropriate incentive (tax deductions) for the greater good.
- *Management.* Management's two goals of maximizing its own compensation while enjoying continued employment may be at odds with shareholders' interests. This conflict, called an "agency problem," arises out of the fact that the typical U.S. corporation is owned by a

Table 5.2 Funding Asset Allocations and Associated Risks

Funding/Asset Allocation	Budgeted Capital	Risk to Participant	Risk to Shareholder
Pay as you go	$0	Will the company be around to pay benefits?	Future shareholders must pay benefits.
Balanced (60/40) asset	$450	Will the company be able to make up any shortfall?	Possible shortfall must be met by future shareholders. Possible surplus will be enjoyed by future shareholders.
Immunized bond portfolio	$600	Very small	Larger up-front contribution and minimal possibility of surplus.

large group of shareholders, with no single dominant owner. Also, one needs to clarify how various levels of management view risk and communicate the issues at the appropriate level (see Table 5.3).

Identify Risk

After identifying the stakeholders, pension plan managers should next identify the particular risks they are facing. Today, in the United States, the pension risk includes:

- *Political/regulatory risks.* With the PBGC's deficit skyrocketing in the past several years (including taking over the recent United Airlines pension plans), the PBGC premiums that all plan sponsors pay to participate in the program will be increasing. It is only a matter of how high and how fast. In fact, most pension professionals believe that the PBGC cannot exist long term as currently organized because of flaws that violate the basic tenets of any insurance market.
- *Risk-based premiums.* Premiums charged do not properly reflect the risk being transferred to the PBGC. Since the PBGC cannot change its premium structure without Congress, it has been unable to charge a true risk-based premium, i.e., charge more for plans with higher probability of a claim on the PBGC. This would be analogous to the government telling all car insurers to charge one rate to both good and bad drivers.
- *Moral hazard.* This is an insurance term to describe the situation where insurers can manipulate their insurance coverage (i.e., claims) to their own advantage. In the PBGC context, this moral hazard occurs when plan sponsors adopt expensive plan amendments knowing full well that if the economy does great, they will have money to pay for these amendments. However, if the economy does poorly, the PBGC will guarantee these benefits. This moral hazard is very apparent in the recent airline industry bankruptcies.

Table 5.3   Management Perspective and Roles Which Typically Occupy That Perspective

Perspective	Role
Control	Functional leaders (human resources, treasury, controller)
Efficiency and stability	Chief financial officer
Growth and opportunity	Chief executive officer

(continues)

(continued)

- *Accounting risk.* The FASB has indicated that it will be adopting new pension accounting rules that will mark-to-market both assets and liabilities. This will be a continuation of the general trend of convergence of accounting standards across the globe.
- *Cash contribution/deficits.* Many plan sponsors, for example, private companies, may not be as concerned about accounting risk. However, they may be very concerned about any cash contribution requirements due to large deficits.
- *Surplus risk.* Under current tax rules, if a pension plan develops a surplus (i.e., assets in excess of liabilities), the company cannot pull the money out of the trust. If the company does so, it will pay a combined tax rate approaching 90 percent (income plus an excise tax). With such a draconian tax, an unintended consequence has been for companies to not fully fund their plans. In essence, their employees then have a free call on the assets of the pension plan: If the assets do well, employees will benefit because the employer cannot get the assets out and will most likely increase benefits. If the assets do poorly, the company will have to contribute more. Such "free" calls due to regulatory influence increase the overall cost of running pension plans.
- *Mortality and other demographic risk.* What are the risks associated with our employees' demographics? Are they living longer? Do other risks like health insurance impact the cost of pension plans?

Quantify Risk

Now comes the harder part of identifying stakeholders and risk—how to quantify each of these risks for all parties involved. For most, if not all, of these risks, you may want to employ several different methods of estimation, including:

- *Best guess.* Just use a best guess estimate of the risk, nothing more than scratching down your ideas.
- *Ignore.* You may decide that the risk is there but that it is so small it is not worth the time it takes to estimate the value. Be careful before you place a risk in this category, because a risk you face now may appear small, but could grow more significant in the future.
- *Scenario testing.* Using various scenarios (e.g., high inflation and high investment returns versus low inflation and low investment), estimate the risks. This is sometimes called deterministic forecasting since you "determine" the assumptions/scenarios ahead of time.
- *Stochastic forecast.* A more sophisticated way for you to estimate the value of risk is by performing a stochastic forecast. Here, you quan-

tify the risk using random variables and provide answers like "We have a 60 percent chance of a $1 million contribution within three years."

Risk Separation and Manager Risk

Now, after all this work, you come to the point of having to make a decision about what risk you want to bear and what you want to pass off onto others. Some of the risks—political, accounting, and so forth—cannot be passed off onto others at all. However, some of the other risks faced by pension plans can be passed to others. In your decision-making process, you should evaluate this alternative.

In support of this evaluation is a key tenet of risk management derived from modern portfolio theory that says you only get "paid" for bearing nondiversifiable risk. In other words, if an efficient market exists for a particular risk, a company would be better off to pass the risk on to this efficient market, and only keep those risks that are nondiversifiable and that they can manage to produce a superior profit.

During this stage of risk separation, do not forget to look at the impact on various stakeholders. For example, a common exercise—especially given the recent investment returns—is for plan sponsors to focus on the investment risk in their retirement plans. The first question is, "Who should bear this risk?" In a DB plan, this risk resides with the plan sponsor. With a defined contribution (DC) plan, this risk is transferred to the participant. Moving beyond this first-order question, you should then ask, "Who is best able to bear this risk? Both now and in the future?" Research has shown that when employees make direct investments in a DC plan, they typically perform less well than professional investment managers. This risk shifting becomes asymmetric: It reduces the employers' risk while increasing the employees' risk, but by a much larger amount. Remember to look beyond one single viewpoint to include all stakeholders.

Asset Allocation Question

Combining all this and getting back to the original question—Is the 60/40 asset allocation a dinosaur?—my opinion is that the jury is still out in the near term. In the long term, however, I believe we will see the allocation move to 20 percent equity and 80 percent fixed income for the following reasons:

- *Tax arbitrage.* With current tax rates, holding equities within the pension plan does not optimize corporate capital structure. UBS, in a recent investment research paper, estimated that for every $1 of equities

(continues)

(continued)

sold in a pension plan, a company could produce approximately $0.10 in present value of tax savings by issuing more corporate debt.

- *Accounting change.* Very soon, the FASB will move to a mark-to-market pension accounting that will highlight the true cost of holding equities within a pension plan. As an analogy, consider the current reserving methods for insurance companies, imagining a pension plan as a small insurance company. If an insurance company holds equities, then they must hold higher reserves due to the volatility of the equities (and vice versa, if they hold more bonds, they have a lower reserve requirement). Applied to pension accounting rules, this would mean that if a plan sponsor decided to hold equities, they would, first, record a higher "reserve" (i.e., liability), and second, show a higher expense and therefore lower earnings.

- *Appropriate risk bearing . . . or "de-risking the pension plan."* Our current accounting methods encourage inappropriate risk bearing that eventually the market will eliminate. Consider this example—an investment in shares of General Motors. Are you really making a bet that GM will build better cars than Ford or Toyota or are you betting that GM's pension committee manages its enormous pension plan better than others? It is just like the key tenet of modern portfolio theory that says you are only compensated for bearing nondiversifiable risk. Companies are in business (i.e., they are not diversified), so you should expect a payment for investing in them. Since much, if not most, of the risk of the pension plan can be diversified away, the market says you should not be compensated for these. Plan sponsors should "de-risk" their plans, and take risks where the market will compensate them—in their core business.

- *Frozen defined benefit plans.* Recent studies have documented the trend toward freezing DB plans and replacing them with DC plans. A 2005 study by Watson Wyatt of the Fortune 1000 showed that over 10 percent had frozen their DB plans. All the arguments above apply doubly so for frozen plans.

With all these good reasons, why haven't other companies followed Boots' example? Some industry experts have commented that many CFOs would move to more bonds, but have not done so because they do not want to be "penalized" for being a first mover. Also, companies are moving slowly in this direction with small incremental shifts to fixed-income securities. Studies of asset allocation of companies have shown small (less than 5 percent swings). The recent trend to freezing pension plans is an attempt to reduce employers' risk and slow the bleeding; however, most frozen plans have kept their asset allocation steady.

Ultimately, the catalyst for change will either be from the regulators (FASB changing their accounting rules) or interest rates rising high enough that plan sponsors can terminate their plans with minimal cash contributions.*

---

*From Daniel Cassidy, "Is the 60/40 percent asset dead? . . . Equities in DB plans: Is the traditional 60/40 mix a dinosaur?" *Employee Benefit Plan Review,* September 2005, pp. 30–33.

Defined Contribution Concerns

Since participants bear the investment risk, DC plans must focus their financial governance work on investments. The actuarial and funding tools are not available in the DC environment; however, plan design options are important and will be discussed in the next chapter.

Background

Today, DC plans are dominated by 401(k) plans. These are a type of profit sharing plan that allows employees to save on a tax-deferred basis. With the responsibility for retirement income shared between employee and employer as well as the technology advancement in the financial services firm, 401(k) plans now universally offer participants the right to choose their investments from a line-up of investment options. The investment options are initially selected by the fiduciaries, and then the participants choose which ones they want for their individual accounts. We discussed some of the fiduciary issues in the prior chapter. Now we want to focus on the performance evaluation itself.

Investment Policy Statement

Just like DB plan investment management, it is prudent for clients to adopt an IPS for their DC plans. While most professionals recommend this step, surveys often show that only 70 to 80 percent of plan sponsors have adopted an IPS. A DC plan's IPS is similar to a DB plan's IPS in several ways, but different in many others.

In general, a DC plan IPS can be compared to a DB plan IPS as follows:

- Similar
  - Fund selection and monitoring process
  - Identification of fiduciaries, parties, advisers

- Difference
  - Role of employees in investment choice
  - Desire of fiduciaries to limit their liability for poor participant choices using 404(c)compliance (see next box)
  - Investment education resources

Typically, your 401(k) provider may supply you with a sample IPS for your adoption. We recommend that you independently draft your own IPS since many of these provider IPS's are generally lacking in clarity on the fund monitoring/manager firing area.

Investment Performance Review

We help many clients perform investment performance reviews on their 401(k) plans every year. We have provided a sample report in Appendix E for your review.

In general, our reviews help our clients assess their overall plan performance, including:

- Aggregate impact of all participants' elections
- Individual performance of fund options
- Fees and expenses paid out of plan assets
- Risk and return profile of fund options

We work to communicate our information in graphic format as well as using multiple methods to illustrate similar points. We find our clients, many of whom are human resource professionals with limited investment background, can more easily assimilate material in a graph, rather than a table of numbers.

Some common issues we see in 401(k) plans become apparent when we perform our analysis in Appendix D:

- Overlap of risk/return profile of fund options
  - *Symptom.* If we see multiple funds in one asset class (in bar graphs on page 8 or overlapping plots on pages 12 and 15), we look for reasons why. The most common reason is that the funds are very similar. This often happens in asset classes like large growth.
  - *Cure.* Drop one of the funds and merge assets into the remaining option.
- Skewing of investment elections due to communication material
  - *Symptom.* If we see that one fund has over 15 percent of assets, we question why. Sometimes we find that communication material developed by the provider highlighted this fund as a good option.

The other most common reason offered by providers is that it is due to transition from the prior provider. Sometimes, when funds are mapped over, one fund may get a very large percentage of assets. And since participants do not often change their investment elections, these assets are "sticky" and have not moved to other options.

- *Cure.* Review communication material. Reinvigorate education outreach. Target those participants with balances in that fund or with one single option.

■ High-Risk Fund Option

- *Symptom.* Fund's investment return is competitive, but when you review its risk profile, you find that it took more risk than its peer to get its return. These funds show up in the upper right-hand quadrant of pages 12 and 13.
- *Cure.* Monitor these funds closely. Risk-taking funds may have substantial swings in performance that could quickly deteriorate. Perhaps select a fund in the "best" risk/return trade-off quadrant of pages 12 and 13 (those funds in the upper left), which have lower risk than peers but higher return than peers.

■ High Stock Overlap

- *Symptom.* Related to the overlap of risk/return profile of fund options, this one is typically an issue when your 401(k) has multiple fund options from one fund family. Often you find high overlap in actual stock holding in the various fund options (see page 22).
- *Cure.* Monitor closely and perhaps diversify fund options across fund families.

Closing a Fund Option

Many DC plan sponsors, after having completed an investment performance review, find that one of the fund options is performing badly. Fiduciaries, by nature wanting to act prudently and cautiously, are then faced with the question—Do we shut down this option and switch over to another fund? How will the participants react to the switch?

Some options that plan sponsors take in these instances include:

■ Complete shut down

- Result—Shutting down fund, moving assets to new fund, mapping elections to new fund.
- Advantages—Clean break from past, participants can see fiduciaries taking active measures to monitor plan performance, easy to communicate.

404(C) COMPLIANCE

404(c) compliance, although worthwhile to strive for, is difficult to obtain in practice. To be truly compliant with 404(c) takes many steps. In general, these steps can be broken down into three main categories:

1. *Overall investment selection.* The plan sponsor must provide at least three investment options that vary in their risk return characteristics. Participants must be able to diversify their portfolio to minimize their risk of loss. Even though the plan seeks 404(c) compliance, the fiduciaries are still on the hook for the selection of the funds themselves. 404(c) compliance, in reality, only protects fiduciaries from possible poor choices made by participants.
2. *Participant control commensurate with risk.* Participants must be able to make investment elections commensurate with the riskiness of the investment, but in no case less than quarterly. Most plans with daily valuations comply with this requirement.
3. *Information.* Probably the most difficult area in which to get true 404(c) compliance is the area of required information. A long laundry list of information (prospectuses, asset list, fees and expenses, etc.) is required to be furnished to participants—some automatically and some at their request. Your plan provider is typically the one responsible for making sure this information gets in the hands of participants. You would be well advised to periodically audit compliance with this requirement.

- Disadvantages—Possible negative participant reaction from forced liquidation. "We rode it down, so let us ride it up. By shutting us off, you're forcing us to sell low."
- Freeze with new alternative in same asset class
  - Result—Shutting down fund to new salary deferrals so no new money can go into the fund. Current investor can stay in the fund or elect to invest more assets in other options. New salary deferrals are mapped to new fund offering from same asset class.
  - Advantages—Recognizes concerns about forced liquidation, gives participants choice to move out into alternative.
  - Disadvantage—Gives mixed fiduciary message: fund is not good enough for new money but okay for old money, more complex message to communicate.

- Communicate watch list status
  - Result—Communicate to participants that the fiduciaries are concerned about the performance of the fund and may take further action in near future.
  - Advantages—Up front with participants shows fiduciaries are monitoring plan offerings, gives participants time to make changes if so desired.
  - Disadvantages—May cause undue concern in participants, still does not "solve" problem.

Each situation will be different, but the above are options that you should consider as you make your decision. Additional factors to consider include the size of the assets in the fund, number of participants affected, current alternative fund offerings, and time since last fund changes, among others. Overall, the key thing for fiduciaries in these situations is to document your process, the information you reviewed, and the reasons for any decisions. ERISA is focused more on process than on results. If you maintain a good record of performance monitoring and then take action when necessary, you should be in good shape overall.

Human Resources

Our last topic in the discussion of the governance tools available to managers is the people side—the human resources impact of retirement plan management. In large part, this chapter will focus on the decisions companies make in designing retirement plans. In addition, we will explain participant issues and how to deal with the risks associated with retirement.

Even though we are covering this topic as the last governance tool, in fact, we should have more properly covered this first. Since all the rest of the tools—funding, investment, actuarial, and administration—are all derivative, they assume that a plan exists. In fact, this chapter should have been the first one. Why did we put this last?

We have placed this chapter last because most of you already have an existing program in place. The plan design has been set in stone for 10, 20, even 30 years in some cases. The other tools—like investments—can be deployed with little, if any, formal approval process and/or communication to employees. Plan design changes, however, require substantial employee communication and board approval.

Most plan sponsors look at plan design changes as a generational change, that is, they'll only look at making changes every 10 to 20 years. (Ignore for the moment hourly pension plans that typically index a flat dollar amount and therefore have frequent, perhaps annual, plan design changes. But even with these plans, substantial changes to formula are rare.) For many of the other tools, decisions made there are usually on the order of magnitude of every three to five years.

Human Resources Issues

Why do companies even have a retirement plan? That's the question many chief financial officers and vice presidents of human resources (HR) ask themselves—especially after another "routine" Department of Labor audit. The simple reason is to attract and retain a workforce for the employer. (We discussed the history of retirement plans in Chapters 1 and 2). During the attraction phase, employers must compete with one another for skilled labor. Employers still must provide competitive benefits in order to keep their employees—or risk losing the valuable training and development investment that they have made in the workers..

Economists would look at any retirement program as simply a vehicle for deferring compensation—taking lower pay now in lieu of higher pay/pension later. And employees would be able to evaluate two competing offers such as:

- Offer A—Salary of $50,000 plus profit sharing plan contribution of $5,000
- Offer B—Salary of $45,000 plus defined benefit plan accrual of $10,000

However, no two jobs are ever exactly alike, and most workers are not able to evaluate differences in indirect pay (and employers do not make it easy). However, even with these limitations, retirement plans do impact workers' choices, both in selecting which employer to work for as well as whether to stay employed. In fact, many times retirement plans promote unwanted results—the law of unintended consequences.

Adequacy

The first step in designing any retirement program is to focus on the ultimate goal—providing sufficient retirement income for your employees after they leave employment. This goal, though stated simply in one sentence, will need to be modified and customized to each particular employer. Open questions pertain to:

- *Sufficient retirement income.* What does this mean? What sources of income should be used? The universal three-legged stool of social security, private savings, and employer-sponsored plans comes to mind. See the ensuing box for more information about replacement income analysis.
- *Employees.* Is it employees or employees and spouses? What about other demographic trends like same-sex marriages, second/third families, and elder care and long-term care needs?

- *Employment.* What is employment? Full time for 30 years? Or does the employer only want employees for 5 to 10 years and then have them move on? What about phased retirement issues?

By working through how you feel about each of these questions, you will get a better idea about your ultimate target. This is a critical first step whether you are designing a plan from scratch or looking to amend an existing plan. With changes to all parts of the adequacy question from social security changes to demographics and employment, "correct" solutions arrived at 10 or 20 years ago may not work for your company today.

REPLACEMENT INCOME ANALYSIS

A replacement ratio is a person's gross income after retirement, divided by his or her gross income before retirement. For example, assume someone earns $60,000 per year before retirement. Furthermore, assume he or she retires and receives $45,000 of Social Security and other retirement income. This person's replacement ratio is 75 percent ($45,000/ $60,000).

This study analyzes the replacement ratios employees need to maintain their preretirement standard of living after retirement. Generally, a person needs less gross income after retiring, primarily due to five factors:

1. Income taxes go down after retirement. This is because extra deductions are available for those over age 65, and taxable income usually decreases at retirement.
2. Social Security taxes (FICA deductions from wages) end completely at retirement.
3. Social Security benefits are partially or fully tax free. This reduces taxable income and, therefore, the amount of income needed to pay taxes.
4. Saving for retirement is no longer a goal.
5. Age- and work-related expenses generally decrease at retirement primarily because shelter and transportation expenses decrease. This factor outweighs an expected increase in health care costs.

Table 6.1 shows that a 75 percent replacement ratio is enough to allow an employee earning $60,000 to retire at age 65 in 2004 without reducing his or her standard of living. Because taxes, need to save, and age- and

---

(continues)

(continued)

Table 6.1 Replacement Ratio Example

	Annual Income		
	Before Retirement (1)	After Retirement (2)	Replacement Ratio (2)/(1)
Gross income	$60,000	$45,299	75%
Taxes	(11,574)	(334)	
Savings	(1,945)	0	
Age- and work-related expenditures	(34,194)	(32,678)	
Remaining income	12,287	12,287	

Source: Aon Consulting, Inc. and Georgia State University, *Replacement Ratio Study: A Measurement Tool for Retirement Planning* (Illinois: Aon Consulting, Inc, 2004), 2.

work-related expenses all decrease at retirement, this person is just as well off after retirement with a gross income of $45,299.

Appendix E is an overview of replacement ratios. In Appendix F, Appendix I describes the methodology used to determine needed replacement ratios. Appendix II shows the calculation details for our baseline cases, and Appendix III summarizes the expenditure data used for the calculations.

The primary data source for this information is the U.S. Department of Labor's Bureau of Labor Statistics' Consumer Expenditure Survey (CES). This is essentially the same database used to construct the consumer price index. The CES is done annually, and we used data from the most recent years available—1999, 2000, and 2001. CES data provided information on 9,738 "working" consumer units and 5,642 "retired" consumer units. In total, this represents approximately 80 percent more consumer units than have been available in prior years. Expenditures that are not age or work related are assumed to be the same before and after retirement.

Table 6.2 shows the 2004 study baseline case results. The baseline case assumes a family situation in which there is one wage earner who retires at age 65 with a spouse age 62. Thus, the family unit is eligible for family Social Security benefits, which are 1.362 times the wage earner's benefit. The baseline case also takes into account age- and work-related expenditure changes after retirement, in addition to preretirement savings patterns and changes in taxes after retirement.

Table 6.2   2004 Replacement Ratio Findings

Preretirement Income ($000)	Replacement Ratios		
	Social Security (%)	Private and Employer Sources (%)	Total (%)
$20	65	24	89
30	56	28	84
40	51	29	80
50	48	29	77
60	43	32	75
70	39	37	76
80	35	42	77
90	33	45	78

Source: Aon Consulting, Inc. and Georgia State University, *Replacement Ratio Study: A Measurement Tool for Retirement Planning* (Illinois: Aon Consulting, Inc, 2004), 3.

Table 6.2 illustrates three significant points about the replacement ratio calculations:

1. Social Security replaces a larger portion of preretirement income at lower wage levels. This is by design and has the effect of redistributing income from higher-paid employees to lower-paid ones.
2. Total replacement ratios are highest for the very lowest-paid employees. This is because these employees save the least and pay the least in taxes (as a percentage of income) before retirement. Thus, they spend a higher percentage of their income and need higher replacement ratios to maintain that level of expenditures.
3. After reaching an income level of $60,000, total replacement ratios begin to increase slowly. This is primarily because postretirement taxes increase as income levels increase. Postretirement taxes increase from 0.7 percent of postretirement income for a person earning $60,000 to 9.3 percent for a person earning $90,000. To pay the additional taxes, higher-paid employees need more retirement income.*

---

*From AON/Georgia State University's Replacement Ratio Study. Used with permission.

Focus: The Defined Benefit versus Defined Contribution Argument—Where Do You Want to Target Dollars?

It is in the news today, another large company froze its defined benefit (DB) plan and replaced it with a defined contribution (DC) plan— Hewlett-Packard did it in 2005, IBM in 2004. Watson Wyatt surveyed the Fortune 1000 companies and found that 116 companies have terminated or frozen their DB plans since 2001, 72 of them in the past two years. Watson Wyatt also found that among the Fortune 1000 companies that sponsor DB plans, 44 of 627 terminated or froze plans in 2004, a significant leap from the 28 of 633 that did so in 2003. Why do we hear about these significant plan changes? One, the managers at these companies are making these changes for financial reasons—they want their company's income statement to be less affected by swings in the financial market. Note that I did not say that these companies made these changes because the costs of the DB plan are too high. These managers are smart enough to realize that they will be spending on average about 5 percent of pay on retirement plans. Granted, DB plans have been costing more lately, but do not forget the 1980s and 1990s, when these plans did not have any cash contributions. So, it really is the volatility in costs rather than the absolute level that is the key financial driver behind these freeze decisions.

However, the second key reason is largely a rethinking of the goals of their retirement plans. These companies are asking questions like, "What do we want our retirement plan to do for our employees?", "What does our retirement program say about our values?", and "Who should bare the investment risk associated with retirement plans?" The answers to these questions will help both companies considering changes to their existing programs as well as starting up new plans.

Targeting Your Retirement Dollars

The primary issue of the DB versus DC debate is simply where does the employer want to target its retirement dollars. (For a moment, let's ignore the significant shift of investment risk from employer to employee.) Do you want your dollars spread evenly across the employee base or do you want to target older, longer service employees? Take a look at Table 6.3, which shows the breakdown of where the costs of the typical DB plan are targeted.

As you can see, over 90 percent of the plan costs are attributable to the over age 40 population, which only represents about 60 percent of the group. If you look at only those over age 50, the numbers are more skewed. They get about two-thirds of the dollars, but they make up less than one-third of the group in head count. This reverse age discrimination is the dirty little secret of DB plans. The vast majority of the costs are associated

Table 6.3   Operating Benefit Cost: Current Plan

Group	$ Millions	% Total Costs	% Total Population
Under age 30	0.1	1	14
30–40	0.5	6	23
40–50	2.0	26	32
50–60	4.0	51	26
60–65	1.1	14	4
Over age 65	0.2	3	1
Total	7.9	100	100

with older people, while younger people accrue very little value from the typical DB plan.

So, employers with DB plans are voting with their dollars and saying they want to target older employees and provide larger retirement dollars to them.

The plan freezes, like that of HP, are clear reactions to this skewing. HP actually allowed current employees to stay in the existing DB plan, basically freezing eligibility. For new employees, they will participate in a new DC plan. This type of generational freeze is used because of concerns about changing the "deal" with existing employees and in reaction to the significant negative reaction at other large companies who made changes to retirement plans, for example, IBM's trouble with its cash balance conversion. Ignoring these transitional issues for a moment, the HP change represents a significant change in where HP will be targeting their retirement dollars in the future. By switching to a DC plan, it says that HP will pay comparable dollars regardless of an employee's age. So, for example, a 30-year-old will get a 5 percent of pay contribution and a 60-year-old will also get a 5 percent of pay contribution. Whereas, if these same two employees were in a traditional DB plan, the 30-year-old would accrue a benefit costing 1 percent of pay, whereas the 60 year old employee's benefit would cost nearly 10 percent of pay.

DEFINED BENEFIT PLANS AS WEALTH ACCUMULATION VEHICLES

For many small, closely held firms with owners over the age of 40, this age skewing of DB plan contributions can allow them to shelter significant dollars into a DB plan compared with a traditional DC plan. Figure 6.1 illustrates this difference in the maximum tax deductible contributions of DB and DC plans.

(continues)

(continued)

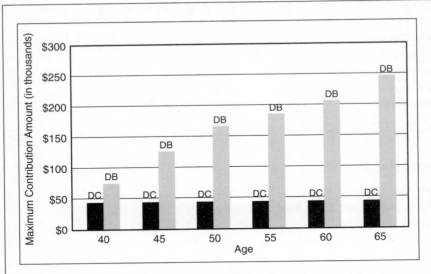

FIGURE 6.1 Comparison of defined benefit versus defined contribution plans: maximum employer contribution amounts

The combination of the age skewing plus the significant dollars that can be sheltered will always make DB plans a part of tax planning for the small, highly profitable employers like law firms, accountants, doctors, and so forth. In fact, if the current trends continue, we predict that the DB plan marketplace with be like a dumbbell—only the large and small employers:

- *Jumbo market.* Large, jumbo employers with multi-billion dollar plans can use sophisticated investment vehicles to insulate them from interest rate risks, and their size makes the administration costs manageable.
- *Small, professional services firms.* These firms will use DB plans as effective tax shelters to provide significant wealth accumulation for partners. These tax concerns will outweigh any administrative cost issues.

The mid-market employers—those with 100 to 2,000 employees—will find the administrative costs plus the financial volatility too burdensome and will terminate their plans. We are seeing many signs of that with plans now freezing. These frozen plans, in most cases, are simply waiting until the cost of termination—either buying annuities and paying lump sums—is small enough. Then they will all wrap up and be completely out of the DB plan marketplace.

Plan Design Modeling

When we work with clients who are looking at their plan design, our approach is to focus initially on their overall goals and objectives. This quickly moves into modeling the current plan and possible alternatives, looking at the impact on sample employees and then in aggregate on the employer. In order to help you get a sense of the tools and methods we use, we have put together three charts that illustrate this process. We use graphs to communicate information and to make it real to our clients. We find they understand information when we present it in graphical format rather than in a big set of tables with numbers.

Defined Benefit Accrual Pattern

We use Figure 6.2 to illustrate how a sample participant accrues his or her DB benefit over time. The line represents the value of the DB plan benefit. The bars represent the change in value at each particular year. Notice, how the DB plan benefit accrues slowly over the early part of this sample participant's career and then quickly accelerates after age 50. Also, you might

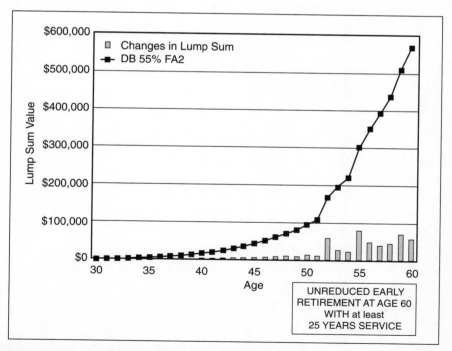

FIGURE 6.2   Company XYZ retirement plan: age 30 new entrant, initial salary $45,000

notice spikes in the accrued benefit at age 52 and age 55. These represent times when various early retirement subsidies are applicable. These "cliffs" or "bounces" in benefit are common in DB plans and sometimes produce unintended HR results—like employees just hanging on until they get to a magic age—a cliff.

DB Plan versus Alternative Defined Contribution Plans

Figure 6.3 illustrates the same DB plan, but with four alternative DC plans that are attempting to replicate the DB plan benefit. Notice that all the DC plans provide substantially more benefits earlier in this sample employee's career. Ultimately, the DB plan catches up to three of the alternatives, while one of the DC alternatives "DC Graded 8/10/12" is estimated to provide a larger benefit at retirement.

This is a type of graph that many consultants would use with a client to illustrate the comparison between DB and DC plans. However, baked into this graph are significant assumptions about future investment returns. In this case, we used 7 percent for future investment returns in the DC plan. This simplistic assumption hides a large part of the DB versus DC comparison—that of the shifting of investment risk from the employer to the employee. In our work with clients, we take this analysis further and do an additional graph.

Stochastic Modeling of DC Plans

Figure 6.4 improves on the simplistic modeling of future DC accumulations by allowing the future investment returns to be more realistically modeled. Using a Monte-Carlo simulation, we have projected the DC plan account balances into the future. Under the simplistic approach above, we assumed that every year the account would earn 7 percent. Here, we allow the future returns to vary every year. We put in the expected mean and variance of different asset classes. The computer then produces 5000 future possible return scenarios—basically rolling the dice 5000 times. This produces, instead of a single line, a set of lines. With this information, you can answer questions like,

- What is the probability that the DC plan will be as good as the DB plan?
- What is the median value of the DC plan—that point with 50 percent chance above and 50 percent chance below?
- What is the 25th percentile value of the DC plan? Or the 75th percentile?

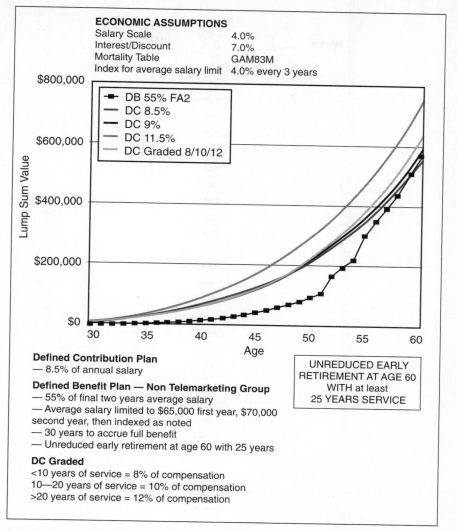

ECONOMIC ASSUMPTIONS

Salary Scale	4.0%
Interest/Discount	7.0%
Mortality Table	GAM83M
Index for average salary limit	4.0% every 3 years

Legend:
- DB 55% FA2
- DC 8.5%
- DC 9%
- DC 11.5%
- DC Graded 8/10/12

Defined Contribution Plan
— 8.5% of annual salary

Defined Benefit Plan — Non Telemarketing Group
— 55% of final two years average salary
— Average salary limited to $65,000 first year, $70,000 second year, then indexed as noted
— 30 years to accrue full benefit
— Unreduced early retirement at age 60 with 25 years

DC Graded
<10 years of service = 8% of compensation
10—20 years of service = 10% of compensation
>20 years of service = 12% of compensation

UNREDUCED EARLY
RETIREMENT AT AGE 60
WITH at least
25 YEARS SERVICE

FIGURE 6.3   Company XYZ retirement plan: age 30 new entrant, initial salary $45,000

This brings home the investment risk transfer. By only modeling a simplistic assumption like 7 percent, you ignore this transfer. With stochastic modeling, you get fuller and richer information about this. With this information, you can then say things like, we want to design a plan that we expect will produce an equivalent benefit 75 percent of the time.

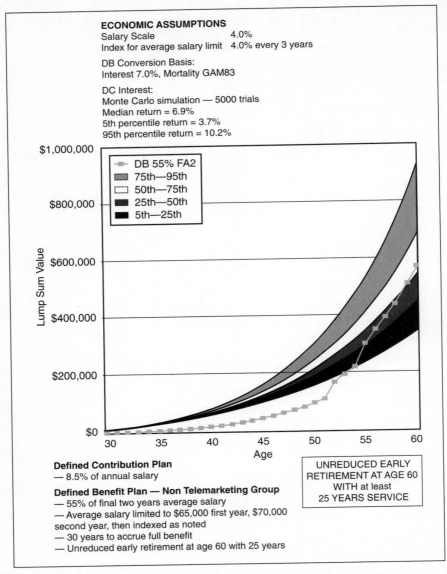

FIGURE 6.4 Company XYZ retirement plan: age 30 new entrant, initial salary $45,000 (defined contribution account balance varying by asset return)

Competitiveness

It is worth spending some time talking about competitiveness. Whenever we work with clients on plan design, they say things like, "What is everybody else doing?" or "We need to be competitive." In general, competitiveness covers more than simply the retirement plan. We will explore some of these issues later when we talk about the relationship to total compensation.

However, when looking at retirement plans, we would recommend that you take a two-pronged approach.

National/Regional Surveys

These surveys, published by major consulting firms, industry associations, and the government, provide a great starting point for any plan design analysis. (See Chapter 9 for some suggested sources.) Each one of these surveys has a particular focus or slant that you need to be aware of when analyzing their results. Be sure to clarify some basics like:

- *Survey group.* Some are focused simply on Fortune 500, smaller employers, industry groups, or geography, for example.
- *Sponsor.* Is the survey sponsor independent or does it represent a potential interest group that could slant the results of the survey?
- *Number of respondents.* Some are broad based surveys with hundreds of respondents while others have fewer respondents.
- *Time series.* We especially like surveys that are repeated year in and year out. If this is the case, we recommend that you request several years worth of results to do your own time series analysis. This is particularly illuminating when you are looking at trends, changes in the marketplace, etc.

We use these surveys to help our clients get a broader perspective on what is available in the marketplace, but not necessarily direct competitor information.

Targeted Competitor Lists

We solve the shortcomings of the general surveys with specific targeted information gathering. At the start of the project, we will ask our client for five or six of their competitors—those companies that the client recruits from, that employees are recruited to, or that the client competes with for market share. Using this, our staff then collects very specific information from these competitors. When we approach companies with these requests, we offer to share results among the respondents. In our experience, we have had very good results, especially with most of this information available electronically.

Using this more detailed information, our clients can see exactly where they match up in all areas of the plans, such as specific match formulas, early retirement provisions, pay definitions, and so forth.

Relationship to Total Compensation

It is worth stressing that retirement plans are just one piece of the total compensation program. When you benchmark your plan versus competitors (especially in large surveys), you need to understand how retirement plans fit into the total pay structure. For our clients, we typically illustrate their retirement plan's competitiveness using both national surveys as well as more focused services. By doing so, our client will have very current market data on their overall competitiveness of "other pay" information. When we turn to look at the retirement plan in isolation, the client can factor in other pieces of anecdotal data more effectively.

For example, our clients would know if they have been losing staff to a competitor based on direct pay, work rules, and so forth. Knowing this, when we show the retirement plan comparison, our clients often say things like, "We know we're higher in direct pay than they are, so we don't mind having a smaller match." This type of real-time, direct feedback is critical as you look to strategically manage your retirement plans.

Special Employee Groups—Executives and Unions

Our focus in this book is on the general employee population, not specifically on either executive compensation issues or union management issues. Both of these groups have specific needs and issues that are not examined in this book. However, I would like to make the following observations:

- *Executives.* The trend toward replacing DB plans with DC plans impacts high-paid employees much more than lower-paid employees. This is explained by two factors:
  - Due to IRS limits, replacement DC plans typically do not provide as significant benefits to highly paid employees as DB plans. Also, the integration with Social Security that is common in DB plans is less so in DC plans and specifically not allowed with 401(k) matching contributions.
  - Many highly paid employees are mid-career hires—recruited to join your organization in their mid-to-late forties. These employees have a difficult time accumulating sufficient DC balances if that is the only retirement vehicle available to them. This issue is exacerbated if the executive is recruited from an employer who had a DB plan.

  Solutions to these issues are usually addressed by nonqualified plans. We would expect that these nonqualified plans will become more common in the future.
- *Unions.* Since retirement plans are subject to collective bargaining, union plan design issues are not in the complete control of the

employer. Unions, overall, are committed to DB plans. They are comfortable with the concept of seniority and the skewing of DB plan value to older employees as well as the security of a DB plan annuity during retirement. Since every management-labor relationship is different, our only advice to management would be to accurately value the retirement plan promises and identify and quantify the financial risks present in the DB plans—both on the asset and liability side. Overly optimistic assumptions can lead to serious financial difficulties like those that the airlines and automobile manufacturers are facing today. This highlights the issue of DB plan sponsors that have large retiree populations and the risks they face. The comparison with insurance companies is also appropriate and something any DB plan manager should consider. If insurance companies have a reputation for being very conservative with their investments, maybe we should be with our DB plan.

Employee Perspective

Examining plan design issues from simply the employer's perspective gives only one side of the equation. The employees are on the receiving end of all the decisions made by the employer. In general, employees are being asked to bear more responsibilities and risk in many areas that were traditionally borne by employers—from the shift to DC plans and elimination of retiree medical coverage to more emphasis on variable pay. As employers ask employees to bear more risk, employers often justify these changes saying, "Employees want choice—they want to be able to select their investments in the DC plan" or "Consumer-directed health care will give employees choice and incentive to manage their own health costs." Implicit in these statements are opinions about what employees think about risk. Many employers sometimes draw conclusions first without digging into what employees actually think. The Society of Actuaries (SOA), the largest worldwide actuarial organization focused on research and education, took on the challenge of finding out what employees actually think about the risks they face. The SOA commissioned several studies examining employees' perception of risk (see Chapter 9 for the SOA web site to get these surveys). For our purposes, we would like to focus on three key risks—investment, longevity, and health—and what the SOA's research shows.

Investment Risk

The vast majority of employers today offer some sort of DC plan, with most offering employees choice in selecting the investments for their individual account. We have dealt with many of the financial and fiduciary issues earlier, but now want to focus on what employees actually would prefer. The decision to offer choice begs the question, do employees actually want to make this decision?

Table 6.4 shows that only 20 percent would like to make investment choices on their own. Over 75 percent would value input from a professional either to actually make all the investment decisions or at least give some input.

This survey information, combined with actual results from 401(k) plan experience, show that employees do not necessarily embrace the idea of choice. For example, many employees are placed in a 401(k) plan's default fund because they never make an investment decision to move out of that default fund. See the Vanguard discussion of default funds in Appendix F.

Moving beyond investment choices while employed, the issue about management of distribution choices is also critical. In the typical DB plan, this choice was simplified to a choice from among several annuities. Many people promoted the idea that shifting to DC plans would give people more control over their distribution options. However, the SOA's study as well as other industry research says differently.

Figures 6.5 and 6.6 echo the same sentiment. Incredibly, 66 percent of workers would like to receive their retirement benefit as a series of payments over their lifetime—the very definition of an annuity. Also, the top

Table 6.4   Preferred Approach to Saving and Investing: Workers

Statement	Percentage Agreeing
You would prefer to look into investing on your own and make your own decisions	21%
You would prefer suggestions from a professional, but often make your own decisions	53
You would prefer suggestions from a professional, and most of the time use their recommendations	16
You would prefer a paid professional to manage your investments for you	7
Don't know/refused	3

Source: LIMRA International Inc., The Society of Actuaries, and Mathew Greenwald and Associates, *Public Misperceptions About Retirement Security* (LIMRA International Inc., The Society of Actuaries, and Mathew Greenwald and Associates, 2005), 22.

Which of the following best descripes how you would like to receive the money from an employer's retirement plan, given that each choice is of equal value/received the money from this retirement program?

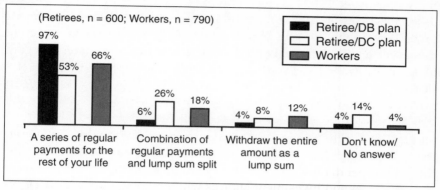

FIGURE 6.5   The vast majority of retirees in both DB and DC plans, in addition to workers, would prefer a series of payments throughout their lives which is consistent with typical defined benefit plans and annuities.

Source: Mathew Greenwald and Associates and The Society of Actuaries. Risks of Retirement—Key Findings and Issues (Mathew Greenwald and Associates and the Society of Actuaries, 2005), 9.

When deciding on what payout option to choose from your retirement plan, how important are each of the following? (percentage saying *very* important)

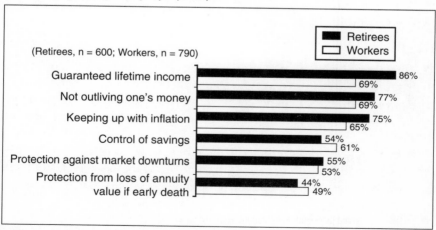

FIGURE 6.6   Both workers and retirees primarily value guaranteed income, such as annuities, throughout their retirement.

Source: Mathew Greenwald and Associates and The Society of Actuaries. Risks of Retirement—Key Findings and Issues (Mathew Greenwald and Associates and the Society of Actuaries, 2005), 10.

two concerns about making decisions is guaranteed lifetime income and not outliving one's assets—both key advantages of annuities. Now with the maturing of 401(k) plans, many recent retirees are faced with the daunting choice of making investment decisions on balances in excess of $1 million. For the vast majority of retirees, this is an unusual sum of money to contemplate and effectively deploy. 401(k) plans are now recognizing this and the trends are to offer annuitization options within 401(k) plans.

Longevity

As identified in the previous section, employees are concerned about outliving their assets. Annuities, by definition, provide a vehicle to manage this risk. However, retirees in the future may have to deal with actively managing their investments. For example, a future retiree may be required to manage assets in an employer 401(k) plan as well as an individual retirement account. These retirees will need to manage these throughout retirement until their death. Critical to this management is the concept of one's life expectancy. The improvement in life expectancy is well known and covered in the popular media, so most people understand that they can expect a longer retirement. However, how well can they estimate this? (See Figure 6.7.)

As you can see, two-thirds of men and over half of women underestimate their life expectancy. One wonders how effective retirees will be in deploying their assets if the vast majority underestimate how long they need the assets to last.

Health

The third, and growing, risk concern is health. As employers shut down their retiree medical programs and face the ever-growing cost of health care in general, they are exposed to significant risk in securing adequate health care. Figure 6.8 highlights the concerns of both workers and current retirees.

With 80 percent of preretirees being either "very concerned" or "somewhat concerned," health risks are a growing issue for workers. Employers may want to explore more options to help retirees manage this risk.

Summary of Risk

Table 6.5 is a summary chart of these risks as well as existing ways to transfer these risks in the current financial services marketplace.

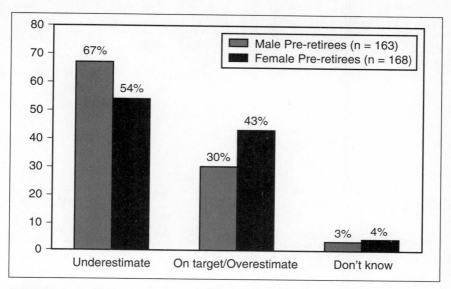

FIGURE 6.7   What age do you think the average 65-year-old male/female can expect to live?

Source: Mathew Greenwald and Associates and The Society of Actuaries. *Risks of Retirement—Key Findings and Issues* (Mathew Greenwald and Associates and the Society of Actuaries, 2005), 8.

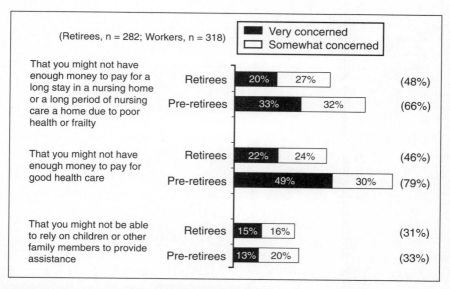

FIGURE 6.8   How concerned are you?

Source: Mathew Greenwald and Associates and The Society of Actuaries. *Risks of Retirement—Key Findings and Issues* (Mathew Greenwald and Associates and the Society of Actuaries, 2005), 13.

Table 6.5   Overview of Postretirement Risks

Risk	Potential Range for Risk	Products for Risk Transfer
Outliving assets	Life spans at age 65 range from 0 years to over 40 years	Annuities, including joint and survivor annuities.
Loss of a spouse	Periods of widowhood of 15 years or more are not uncommon. These are often accompanied by a reduction in standard of living.	Joint and survivor annuities; life insurance.
Decline in functional status	Cost of care on account of frailty can range from $0 to over $2,000,000 for a couple over their lifetimes. Today, nursing home care costs may run $70,000 or more per person per year. Care can be provided at home, in adult day care, assisted living facilities, or nursing homes.	Long-term care insurance helps pay for the cost of care for the disabled. Continuing care retirement communities that provide caps on monthly costs for assisted living and skilled nursing care offer some risk protection as well.
Out-of-pocket medical expenses	Medical costs not covered by Medicare for retirees over age 65 can range from $0 to over $1,000,000 for a couple over their lives.	Medical insurance.
Inflation	Inflation can range from 0% in any year to 10% or more; inflation has been much higher in other countries.	Products with cost-of-living adjustments.

Source: Mathew Greenwald and Associates and The Society of Actuaries. *Risks of Retirement—Key Findings and Issues* (Mathew Greenwald and Associates and the Society of Actuaries, 2005), 3.

THE MICROSOFT QUESTION

At an actuarial conference in California in 2004, Jeremy Gold, a well-known actuary who has prodded the whole industry to update our practice, asked the audience a question. If DB plans are so great, why doesn't Microsoft Corporation sponsor one? He jokingly called this the Microsoft Question. In a roomful of actuaries, he wanted to provoke a conversation in the hopes of rescuing DB plans. If Microsoft Corporation, a company whose management is highly regarded, does not sponsor a DB plan, why would any company do that?

Well, the answer to the Microsoft issue can best be answered by looking at their entire compensation and HR goals: offering stock options and employing the best and brightest who can take care of themselves.

The following three case studies provide you with some real-life examples of plan design projects we have recently worked on with clients.

CASE STUDY #1

A large employer in the publishing industry was gearing up for union negotiations where pension benefits would be on the table. The employer maintains two separate DB pension plans: one for union employees and the other for salaried, nonunion employees. Concerned about the overall cost of the union plan, as well as competitiveness with others in the industry, the employer wanted to do a strategic review of the union plan setup.

Benchmark—Current Status

Our first step in helping this client was to benchmark where it stood with regard to its retirement plans.

OPERATING BENEFIT COST

What cost measure should you focus on when you manage your pension plan? Pension cost as defined by the Financial Accounting Standards Board, minimum contributions level as defined by the Employee Retirement Income Security Act (ERISA), or something else? Well, like a lot of things in life, it depends. However, in general, we recommend our clients try to separate decisions they make on the level of benefits from the decisions about the financing of the benefits.

We recommend that clients view their total pension plan costs as shown in Table 6.6. For example, if a DB plan is in surplus and has no required minimum contribution ($0), then the cost of making a plan change would be understated if you looked simply at the impact on the minimum contribution requirement. In this case, the minimum may stay at zero, but the future costs of the plan have changed.

Table 6.6   Total Pension Costs

Type	Includes	Description
Operating benefit cost	Benefits for active employees only	From a plan design standpoint, managers can only impact the value of benefits to active employees and should focus on its financial impact.
Financing benefit cost	Benefits for retirees and impact from any investment decisions	Liability for retirees is already complete—management cannot change. Investment decisions are made independently of plan design and should remove any impact when analyzing plan design alternatives.

Using our retirement plan framework, we helped our client focus on their overall retirement plan and how it fits within their overall financial program. The management team was confused about what actually drives their overall costs and how they could manage its outcome. They felt defenseless, without much ability to change the costs of the programs beyond just shutting it down. In order to help them begin to get control back, our first step was to make sure they knew where they were. During the initial phase of this study, we isolated the impact of each "lever" at management's disposal—how much investment risk they were taking, how rich were the benefits, where were the benefits dollars being targeted, and so forth.

Based on this initial review, we then focused on the question at hand— how could management effectively propose alternative plan designs that would meet the union members' needs for retirement income, but give the employer more control over the financial impact. Working with management, we helped them organize and prioritize their goals and objectives (top of the list—provide a secure retirement income) and provided a framework within which they could begin to negotiate with the union. As of this writing, these negotiations have begun, but have not been completed. Whichever way the negotiations go, our client felt satisfied because they now understand how to apply the levers to manage the pension plan.

CASE STUDY #2

A mid-sized insurance company had concerns about its retirement program. Established more than 25 years ago, this company maintained both a rich DB plan as well as a 401(k) plan. Management had multiple concerns, including:

- *Adequacy of benefits.* Will the total benefit package allow full-career retirees to maintain their standard of living in retirement?
- *Cost and volatility of pension expense.* The pension expense for the DB plan has been increasing steadily over the past few years. This increase has strained the company's budget.
- *Competitiveness.* How do we compare with our competitors? Is our retirement program an impediment to hiring staff?

This client was financially sound and had recently paid an unexpected bonus to all employees because the company had such a profitable year. Still, the company had concerns about the retirement program. The company formed a working group of finance and HR staff. We facilitated this group and produced analysis of various alternatives. Ultimately, the decision was made to make a change to the program for future hires. All current hires will remain in the current programs with the same level of benefits, while new hires will participate in a souped-up 401(k) plan.

CASE STUDY #3

A medical device manufacturer with operations throughout the world was in financial distress. Adding to the overall decline in revenues was a sharp increase in pension expense due to low interest rates and decline in the equity market, pushing the pension plan's assets lower. Faced with making substantial pension plan contributions over the next few years, this company reviewed its options. Given the typical objectives of providing for an adequate retirement savings vehicle, this company's cash crunch was paramount. How could it redesign the retirement program, save cash, and still provide an adequate retirement income for employees?

After a review of alternatives, this client chose the following course of action:

- *Freeze the DB plan.* This stopped the bleeding on the pension plan by substantially reducing cash contributions in the future. The client elected not to terminate the program given the low-interest environment. It will continue to monitor the "termination" cost in future and will most likely terminate when cost is affordable.
- *Augment existing 401(k) plan.* Using an existing 401(k) plan that included a common matching provision of 50 percent match on the first 6 percent of employee salary deferral, this client doubled the match to 100 percent match on the first 6 percent.

This decision to freeze and change to a completely matched program is a huge strategic change for this employer. It went from a 100 percent employer paid DB plan that provided the bulk of the retirement dollars to a program that requires employees to save to get any employer dollars. This client reviewed alternative DC programs, including an automatic employer contribution at a modest level (2 percent). However, in a major change in strategic direction, it wanted a shared responsibility between employee and employer to be the top priority—hence the new program. This new strategy dovetailed with other pay and benefit issues that were also being communicated to employees at the same time.

WHEN CULTURES COLLIDE: MERGING TWO PENSIONS PLANS

In today's business world, mergers and acquisitions are the fastest way to achieve corporate goals of growth, both in terms of earnings and market share. Wall Street demands annual double-digit rates, leaving corporate executives few choices. Many seek higher returns through acquisitions.

(continues)

(continued)

But although the objectives of acquisitions are financial, the implications are personal. Nevertheless, deal makers focus only on the balance sheet, economies of scale, and market share, with very little discussion of the impact on the people of both organizations. No wonder that as people look back at deals completed in the past decade, not that many have succeeded as planned.

Although it is true that the failure of these mergers derives from many causes, including unforeseen marketplace changes, debt load, and other factors, the most often overlooked cause— the human element— is frequently the real culprit. That is because the merging of two cultures is a lot harder to do than people think.

THE HUGE ISSUE OF CULTURE

Defining culture is just as difficult as trying to manage it. Teamwork, vision, pay, benefits—these all affect a company's culture. Organizations such as the Great Place to Work Institute in San Francisco actively examine what makes a company tick, using multiple surveys and in-depth interviews to evaluate all areas of culture. These may include a company's credibility, respect, fairness, and other factors.

Many of these aspects revolve around the concept of trust: Do employees trust each other and their managers to "do the right thing"? And although many businesspeople may believe that culture and trust do not really matter, *Fortune* magazine has found that firms listed in its annual "100 Best Places to Work" produce profits as high as 36 percent over a 10-year period, such as the one that ended December 2000. The Standard & Poor's 500, by contrast, returned only half that in the same period. So it pays to have a great culture.

WHY PENSIONS ARE UNIQUE

Pension programs are a unique part of every business culture. You can, in fact, discover quite a lot about a company just by examining how it helps its employees save for retirement. The following are common features of standard pension plans with a description of how each can affect a culture:

- *Compensation.* The actual money touches employees and retirees directly in their pocketbooks.
- *Visibility.* All employees talk about their plan and how it affects them.
- *Communication.* How the company communicates its pension plan speaks legions about its commitment, focus, and investment in its employees.

- *Fairness.* Does the plan allow for the same percentage of pay for all employees, or do certain employees get more and others less?

Executives must be aware of these perceptions and manage them while operating their businesses. Within a merger, these issues only become magnified and more apparent. Manage them well, and your company will move beyond the transaction. Manage them poorly, and employee moral (and integration) will surely suffer.

MERGER OVERVIEW FROM 10,000 FEET UP

No two mergers are alike. They may often start out the same, but they will usually follow different paths and experience different outcomes as the process moves along. However, they are transactions that usually break down into four principal stages: (1) Initial interest and due diligence, (2) contract negotiations, (3) closing, and (4) integration.

These stages can occur separately or in combination with each other, and they might happen very quickly or with long delays between stages. Let's first (and briefly) explore the first three phases, then delve in-depth into the all-important final integration phase.

1. *Initial interest and due diligence.* During this initial curiosity and due diligence phase, a buyer looks closely at the seller's business, focusing primarily on financial assets and liabilities. During this phase, buyers should direct particular scrutiny to potential liabilities from the seller's pension and other benefit plans. Parties typically limit the number of people involved at this stage due to concerns about confidentiality, and this usually means excluding HR personnel. Rethink such detachment of HR, because earlier involvement from HR could actually yield significant benefits, including assisting in uncovering potential liability, analyzing compensation costs and employee structure, uncovering the "soft issues" of seller's value, and increasing speed of integration at later stages, to name just a few. Although the desire to keep the due diligence team small seems sensible, inclusion of HR will probably not substantially increase the number of people involved. Plus, HR is used to working with confidential data. For such reasons, acquiring firms could realize significant gains throughout the entire merger and integration period if their HR departments become involved early in the process.

2. *Contract negotiations.* After due diligence has been completed, HR definitely should be at the table to provide input into the final purchase and sale agreement. Areas to focus on at this point include representations made by both seller and buyer, especially the following:

(continues)

(continued)

- *Employees.* How will the merger affect employees? Are any layoffs considered at this point? Are there any unionized employees?
- *Compensation.* What are the buyer's initial thoughts about compensation levels and expectations?
- *Pension plans.* What plans are out there? Which ones will survive? What level of funding do they have? Who is responsible for any unfunded liabilities? Are the plans in compliance with legal rules? Who will take care of retirees? These are just a few of the pension-related questions.
- *Executive plans.* What is out there now? Will any payments accelerate due to the transaction? Are there any "handcuffs" on sellers' executives?

    You can see how, without HR's direct input, these kinds of matters would be hard to address.

3. *Closing.* Up until this point, the two parties have typically dealt only with each other through lawyers and investment bankers. After the signing and before the closing, the parties will organize transition teams, and HR departments from both companies can now begin to deal directly with each other. The parties should deal with any amendments or clarifications to the agreement now, and HR should not be afraid to suggest changes. Of particular concern would be the immediate needs affecting merged employees, such as payroll and medical benefits. HR can deal with other less pressing issues after the closing at a more leisurely pace.

POST-MERGER INTEGRATION: THE REAL WORK BEGINS

When the deal makers have left, the real work of integrating two companies and their unique cultures must start. At this point, those high-level decisions about business strategy, structure, and goals will be about as useful as Horace Greeley's old advice, "Go West, young man." Yes, managers now know where they are going, but they do not necessarily know what to do next. Managers must assess their situation and plan their first move (of many moves) in a generally westerly direction. What would be of particular use to them would be a road map (if they can find one or figure one out) to help them along the way.

To construct such a road map, both companies, during the integration phase, should work through the following steps to integrate their pension plans successfully. Doing so will provide them with that much-needed map:

1. *Assess current cultures.* This means evaluating the cultures of each organization, including how each developed, how it now manifests

itself, etc. Is one company a very paternalistic company and the other a world of "every-man-for-himself"?

2. *Describe cultural goals.* Where do you see the finally merged company: maintaining one firm's culture—the buyer's perhaps, with the seller's having to adapt? Or is the plan to try to take the best from each—in other words, mix-and-match features?

3. *Identify conflicts.* Does the cultural vision of the two merging parties conflict with any existing cultural items? Say a newly merged bank wants to change its employment habits to encourage shorter tenure, employees staying with them for only 5 to 10 years rather than fostering "life-long employment" as had been the tradition of both these merged banks. Previously, in other words, managers at both institutions had spent lots of time moving employees around like so many chess pieces just to keep them employed, even when employee skills did match well with the "new" position. The new cultural vision would force managers to now hire more people from the outside who possess exactly the skills required to carry out the job at hand. Here a conflict might arise if the pension plan in place is "service weighted," in other words, the plan effectively encourages employees to remain with their employer no matter what. The merged bank would have to realign such a formula with its "people strategy."

4. *Review pension plans.* Benchmark pension plans against cultural goals: Is there a fit, or is some modification necessary? (See next section below for a more detailed discussion of useful criteria for making these decisions.)

5. *Discuss integration issues, including potential winners and losers.* After benchmarking and deciding on any changes, the implementation team should assess the impact on total compensation, typically with an analysis of any "winners" (people who will earn more benefits) and "losers" (people who will earn fewer benefits).

6. *Communicate.* Whatever is decided, the implementation team must communicate decisions to all affected employees. This is a great opportunity to reinforce three things: the overall goals of the merger, the shared vision of the future firm, and any concrete impact on employees' pay and benefits.

CRITERIA TO EXAMINE

As we have discussed, part of your road map will include the need to review the effectiveness of the current pension plans in light of the newly merged organization. Criteria worth examining include:

(continues)

(continued)

- *Cost.* What levels of benefits are competitive in your industry? Where do you want to be ranked in terms of total compensation—average, above average, etc.?
- *Flexibility.* Many companies that make acquisitions want their plans to be flexible enough to handle future mergers and sales with ease. For example, a DC/401(k) plan will be more flexible than a DB plan. Thus, the type of plan you choose is an important consideration.
- *Legal.* Legal compliance is a necessary evil with pension plans. To maintain the tax deductibility of both past and future contributions, companies must be sure their plans comply with all rules and regulations. The risks of merging a plan with a bad legal history are high.
- *Employee ownership.* Is employee ownership a goal of the organization? If so, how should you put the fiduciary structure in place to protect employee savings? Remember Enron!
- *Corporate viewpoint.* Is it paternalistic or entrepreneurial? In other words, how does the corporation feel toward its employees? Is the culture one of everyone for themselves, or is it a team-oriented, we're-all-in-this-together organization?

Other issues often crop up in merging two cultures and their pension plans that the parties usually identify during the due diligence phase. These could include old orphaned plans from previous mergers/sales, controlled group issues with nondiscrimination rules, delinquency in maintaining proper plan documentation, and so forth. Whatever such issues may be, it is imperative that you deal with them.

Although the initial deal makers usually dismiss "soft" and "people" issues as less essential, they in fact will often be "company breakers" down the road. Addressing them early in the game and life will be easier, and more profitable, when the merged firm's rubber meets the road.*

---

*From Daniel Cassidy, "When Cultures Collide: Merging Two Pension Plans," *Handbook of Business Strategy 2003* (Bradford, W. Yorkshire, England: Emerald Group Publishing, Ltd., October 2002), 143–146.

How to Hire the Right Consultants

Technology has changed the way companies do business. As such, it has changed the way consultants dispense their expertise. Without a thorough reevaluation of the technology versus consultant ratio, companies are likely to squander funds and waste valuable resources and opportunities.

Following World War II, companies started offering a plethora of company-sponsored benefit plans. As these plans grew in complexity, consultants became valuable for their experience and expertise. With stretched resources and companies expected to do more with fewer employees, human resources (HR) outsourcing has become a nationwide trend.

With this came many opportunities for consultants. With all these prospects come situations where technology could be leveraged to complete projects better or in a more cost-effective manner than consultants. With the advent of the Internet, companies can leverage existing tools and services to do what a consultant does for a fraction of the cost. The value of a good consultant may be how he or she interacts with and augments face-and-brain time with technology. The following box proposes that understanding and evaluating the return on investment of outsourcing consulting services in light of the new role of technology are vital for companies and their budget.

How do you determine which set of consultants best fits your needs? Does your consultant proactively and independently bring solutions to you that spend your "discretionary" budget dollars wisely? How quickly and effectively have your consultants adopted technology solutions that should replace low-value, administrative tasks?

Surveys indicate that companies use a variety of consultants for all types of benefit issues. Tables 7.1 and 7.2 and Figure 7.1, taken from surveys performed by Diversified Investment Advisors, illustrate the penetration of consultants by type of service (defined contribution plan design work), trends, and size of organization.

Especially in today's tight fiscal environment, companies should reconfirm the "value-added" role their consultants play and challenge whether current processes and solutions effectively leverage technology to manage information and company costs.

Table 7.1 Sources of Guidance for Plan Sponsors When Making Changes to Defined Contribution (DC) Plan

	All Employers Offering a DC Plan
Benefits consultant	58%
Benefits broker	31%
Securities broker/dealer	21%
ERISA attorney	26%
Accounting/audit firm	31%
Other	4%
None of these	5%

Source: Diversified Investment Advisors, *Report on Retirement Plans 2005* (New York: Diversified Investment Advisors, 2005), 17.

Table 7.2 Outside Advisers Consulted by Number of Eligible Employees

	Less than 100	100–499	500–999	1,000–4,999	5,000–9,000	10,000 and over
Benefits consultant	41%	43%	61%	70%	71%	75%
Benefits broker	53%	34%	21%	26%	21%	13%
Securities broker/dealer	6%	17%	7%	10%	8%	13%
CPA	6%	11%	4%	3%	5%	44%
Attorney	6%	14%	20%	29%	24%	50%
Current provider	6%	24%	14%	21%	21%	21%
Other	0%	18%	16%	16%	16%	13%

n=351.
Source: Diversified Investment Advisors, *Report on Retirement Plans 2005* (New York: Diversified Investment Advisors, 2005), 18.

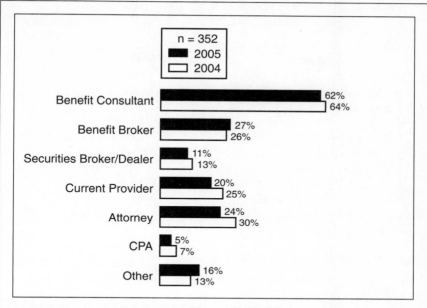

FIGURE 7.1   Outside advisers consulted—trend
Source: Diversified Investment Advisors, *Report on Retirement Plans 2005* (New York: Diversified Investment Advisors, 2005), 18.

Let's look at the benefits field as an example. We have come a long way since the earliest days of benefits procurement. Technology has now changed the entire picture. Without a thorough reevaluation of your technology versus consultant ratio, you are likely to squander company funds and waste both valuable potential resources and golden opportunities.

BENEFITS PLANS BECOME ESSENTIAL

Following World War II, companies began offering insurance benefits to help protect their employees from financial hardship if they were unable to work (death, injury, disability, or retirement). Over time, company-sponsored benefit plans became "needed to play," although some companies may argue that it is their overall package of benefits that foster a true competitive advantage in hiring and retaining employees. Regardless, it is a given in the United States that businesses provide core benefit plans to its full-time employees. Without these, a firm would be effectively out of contention.

(continues)

(continued)

More and more, however, employee benefit programs have grown into "complexity monsters"; that is, they are so administratively complicated and legally challenging that they are all but out of control. For example, employee benefits are the second largest employee cost, following salary. Annually companies spend $5,000 to $10,000 per employee, a cost that increases automatically by 10 to 15 percent each year.

To best meet the challenges created by these benefit programs, many companies will bring in outside consultants or insurance brokers to facilitate the purchasing and management of these programs. With widespread downsizing of HR departments and of many businesses in general, directives to outsource noncore business functions have exploded, accelerating the use of and reliance on consultants for maintenance of these services.

ROLE OF THE CONSULTANT

But what is the role of the consultant, or what should it be? What exactly are consultants asked to do and to keep doing? And how does one determine if a consultant or broker is offering added value?

The definition of value-added consulting support is formulated by each buyer. What *value-added* means to one firm may not mean the same to another. Nevertheless, certain commonalities have evolved. Traditionally, companies have utilized consulting support in the following variety of ways:

- *For technical and legislative expertise.* Employee benefit specialists such as actuaries, attorneys, and other benefit strategy specialists develop deep expertise and thought leadership positions.
- *For market knowledge.* Keep up-to-date on the various benefit vendors, products, pricing, and target market knowledge to best fit the vendor with client needs.
- *For special projects.* Infrequent projects that have a defined duration and require more than an average level of experience available in-house. Examples include mergers/acquisitions due diligence, system/software implementation, and interpretation of new legislative or accounting rules.
- *For project management.* Accelerate timetable to implement cost-effective changes typically involving multiple departments or outside vendors.
- *For annual plan management.* Collecting and negotiating insurance vendor renewals, sending out requests for proposals, collecting and analyzing claim data, and managing and updating communications, policies, and SPDs.

- *For additional staffing.* Staff reduction, maternity or other extended time leave of absence, work back-log, and staff pulled to another project and away from benefits work.

With so many business reorganizations and business process reengineering initiatives over the past decade, thereby pushing companies to do more with less, outsourcing services that had previously been internal functions has been a leader in the HR department's space. Since professional service firms providing these outsourced services have changed as well during these times (to meet customer demands as well as to preserve revenue), there is a widespread lack of knowledge or understanding of how these services are performed. This makes it more difficult for companies to determine whether these services are value-added or not.

Also, it can be difficult to determine whether or not there are more efficient approaches available than what any one firm is familiar with. If you have not heard about something new on the scene, it might as well not exist. And can you trust your consultant to tell you about it?

For example, scan this list of HR outsourcing options that dominate the scene today:

- Payroll administration
- Pension investments
- Vendor billing
- Compliance, legal
- Vendor selection
- Actuarial services
- Vendor performance evaluation
- Benefit communications
- Retirement plan administration
- Enrollment
- Benefit surveys
- Plan renewals

As you might imagine from reviewing this list, there are many opportunities for consulting firms to fill if they only step up to the plate and proclaim their proficiency. Thus, many consulting firms have become "multidisciplined service providers" so as to both respond to customer requests and maintain and increase their own revenues. Logically, from a revenue perspective, cross-selling services within a solid distribution network would be a prime goal.

With such one-stop shopping so increasingly important, it is easier than ever to locate consulting services with multiple service offerings

(continues)

(continued)

(and multiple products) under one roof. This development has unfortunately spawned previously little-seen problems, in the form of real or at least perceived conflicts of interest.

POTENTIAL CONFLICTS OF INTEREST

Many large banks, for example, have taken up managing 401(k) assets, but have also added third-party consulting arms to help companies make initial decisions about what to do with such assets. Is it any surprise they would end up guiding their client companies toward certain choices about 401(k) asset management that send them into the arms of their own banks' 401(k) services? Now the banks get to play the role of retirement consultant, banker, investment services, outsourcing adviser (i.e., how to find a good outsourcing solution), and outsource provider (i.e., that very same "good" outsourcing solution) all at once.

Mellon Bank, for example, will be happy to help you take a look at how best to manage payroll and benefit programs, as well as to answer this question for a client: "Should we in-source or outsource it?" In such situations, we might be forgiven if we assume the "adviser" is not likely to be as up front about all available options as a more independent adviser might (and should) be. Although perhaps best recognized for its banking and asset management services, Mellon Bank also owns mutual fund company Dreyfus and Buck Consulting [including asset performance review, 401(k) vendor selection services, and HR outsourcing consulting services], and recently purchased HR Outsourcing Services (formerly known as PwC/Kwasha).

Another example is Hewitt Associates. Traditionally an actuarial firm, it is now a major player in HR outsourcing and has in recent years greatly expanded its consulting work, advising clients on outsourcing options. Most recently, it has also added to these services the ability to provide one of the major outsourcing needs on the list—payroll administration—by purchasing a payroll company.

There are countless other examples of the new business combinations that have emerged in the past few years:

- Fee-for-service consulting plus insurance brokerage plus benefit outsourcing
- Employee benefits plus property and casualty insurance brokerage
- Executive compensation consulting plus insurance product brokerage
- Retirement actuarial, administration, investment manager plus vendor selection
- Claim administrator plus insurance brokerage

These combinations have developed because of the hesitation practiced by consultants to adopt or augment their services via technology. Software and the use of the Internet have evolved significantly throughout most of the business world over the past five years, continuing to evolve at a rapid pace, and have gotten better and better at promoting major efficiencies.

But the advantages realized by this trend have generally not been integrated into the company/consultant working relationship, especially when HR departments are involved. Quite simply, because of a perceived threat on the part of the consultant, and the lack of understanding of how things could be on the part of the company, technology and consultants have not proven the best of partners.

When a client shows a need, for example, consultants typically prove quite adept at helping them understand what their current and future needs may be. The trouble begins when evaluating pros and cons of developing a solution internally versus purchasing a supplier's product. Furthermore, when such a need is identified by (or for) a client, the consultant's natural reaction is to tell a client, "We can figure this out for you" and/or, "We have to develop the solution for you because no one knows your needs the way we do." And when a firm charges $500 or more an hour, it typically harbors (or at least expresses) a lot of confidence that these statements are absolutely true, even if they know little or nothing about the situation at hand.

It is an old consultant's axiom to never say no to a potential consulting project, even if expertise is somewhat lacking. One, after all, can always learn. Thus, the effect of such widespread overconfidence manifests itself in the fact that a more technical expert, say a software developer, might charge as little as $50 an hour to solve the problem versus 10 times as much with the established consulting firm. The software expert might even be capable of delivering far better service than the less knowledgeable, higher-priced consultant could or would. In fact, the odds of this are quite good.

Will things change as younger consultants come up the ranks? Possibly not, since conflicts of interest reign in this area as well. For every veteran strategic benefits consultant, there may be typically 5, 10, or 50 junior consultants in training, a percentage of which will emerge as the strategic consultants of tomorrow. They approach things differently, of course, being raised on such software staples as spreadsheets, word processing, and data management. Also, junior consultants' time may make up 50 to 90 percent of the project fees (time × rate), which may turn out more costly than drawing upon readily available software solutions not based on hourly fees.

(continues)

(continued)

Although they may be learning well the technical aspects of their craft, sometimes the technological expertise of junior consultants (i.e., making consulting processes more efficient), ends up counterproductive to the goals of their training and development. For example, commonly used tools in consulting at the junior consultant level continue to be spreadsheets, database software, and word processing. These tools are excellent for helping to evaluate and present qualitative data on a client-specific basis, but when a larger-scale solution needs to be developed, it may not matter much how advanced the consultant is at Excel. This is especially true when programming in another software may more likely produce the best result of all options and at a fraction of the cost.

INTERNET TO THE RESCUE, OR NOT

The Internet has created a whirlwind of opportunities to enable companies to solicit proposals and negotiate directly with suppliers. Many excellent applications have been developed for purchasing supplies and raw materials, but how well this translates into the HR procurement needs of a company is still evolving. Surely, if applying the same procurement techniques increasingly in use in the supply purchasing side can also return favorable results in the HR space, a winner will have been born. But by and large, the jury is still out.

Potential answers to this issue have emerged, however. Three approaches in particular have surfaced in the HR benefits procurement space.

Consultant-Developed Tools and Solutions

These are often driven by their largest and most influential clients, and heavily influenced by historical approach to benefits consulting.

An example: In the 1990s, HR and benefit outsourcing was the train every HR consulting firm had to be on. Leading companies such as IBM, Raytheon, and Dupont challenged the market by asking, "Will outsourcing our benefits be more efficient?" Many of the benefit consulting firms answered these questions by saying, "Yes, and here is our solution." They then used their own consultants (and junior consultants) to replace the HR in-house folks when they accepted the outsourcing assignments. They would also build a systems/technology that their "smarter" staff would use, theoretically saving money overall on well-trained and technologically equipped staffers.

Today, however, after investing hundreds of millions of dollars in technology and learning so that HR customer service calls can be answered by a well-trained person (rather than a $100,000/year consultant), only a handful of consulting firms have weathered the storm and remain committed to this market. Most lost too much money, exiting the business once they realized their consultants did not do administrative work all that efficiently and the cost to develop the helping technology proved just too high.

Firms Targeting Insurance Brokers and Consultants

Some companies have developed systems that connect employee benefit professionals so as to streamline the purchase, distribution, and service of employee benefit products for brokers, consultants, and insurance carriers.

Example: BenefitPoint makes it easier for employee benefits professionals to buy, sell, and manage benefits by providing the industry's leading Web-based platform for client data management and procurement. Its customers realize expanded business opportunities and operational efficiencies, and a greater ability to deliver quality information and services to their clients via access to a complete range of such employee benefits products as medical, life, disability, dental, vision, stop loss, and third-party administration.

Firms Targeting Employers

Some companies have developed HR procurement and data management tools that put the control back in the hands of employers so they can minimize time spent on procurement and renewal activities that otherwise may take months to complete (and hundreds of thousands of dollars in low-value consulting fees).

Example: IE-Engine has developed related products to accumulate client data, vendor contract and performance evaluation data, and employee survey tools leveraged through their "Human Resource Cost" management software solutions. Thus, time spent is drastically reduced, as is cost.

WISE USE AND RETURN ON INVESTMENT

Although technology is advancing in such a way as to outdistance the time and costs traditionally expended on company activities and consulting services, the goal as yet is not to eliminate company activities or consultants entirely. Value added of a good consultant today may be how he or she interacts with and augments face and brain time with technology. When all is said and done, there is still the need for brainstorming, deliberating, soliciting feedback, and obtaining an experienced point of view. When technology is used to erase the drudgery of

(continues)

(continued)

benefits procurement, the time and attention left can be used for reflective decision making.

Understanding ROI when using consulting services is now more critical than ever, especially at a time when many firms are eliminating benefit advisory services altogether. This rush to meet short-term financials may lead to higher long-term costs with no one at all left to offer a seasoned point of view.

The poor economic conditions we have been experiencing the past few years have put a great strain on "discretionary" budgets. At the same time, while budgets for outside advisers are being cut, the attention, scrutiny, and accountability attached to employee benefit plans has never been higher. Fortunately, how the Internet and other technology developments continue to impact these services on a positive cost-effective basis will be increasingly felt.

By attending to wise use of consultants, in conjunction with advancing new technology, you can ensure that your firm reaps truly value-added service from your consultants as well as utilizing technology as a measurable solution for managing benefits costs. The platform is before us, and it is beckoning us to climb aboard.*

---

*From Daniel Cassidy, "How to Hire the Right Consultants: Value-Added Benefits Consulting Can Save the Day," *Handbook of Business Strategy 2005* (Bradford, W. Yorkshire, England: Emerald Group Publishing, Ltd., October 2004), 225–229.

SPOTLIGHT: IE-ENGINE

Q&A with Brent Bannerman, Founder and Vice President for Business Development and Marketing, IE-Engine (www.ie-engine.com)

Buying health care has always been a process that is lengthy, frustrating, labor intensive, and extremely expensive. IE-Engine is the leader of a small but growing group of new firms providing software tools to speed up and make more efficient this traditionally painful process of health care procurement. IE-Engine's customers include Ford, Dow Chemical, Lucent, Staples, Pitney-Bowes, and Owens Corning. Here are comments from IE-Engine's founder Brent Bannerman on where this trend is heading:

Q: Why do you believe HR/benefit programs have been slow to adopt technology advancements?

A: Bannerman: They haven't had to because the insurance carrier market is slow to adopt technology. The suppliers don't really adopt technology. There hasn't been a major pressure on organizations to get real effective HR and employee benefit programs in place. Up until the rise in cost, HR and benefit programs have always been a backwater issue and HR has been able to handle programs as they want, and have not been held accountable. Now, with the lingering effects of recession and rising costs, companies need every dollar and are looking to save every last penny.

Q: How do you compare/contrast opportunities in HR/benefit space that have likely been achieved in other areas of the organization through technology (e.g., procurement, contracts)?

A: Procurement protocols, audit strategies, total quality measures (e.g., six sigma) have been adopted throughout corporations to reduce defects. Heretofore, HR has not been held accountable and required to work under the same guidelines as the rest of the company because HR is a people business, and CFOs did not understand how it worked. Now, with the rise in costs, companies are forcing HR to adopt the same protocols and apply the same principles to purchasing health care that they apply to the purchasing of raw materials.

Q: How does your technology integrate with and/or complement value-added consulting?

A: The IE-Engine technology allows companies (and their consultants) to reduce the amount of administrative time, paperwork, and resources associated with many of the repetitive and costly processes, and to focus more energy on value-added, strategic program initiatives. In addition, key areas of vendor performance and contractual elements are collected and monitored by the software for ongoing review and compliance with contract terms. Within HR and employee benefits, this is typically a very time-consuming process and often goes unmonitored.

General Trends

S tepping back for a moment from thinking about management of your
own retirement plan, we wanted to spend some time to discuss some
of the underlying currents and megatrends in the retirement arena. We
have touched on some of these trends earlier, but wanted to fully explore
them here together.

As we see it, the retirement industry is being driven by the following
megatrends:

- Asset-based solutions—including "portable alpha" strategies
- Globalization
- Death of defined benefit (DB) plans, followed by DB-ification of 401(k)
  plans
- Bundling of service providers
- Enterprise risk management
- Demographics

Asset-Based Solutions—Portable Alpha

For DB plan sponsors, the trend over the past 20 years has been to look to
the liability side of the balance sheet for solutions. If the plan was "too expensive," a plan sponsor would begin a plan design study rather than
look to the asset side to solve the problem. Combine this with the seem-
ingly constant regulations coming out of Washington calling for required

plan design changes, most plan sponsors spent an enormous amount of time on the plan designs. The major consulting firms, like Hewitt, Towers Perrin, Mercer, and others, blossomed during this period to help their clients manage this process. The primary example of the significance of liability side management has been the conversion of many DB plans to cash balance plans—a hybrid DB plan design (see Table 8.1). Various surveys highlight the prevalence of these new designs: One-third of the Fortune 100 and 19 percent of employers with more than 1,000 employees have now converted their plans to cash balance plans.

The U.S. government and courts have struggled with the issues surrounding the cash balance conversions. This uncertainty has put a stop to the conversions for the most part. Besides this uncertainty, some employers have frozen their plans altogether. Watson Wyatt's 2005 survey of the Fortune 1000 showed that 116 froze or terminated their DB plans since 2001.

All of these attempts—either cash balance conversions or plan freezes —are liability side methods to manage retirement plan costs. For those employers who remain committed to DB plans, the only realistic area to look at now to manage their costs is on the asset side.

We mentioned in Chapter 5 one of the asset side methods some plan sponsors are looking at—that of extending the duration of the fixed-income portfolio to better match the duration of the liabilities. Another method that is being discussed is called "portable alpha strategy." Both of these methods require the use of derivatives and other investment vehicles that some plan sponsors may not be comfortable with. However, we see this trend continuing and would recommend that all plans sponsors

Table 8.1 Comparison of Typical Plan Features

	Defined Benefit Plans		Defined Contribution Plans
	Regular	Cash Balance	401(k)
Participation	Automatic	Automatic	Voluntary
Contributions	Employer	Employer	Employer and employee
Investment risk	Employer	Employer	Employee
Disability coverage	Yes	Yes	No
Loans	N/A	N/A	Allowed
Distribution form	Annuity	Lump sum	Lump sum
Benefit guaranty	PBGC	PBGC	N/A

PBGC, Pension Benefit Guaranty Corporation.

get comfortable with the use of derivatives to help control the risk of their pension plans.

Modern Portfolio Theory—Basics

To understand portable alpha strategies, you need to get comfortable with some basic concepts from modern portfolio theory. Investment return from any actively managed portfolio can be broken into two pieces, as shown in Figure 8.1.

Beta is defined as the investment return generated from market exposure and is essentially the return earned for bearing the risk of being invested in the market. Alpha, on the other hand, is the excess return—either positive or negative—that a fund manager generates from the active management of the portfolio. The holy grail of any investment manager search is to find those managers who can produce alpha.

Traditional Investment Manager Searches

Historically, pension funds have attempted to find these alpha-generating managers through traditional investment management searches looking for the best investment manager in various asset classes. So, for example, a pension fund would determine its asset allocation—say 15 percent or $15 million—targeted to the U.S. long bond asset class. The fiduciaries would then hire an investment consultant to help them find the best manager in that particular asset class. After a search, the fund would give the entire $15 million to the investment manager, who would then deploy the dollars according to their strategy. The investment manager would be compensated at a level—say 50 basis points—on the entire $15 million or $75,000. The fiduciaries would sit around and hope that this manager could replicate his or her past performance and in fact produce positive alpha while being exposed to the asset class's beta.

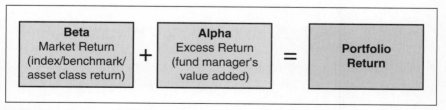

FIGURE 8.1   A portfolio's return is a combination of beta (the return of the market) and alpha (the excess return, or fund manager's valued added).

Portable Alpha Process

Compared with the traditional investment model just described, portable alpha strategies divorce the search for alpha from beta. The following example provides more detail on how strategy is deployed (see Figure 8.2).

Sample Scenario

Using the same example above with a $15 million desired allocation to U.S. long bonds, the fiduciaries have confidence in a European equity manager and believe they will produce significant alpha in the near term. In addition, the expected alpha of the European equity manager is significantly higher than the expected alpha of the current U.S. long bond manager. The fiduciaries, however, do not want to be exposed to the European equity market. So, they adopt a portable alpha strategy as follows:

1. Allocate fund to the European equity manager seeking high alpha.
2. Use derivatives to "short" the European equity market (i.e., sell futures of the Japanese market).
3. Use derivatives to "long" the U.S. long bond market (i.e., buy futures of the U.S. long bond market).

Some key benefits of a portable alpha strategy include:

- Separates the search of alpha from the search of beta (asset allocation exposures).
- Targets investment management fees to alpha sources and reduces investment management fees for beta sources.
- Can diversify across multiple, uncorrelated alpha sources while maintaining pension plan's asset allocation exposures.

Some challenges of executing a portable alpha strategy include:

- Plan sponsor must find alpha sources on a consistent basis.
- Successful coordination between alpha generators and the porting process is critical.
- Plan sponsor must be comfortable with entering into the derivative marketplace. Many pension plan IPS's specifically exclude derivatives from allowable assets.

Overall, portable alpha strategies can be very appealing to pension plan sponsors as they look for ways to control the risks in their pension plans. And more important than specifically portable alpha strategies, we

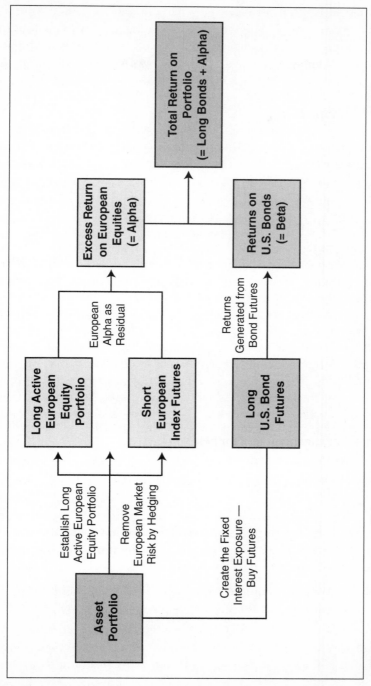

FIGURE 8.2 Using the portable alpha strategy, a manager's alpha in one market can be transferred to another market.

see a trend of plan sponsors being more accepting of entering the derivative market. The traditional methods of only using long asset positions is comparable with using only one hand in a boxing match. By allowing the full spectrum of investments available today in the global marketplace, plan sponsors can dial in the risk level they want to take in their plans.

Globalization

By globalization, we include all types of changes to our world from financial service industry to accounting requirements to employment to government barriers. Many of these changes may only apply to multinational corporations; however, all employers, regardless of size, should consider the ramifications for their organizations.

Financial Service Industry

The world is getting smaller, and the ability for global capital to flow between countries has never been greater. Retirement plans can now get exposure to emerging markets in an efficient manner like never before. Investment managers now compete on a worldwide basis, and investment firms compete to attract their talent anywhere in the world. Hedge funds have exploded in numbers as investment managers attempt to exploit inefficiencies in the marketplace—anywhere in the world. Costs of operating these financial instruments will continue to drop, putting more sophisticated vehicles in the hands of the average investors. This will require significant investment in education and dissemination of knowledge to allow investors throughout the world to assess the risk/return trade-off of the particular vehicle.

Accounting Requirements

In the past, each developed country had their own specific accounting standards that would apply to any publicly traded company. The British, Canadian, French, German, and Japanese financial industries each developed their own standards. In the past several years, however, the push has been to establish common international accounting standards. Two major benefits of robust international standards include:

- Companies need only comply with one standard rather than multiple standards—one for each country where their stock is traded.
- Investors can more effectively compare financial records based on a single method. Currently, adjustments are required to compare companies traded in the United States versus Germany, for example.

While the benefits are clear, the speed by which individual countries adopt the international standards is slow. Convergence will happen, but it will be incremental and take 10 to 20 years.

Employment

No matter whether it is companies operating globally, outsourcing operations to lower-cost countries, or smaller companies attracting talent regardless of location, employment opportunities and their complexities will continue to increase over time. Retirement plan solutions will continue to include offshore pension arrangements that move beyond national borders. An example of this is shown in the survey Argus Consulting Ltd performed for the nongovernmental organization (NGO) industry, showing the increased use of offshore retirement vehicles (see Appendix G).

Death of Defined Benefit Plans Followed by DB-ification of 401(k) Plans

The slow decline of DB plans has been well documented and is quickly accelerating (see Figure 8.3). As mentioned earlier, we predict that the DB marketplace will continue its path and eventually be dumbbell shaped. The only companies that will have DB plans will be either small, closely held firms using DB plans for tax avoidance, and jumbo companies with DB plans that will continue to exist and never close. (We include large public plans in the jumbo definition.) Mid-size organizations will continue to freeze and terminate their plans (see Table 8.2).

Small organizations that initially adopt a 401(k) will not adopt DB plans when they grow in size for fear of the financial uncertainties. You can hear people say, "If Microsoft doesn't adopt a DB plan, there must be something wrong with them."

This slow death of DB plans will be accelerated by two things:

1. Rise in interest rates that will reduce the cash required to terminate any DB plan—whether it is frozen already or not. We predict that if interest rates rise by 200 basis points, you will see a flood of DB plans terminate. This will reduce the number of plans from today's 30,000 to under 10,000. This reduction in private DB plans will exacerbate the current problems with the entire pension system, since the insurance system guaranteeing DB plans is self-funded.

2. The government's inability to control the skyrocketing liabilities being pushed onto the Pension Benefit Guaranty Corporation (PBGC) —the quasigovernment agency responsible for insuring DB plans— will also force plan sponsors to terminate their DB plans. The PBGC

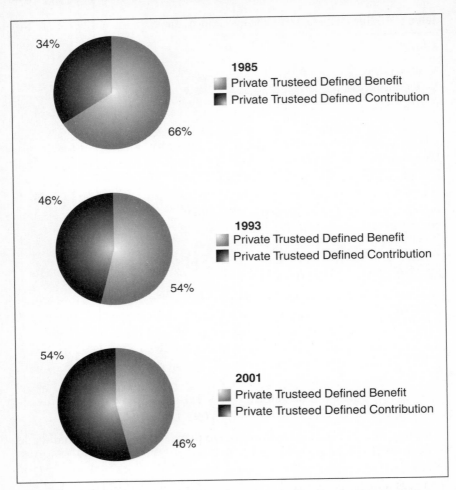

FIGURE 8.3   From 1985 to 2001, the percentage of assets in private trusteed defined benefit plans fell 20% to 46% of plans, while the percentage of assets in private trusteed defined contribution plans increased by 20% to 54% of assets.

Source: "EBRI Research Highlights: Retirement Benefits" *EBRI Special Report,* 258 (2003): 8.

insurance program is seriously flawed and promotes bad behavior on financially distressed organizations. Since healthy DB plans pay for the unhealthy ones, if the number of DB plans continues to fall, the PBGC premium income will spiral down and the system will crash

Table 8.2   Recent and Possible Future Plan Changes

Plan Actions Considered in the Past 12 Months

Bundle defined benefit plan services with a single provider	34%
Move from a traditional defined benefit plan to a cash balance plan	31%
Move from a traditional defined benefit plan to a pension equity plan	30%
Reduce plan benefits	21%
Terminate the defined benefit plan	20%
Freeze the defined benefit plan	19%
Make other plan design changes	29%

Potential Changes to Consider in the Next 12 Months

Move from a traditional defined benefit plan to a pension equity plan	26%
Terminate the defined benefit plan	25%
Reduce plan bnefits	24%
Freeze the defined benefit plan	23%
Move from a traditional defined benefit plan to a cash balance plan	20%
Bundle defined benefit plan services with a single provider	19%
Make other plan design changes	40%

Source: Diversified Investment Advisors, *Report on Retirement Plans 2005* (New York: Diversified Investment Advisors, 2005), 26.

From the ashes of the demise of DB plans, we now see 401(k) plans adopting many of the best features of DB plans. These changes that we see now in 401(k) plans are being made to fix many of the problems the 401(k) plans have in actual operation. The following runs through some of these changes that have happened and some that we predict will happen.

I.   Participation
    A. Problem—Many 401(k) plans have very low participation rates, especially among the employees who most need assistance saving for retirement.
    B. Fix—Automatic enrollment and/or negative elections. These two features both work to force employees into the plan immediately upon hire. It works by automatically enrolling employees at a set rate, say 3 percent, upon employment. If an employee does not want to participate, he or she can elect to do so; however, research shows that such employees are very unlikely to do so. DB plans always had automatic enrollment and this problem was never an issue (see Table 8.3 and Figure 8.4).

Table 8.3 Percentage of Plans with Automatic Enrollment

1999	2000	2001	2002	2003	2003
4.2	8.1	9.1	7.4	8.4	10.5

Source: The Profit Sharing Council of America, *43rd Annual Survey of Profit Sharing and 401(k) Plans* (Illinois: Profit Sharing Council/401(k) Council of America, 2000), 34.

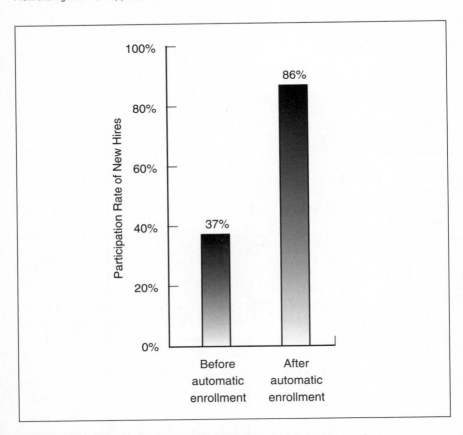

FIGURE 8.4 Automatic enrollment and participation rates

Source: Stephen P. Utkus and Jean A. Young, *Lessons from Behavioral Finance and the Autopilot 401(k) Plan* (Pennyslvania: The Vanguard Group, 2004), 5.

II. Participants Do Not Make Any Investment Elections

   A. Problem—Many participants do not make any investment elections after they join the 401(k) plan. The plan then invests their account in the default fund—which was typically a money market fund. Now plan sponsors are looking more closely at this default choice because they see that participants never shift out of the money market fund—which will not keep pace with inflation (see Table 8.4).

    B. Fix—Plan sponsors select funds with balanced equity and fixed-income exposure, including balanced or asset allocation funds that may change risk profile based on the participant's age. DB plans never had investment choice, and 401(k) plans continue to struggle with participants who do not want to make investment elections for their accounts (see Figure 8.5).

III. Distribution Options

    A. Problem—Most 401(k) plans provide for lump sum distribution of the account upon retirement. Many participants are troubled

**Table 8.4   Inertia in Participant Decision-Making
Participants Intended versus Actual Behaviors**

Action	Planned Change	Actual Change
Enroll in 401(k) plan	100%	14%
Increase contribution rate	28%	8%
Change fund selection	47%	15%
Change fund allocation	36%	10%

Source: Stephen P. Utkus and Jean A. Young, *Lessons from Behavioral Finance and the Autopilot 401(k) Plan* (Pennsylvania: The Vanguage Group, 2004), 5.

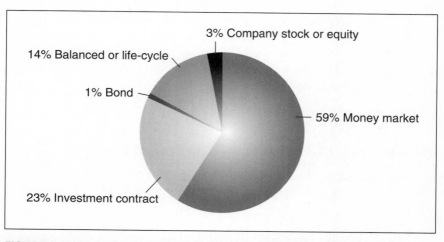

FIGURE 8.5   Default funds for defined contribution plans 2003 (n = 1,694 plans)

Source: Stephen P. Utkus and Jean A. Young, *Lessons from Behavioral Finance and the Autopilot 401(k) Plan* (Pennsylvania: The Vanguage Group, 2004), 3.

when faced with making investments that will impact their retirement years.

B. Fix—Many 401(k) plans are now exploring annuities and other payout options that give the participants additional choice that will guarantee monthly income throughout their remaining lifetime. A recent (2005) Hewitt survey highlighted this increase. Hewitt found that 20 percent of companies now offer annuities as a form of payment for final distributions, which is up from 17 percent in 2003. When available, 6 percent elected an annuity, which is up from 2 percent in 2003.

IV. Disability

A. Problem—Since the driving force in 401(k) plans is the employee's own salary deferrals, when a person is not employed due to a disability, his or her retirement savings can be significantly reduced. Most long-term disability plans do not contemplate these lost contributions and/or provide insufficient income for employees to continue to make 401(k) contributions during a time of high medical costs (see Table 8.5).

B. Fix—Provide disability coverage directly within the 401(k) plans. Participants can select an option, just like other investment options, that provides for continuation of 401(k) contributions in the event of a participant's disability. This insurance option, though not commonplace today, will become more popular as 401(k) plans become the only plan for most employees. IBM has begun to offer this insurance, and major insurance companies (UnumProvident, MetLife, AIG) are working to include it in their offerings. DB plans typically included disability provisions that provided for continued accrual of benefits, as well as early commencement of benefits.

Table 8.5   Lost 401(k) Balances by Age When Disability Occurred

Age When Totally Disabled	$6,000 Annual Contribution	$14,000 Annual Contribution
30	$887,481	$2,070,788
35	$606,438	$1,415,023
40	$406,059	$947,471
45	$263,191	$614,112
50	$161,328	$376,433
55	$88,702	$206,970

V. Deferred Annuity Options

    A. Problem—Investment risk is the number one risk being shifted to employees with 401(k) plan design. Many employees are not suited either by education or desire to make investment choices. This indecision shows up in many studies in the form of poor asset allocation, no investment choice being used, and other inactivity.

    B. Fix—Provide an option within the 401(k) plan that purchases units of deferred annuity with each salary deferral contribution. This "new" concept was developed decades ago when insurance companies dominated the retirement plan package. Today we see this option when insurance companies provide the bundled administration and investments for a plan. New York-based MetLife has introduced a deferred fixed annuity that converts into an immediate fixed annuity upon retirement. It works like this: An investor can put money into the annuity in increments. And with each investment, he or she is locking in an interest rate for that sum of money. That means when the investor retires and the deferred annuity converts to an immediate one, the payouts are based on the rates at the time of the investments. With a traditional fixed annuity, the return would be based on the rate at the time of conversion. We see it moving beyond insurance company–based models and into all 401(k) plans, even those managed by mutual fund companies. DB plans always focused on the ultimate benefit paid to participants, so it would not expose them to investment risk.

See Appendices F and H for some research on these topics performed by Vanguard. Overall, we applaud the changes that 401(k) plans are adopting to solve real problems with the actual operation of their plans. These changes address many of the shortcomings in 401(k) plans. However, participants still bear the investment risk associated with these plans. We believe the financial services industry will continue to work to bring cost-effective solutions that will help participants shift risk to organizations more suited to handle these risks, such as insurance companies.

Bundled Service Providers

In the small and mid-size marketplace, providers are pulling together all functions associated with retirement plan management. And in many cases, they are also providing bundled services for both defined contribution and DB services. These changes are being driven by both plan sponsor demand, as well as technological developments (see Table 8.6 and Figure 8.6).

We see this trend continuing and, in fact, accelerating, with service centers moving offshore to lower-cost countries. The advantages to employers are significant, with cost reductions paramount.

In addition to the continued dominance of bundled providers, we predict that you will see an increase in the use of independent fiduciaries and retirement advisers (see Table 8.7).

Table 8.6   Interest in Total Benefits Outsourcing

Interest in Total Benefits Outsourcing by Plan Type

		Employers Offering	
	All Employers Offering a DC Plan	Stand-Alone DC Plan	Both DC and DB Plans
We have never seriously considered it	40%	54%	33%
We have considered it but decided against it	27%	30%	26%
We are currently considering it	22%	8%	29%
We have considered it and have either implemented it or are currently in the process of implementing it	11%	9%	11%
Total	100%	101%[a]	99%[a]

[a]Numbers may not add up to 100% due to rounding.

Interest in Total Benefits Outsuorcing by Employee Size Group

	1,000– 2,499	2,500– 4,999	5,000– 9,999	10,000– 24,999	25,000+
We have never seriously considered it	46%	34%	23%	33%	27%
We have considered it but decided against it	26%	34%	20%	26%	31%
We are currently considering it	20%	21%	37%	24%	19%
We have considered it and have either implemented it or are currently in the process of implementing it	7%	11%	20%	17%	23%
Total	99[a]%	100%	100%	100%	100%

[a]Numbers may not add up to 100% due to rounding.
DB, defined benefit; DC, defined contribution
Source: Diversified Investment Advisors, *Report on Retirement Plans 2005* (New York: Diversified Investment Advisors, 2005), 27.

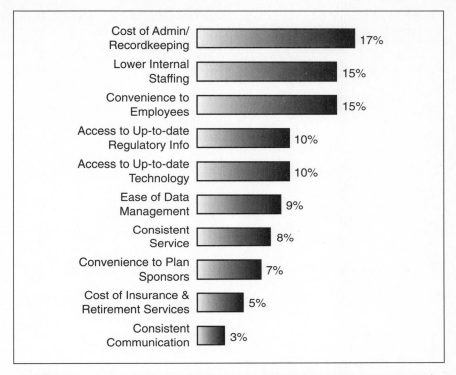

FIGURE 8.6   Single biggest advantage to total benefits outsourcing

Source: Stephen P. Utkus and Jean A. Young, *Lessons from Behavioral Finance and the Autopilot 401(k) Plan* (Pennsylvania: The Vanguage Group, 2004), 31.

With all the retirement plan services bundled with one company, fiduciaries are exposed to increases from the concentration with a single source. While many of these bundled providers include additional services such as performance monitoring, access to legal counsel, and actuarial consultants to help plan sponsors manage their fiduciary duty, we see an increased demand by plan sponsors for independent advice. We predict that you will see a substantial increase in the use of independent fiduciaries and investment consultants as a direct result of the move to total retirement outsourcing.

Enterprise Risk Management

As mentioned in earlier chapters, we see all our clients looking at their retirement plans in a new light. They are starting to look at their plans in re-

Table 8.7 Preferred Sources of Total Retirement Outsourcing

Preferred Sources of Total Retirement Outsourcing by Plan Type
Percentage of Companies Rated 4 or 5 Where 5 Is "Very Well Positioned"

	All Employers Offering a DC Plan	Employers Offering	
		Stand-Alone DC Plan	Both DC and DB Plans
Nationally recognized benefits consulting firm	62%	63%	62%
Provider of retirement benefits such as an insurance company, mutual fund, or bank	54%	60%	52%
TPA with a specialty or subspecialty in outsourcing	30%	35%	28%
Provider of health care benefits	24%	20%	26%

Preferred Sources of Total Retirement Outsourcing by Employee Size Group
Percentage of Companies Rated 4 or 5 Where 5 Is "Very Well Positioned"

	1,000– 2,499	2,500– 4,999	5,000– 9,999	10,000– 24,999	25,000+
Nationally recognized benefits consulting firm	65%	63%	51%	51%	58%
Provider of retirement benefits such as an insurance company, mutual fund, or bank	51%	71%	51%	46%	48%
TPA with a specialty or subspecialty in outsourcing	24%	40%	29%	37%	50%
Provider of health care benefits	17%	37%	29%	32%	35%

DB, defined benefit; DC, defined contribution.
Source: Diversified Investment Advisors, *Report on Retirement Plans 2005* (New York: Diversified Investment Advisors, 2005), 28.

lation to their entire business. In addition to retirement plans, other employee benefit programs are also scrutinized to see how they impact the overall risk of the employer. Medical programs—both for active employees and retirees—top the list of companies' focus points. Companies are starting to talk about what risk they want to hold and what risk they can transfer to employees or onto other financial markets. Enterprise risk management (ERM) is defined by the Casualty Actuarial Society as:

> The discipline by which an organization in any industry assesses, controls, exploits, finances, and monitors risk from all sources for the purpose of increasing the organization's short- and long-term value to its stakeholders.

ERM should force companies to be more educated about where they can provide a competitive advantage and therefore should keep the risk, or where it is more efficient to transfer the risk in order to reserve "risk capital" for other projects. This ERM trend has been spurred on with the passage of the Sarbanes-Oxley Act, which forces companies to take a risk control perspective throughout their organizations. No longer can executives simply "get the numbers right"—they need to put in place controls that will catch any problems before they happen. This is risk management at its core.

For retirement plans, ERM means that employers will no longer look at their retirement plans as silos, but as part of the broader organization. Managers will consider the impact of the business's life cycle—whether they are in a growth phase, maturity, decline, etc.—and how that intersects with the life cycle of the retirement plan. This disconnect is apparent when one considers the automobile industry, where some manufacturers have three retirees for every one of their workers. Is this a sustainable business model? Combine the business life cycle concerns with strategic concerns such as competitiveness within an industry such as we have seen with the airline industry recently. The new lower-cost carriers do not have high-cost DB plans; therefore, they have lower operating expenses. For all of these reasons, we predict that companies will continue to increase to use ERM techniques to manage their retirement plans in the future.

Demographics

The demographics facing the United States are well documented in the media. The aging of our population, the baby boomers starting to enter their retirement years, and a reduction in the birth rate will all have a tremendous impact on our society. The never-ending debates about how to solve the social security problem seem to flare up with each new presidential administration. For our purposes, we would like to highlight three areas that employers can focus on now that will help them navigate their organizations through these huge demographic changes.

Employees Working Longer

The image of people taking early retirement and moving to Florida to live out their golden years will not be and probably was not reality. Employees, for better or worse, understand that they can probably expect to work longer than their parents did. Whether it is because of financial needs or desire for social interaction, employees today do not expect to retire at 65. Other societal changes also impact this—such as people getting married later in life, having children later in life, having second or third marriages (some combined with new children)—and all contribute to the understanding that employees will have to work longer. Improvement in life expectancies coming from fantastic improvements in cancer and cardiovascular treatments has enabled many people to be productive after the initial onset of these once dreaded diseases. Granted, cancer and heart disease still are the leading causes of death in America, but improved medical treatment today extends both people's working lives and their lives in retirement (see Figures 8.7 and 8.8).

Phased Retirement

Combined with the expectation of people working longer, older workers are exploring ways to work that are outside the normal full-time commitment. Our government still puts up certain roadblocks for retirement plans to fully support this phased retirement, but many special interest groups are actively pursuing these changes.

Probably one of the biggest factors for employees looking to continue working in some fashion is access to medical care. As you can see from Figure 8.9, the top two concerns of employees during retirement are not actually related to retirement income, but rather their health status.

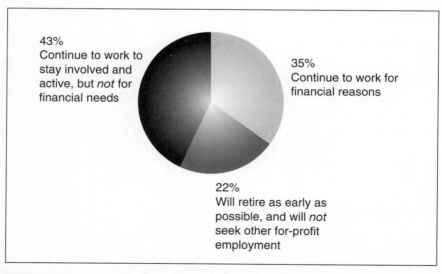

FIGURE 8.7 Expectation of continuing employment after retirement age

Source: Towers, Perrin, *Back to the Future: Redefining Retirement in the 21st Century* (Towers Perrin: 2004), 3.

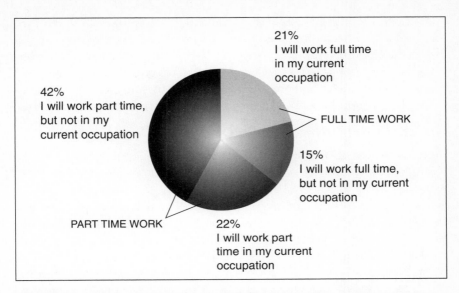

FIGURE 8.8   Nature of continuing employment after retirement age

Source: Towers, Perrin, *Back to the Future: Redefining Retirement in the 21st Century* (Towers Perrin: 2004), 4.

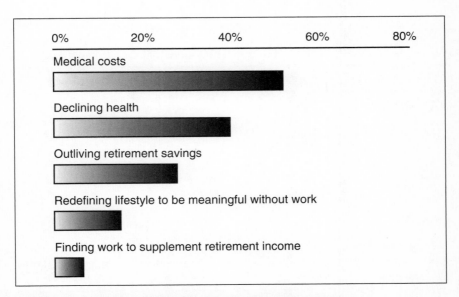

FIGURE 8.9   Employees' top concerns in retirement

Source: Towers, Perrin, *Back to the Future: Redefining Retirement in the 21st Century* (Towers Perrin: 2004), 9.

With the medical system in the United States tied to employment, we see this tension continuing. Left alone, we do not believe the medical system in the United States will change. Only through government intervention will any major structural changes occur that could reduce this tension. Given the current environment in Washington, DC, we do not believe there is enough willpower to make the tough choices to change this.

Generational Differences in Outlook

Employers need to recognize that the multiple generations within their workforce look at retirement planning significantly differently (see Table 8.8).

As you can see, younger people do not believe that Social Security will be there when they reach retirement age. This is a troubling thought, because one of the key tenets of Social Security is that it should cover every worker in the U.S. economy. This tenet of universal coverage was crucial when President Franklin D. Roosevelt proposed the program so that Social Security was not viewed as welfare. If the poor were the only ones to receive Social Security benefits, then the remaining people would only view it as another welfare payment. By insuring that all workers were covered and would receive Social Security, FDR believed that he would have broader support throughout the country.

Table 8.8   Expected Sources of Retirement Income (In Order of Importance)

All Employees	Age 18–34	Age 35–49	Age 50–59
401(k)/403(b) plans	401(k)/403(b) plans	401(k)/403(b) plans	Social Security
Social Security	Personal savings/investments	Social Security	401(k)/403(b) plans
Personal savings/investments	Social Security	Personal savings/iinvestments	Company pension
Company pension	Company pension	Company pension	Personal savings/iinvestments
Part-time employement during retirement	Part-time employement during retirement	Part-time employement during retirement	Part-time employement during retirement

Source: Diversified Investment Advisors, *Report on Retirement Plans 2005* (New York: Diversified Investment Advisors, 2005), 5.

If the younger population loses confidence in the system, overall support for Social Security will be reduced. If this trend continues, at some point in the future, the confidence and expectation of Social Security will be so low that our society as a whole will stop supporting it and we will revert back to a system based on personal employment–based savings only.

Demographically, as the baby boomers continue to retire, this bugle of Social Security beneficiaries will move through the system like a pig in a python. Once this "pig" of baby boomers is complete, if Social Security does not maintain the confidence and commitment of the remaining population, we could see it quickly dwindle and be eliminated. We would then be back to a welfare system supported by general tax revenues. That is certainly not what FDR envisioned in the 1930s.

Where to Go for Help

Resources

United States Government Sites

Bureau of Labor Statistics: http://www.bls.gov/blshome.html

Code of Federal Regulations: http://www.access.gpo.gov/nara/cfr/cfr-table-search.html

Department of Labor: http://www.dol.gov

Internal Revenue Service: http://www.irs.gov

Pension Benefit Guarantee Corporation: http://www.pbgc.gov

Securities and Exchange Commission: http://www.sec.gov

Social Security Online: http://www.ssa.gov/

Other Sites

AARP: http://www.aarp.org

American Academy of Actuaries: http://www.actuary.org

American Benefits Counsel: http://www.americanbenefitscouncil.org/

BenefitsLink: http://www.benefitslink.com

Boston College's Center for Retirement Research: http://www.bc.edu/centers/crr/

Canadian Institute of Actuaries: http://www.actuaries.ca/

Employee Benefit Research Institute: http://www.ebri.org

ERISA Industry Committee: http://www.eric.org/forms/documents/ Document FormPublic/

401(k) Help Center: http://www.401khelpcenter.com/

FreeErisa: http://www.freeerisa.com

International Foundation of Employee Benefit Plans: http://www.ifebp .org/

Pension Research Counsel: http://prc.wharton.upenn.edu/prc/prc.html

PlanSponsor: http://www.plansponsor.com

Profit Sharing Council of America: http://www.psca.org

Society of Actuaries: http://www.soa.org

Tag Data: http://www.tagdata.com/home.htm

Studies and Surveys

Argus Consulting Ltd., NGO Retirement Plan Survey: http://www. arguscl.com/2005%20NGO%20Retirement%20Survey%20Summary .pdf

Employee Benefit Research Institute, EBRI Research Highlights: Retirement Benefits: http://www.ebri.org/pdf/briefspdf/0603ib.pdf

Georgia State University/AON, Replacement Ratio Study: A Measurement Tool for Retirement Planning: http://www.aon.com/about/pub lications/issues/2004_06_replacement_ratio_study.jsp

Hewitt Associates, Current Retirement Plan Challenges: Employer Perspectives 2003: http://was4.hewitt.com/hewitt/resource/rptspubs/ subrptspubs/pdf/curr_ret_plan_2003.pdf

Hewitt Associates, Financial Insecurity: Facing America's Healthcare and Retirement Crisis: http://was4.hewitt.com/hewitt/resource/spkrs conf/subspkrsconf/upcoming/pbs_documentary.pdf

Hewitt Associates, Global Survey of Retirement Plan Accounting Assumptions: http://was4.hewitt.com/hewitt/resource/rptspubs/sub rptspubs/pdf/global_survey_2005.pdf

Hewitt Associates, Total Retirement Income at Large Companies: The Real Deal: http://was4.hewitt.com/hewitt/resource/rptspubs/subrpts pubs/total_retirement.pdf

Mellon, Is Severance the Right Solution for Your Company: http://www .mellon.com/hris/pdf/Severance_091404.pdf

Mercer Human Resources, Benefits Outside the Square Report: http://www.mercerhr.com/summary.jhtml/dynamic/idCon tent/1178605

Mercer Human Resources, Eye on Accounting Trends FAS 87 Report: http://www.mercerhr.com/summary.jhtml/dynamic/idContent/ 1172825

Mercer Human Resources, Market Issue Survey Choice of Fund: http://www.mercerhr.com/summary.jhtml/dynamic/idContent/ 1180545

Mercer Human Resources, Review of Retirement Programs Sponsored by S&P 500 Companies: http://www.mercerhr.com/summary.jhtml/dynamic/idContent/1193815

Profit Sharing Council of America, 48th Annual Survey of Profit Sharing Plans: http://www.psca.org/DATA/48th.html

Society of Actuaries, 2001 Retirement Risk Survey: http://www.actuary.org/newsroom/pdf/survey_25feb02.pdf

Towers Perrin, Back to the Future Redefining Retirement in the 21st Century: http://www.towersperrin.com/hrservices/webcache/towers/United_States/publications/Reports/Redefining_Retirement/ 2003_redefining_ret.pdf

Towers Perrin, FASB Proposes Guidance on Accounting for Post Retirement Medical Benefits after the Medicare Modernization Act: http://www.towersperrin.com/hrservices/webcache/towers/United_States/publications/Reports/Update_FASB/Update_FASB_3-25.pdf

Towers Perrin, The Fortune 100 Pension Funding Shortfalls Decline but Deferred Costs Continue to Rise: http://www.towersperrin.com/hrservices/webcache/towers/United_States/publications/Reports/2004_Fortune_100_Pension/Fortune_100_2004_pension.pdf

Towers Perrin, Managing Pension Plan Financial Performance Worldwide: http://www.towersperrin.com/hrservices/webcache/towers/United_States/publications/Reports/Global_Actuary/Global_Actuary_Brochure.pdf

Towers Perrin, Pension Plans Financial Results Come Under the Corporate Microscope: http://www.towersperrin.com/hrservices/webcache/towers/United_States/publications/Reports/2003_CFO_Survey/2003_CFO_Survey.pdf

Towers Perrin, A Towers Perrin Proposal for Pension Funding Reform: http://www.towersperrin.com/hrservices/webcache/towers/United_States/publications/Reports/Pension_Fund3/pension_funding.pdf

Towers Perrin, A Towers Perrin Proposal for Pension Funding Reform: http://www.towersperrin.com/hrservices/webcache/towers/United_

States/publications/Reports/Pension_Funding_Reform/Pension_
Funding_Reform.pdf

Towers Perrin, TP Track M&A Report: http://www.towersperrin.com/
hrservices/webcache/towerUnited_States/publications/Reports/TP_
Track_MA/TPTrack_MA.pdf

Towers Perrin, TP Track Shifting Investment Risk to Employees—The
Landscape Changes: http://www.towersperrin.com/hrservices/web
cache/towers/United_States/publications/Reports/TP_Track_Shift
InvstRisk/TP_Track_ShiftInvstRisk.pdf

Towers Perrin, Worldwide Benefits Management Survey: http://www
.towersperrin.com/hrservices/webcache/towers/United_Kingdom/
publications/Reports/2004_WWBM/WWBM2004.pdf

U.S. Chamber of Commerce, The 2003 Employee Benefits Study: http:
//www.uschamber.com/NR/rdonlyres/eo2knri5wjdblcrmfnyld
hrwsrr3gawv6lp4ndpzrtwlbgdtqu7oonimwafsckhh4dpogejbbf5bed/2
003EBSBrochureforweb.pdf

The Vanguard Group, Automatic Enrollment: Vanguard Client Experience: https://institutional3.vanguard.com/iip/pdf/CRR_automatic_
enrollment_clientexp.pdf

The Vanguard Group, Lessons From Behavioral Finance and the Autopilot 401(k) Plan: https://institutional4.vanguard.com/iip/pdf/crr_
autopilot.pdf

The Vanguard Group, Selecting a Default Fund for a Defined Contribution Plan: http://www.vanguard.com.au/library/pdf/defaultfunds
.pdf

Watson Wyatt, Adopting Hybrid Pension Plans Financial and Communications Issues: http://www.watsonwyatt.com/research/white papers/
wprender.asp?id=wp01

Watson Wyatt, The Effects of Pension Nondiscrimination Rules on Private
Sector Pension Participation: http://www.watsonwyatt.com/research/
whitepapers/wprender.asp?id=wp-05

Watson Wyatt, The Emergence of Hybrid Plans and Their Implications for
Retirement Income Security in the Twenty-First Century: http://www
.watsonwyatt.com/research/whitepapers/wprender.asp?id=wp-04

Watson Wyatt, An Empirical Analysis of the Transition to Hybrid Pension
Plans in the United States: http://www.watsonwyatt.com/research/
whitepapers/wprender.asp?id=wp-02

Watson Wyatt, ERISA Motivations, Provisions, and Implications for Retirement Security: http://www.watsonwyatt.com/research/white papers/wprender.asp?id=wp-06

Watson Wyatt, Risk Sharing in Employer Pensions Provision: http://www.watsonwyatt.com/research/whitepapers/wprender.asp?id=eu6 43

Watson Wyatt, Structural Impediments to Phased Retirement: http://www.watsonwyatt.com/research/whitepapers/wprender.asp?id= wp-13

Watson Wyatt, Taking the Subsidy Out of Early Retirement: The Story Behind the Conversion to Hybrid Pensions: http://www.watson wyatt .com/research/whitepapers/wprender.asp?id=wp-03

Company ABC— Request for Proposal: 401(k) Savings Plan

Company Background

Since its founding in 1959, Company ABC has led the rapidly evolving markets of clinical diagnostic systems. Company ABC's renowned medical technology is used every day in hundreds of hospitals and laboratories around the globe. It is Company ABC's focus on its customers—and on the patients whose lives are touched by its products—that is guiding the company into the next century. For information, visit http://www.CompanyABC.com.

Retirement Program Goals

Company ABC has recently frozen its defined benefit plan and increased its company match for the 401(k) savings plan. Company ABC has identified the following goals:

- *Investment fund options*
  - Competitive mutual funds with proven track records of performance are required of the new provider.
  - "Lifestyle" funds—Company ABC is very interested in offering lifestyle options and is concerned about issues such as default option and impact on communication.
- *Account service.* Proactive, efficient, and high-quality service is required of the provider. This will include, but not be limited to, compliance

issues, scheduled employee and sponsor meetings, and ability to rectify problems (as they arise).

- *Employee meetings.* Quarterly meetings at two primary locations (Boston and San Francisco) and a yearly meeting for field staff at a location to be determined.

- *Plan provisions.* No changes anticipated.

- *Time line.* Company ABC is flexible on an implementation date but would prefer completion by September 30, 2005.

Other Assumptions

- *Fees.* Please include in your fee proposal an annual ERISA reimbursement account equal to 10 basis points (roughly $35,000) to be used by Company ABC at their discretion for ERISA qualified plan expenses (audit, investment performance monitoring, legal, etc.).

- *Commissions, other adviser fees.* None.

- *Payroll.* 26 pay periods per year. One payroll vendor—ADP.

Request for Proposal

We are requesting proposals from select vendors to provide 401(k) administration services for the Company ABC 401(k) Savings Plan. Please submit your response by April 2.

COMPANY ABC will adhere to the following schedule for the selection process:

Date	Description
3/17/05	Argus issues RFP
4/2/05	Vendor proposals due
Week of 4/12/05	Notification of finalists (maximum of 4)
Week of 4/26/05	Finalist interviews
Week of 5/03/05	Vendor selection and notification
10/1/05	Effective date of consolidated plan

Please direct all correspondence to Argus Consulting at the following address:

Argus Consulting Ltd
66 Commonwealth Avenue
Concord, MA 01742
phone: 978 371 8029
fax: 978 371 8028

Attachments

To assist in the development of your proposal, we have provided the following data:

Description	Comments
Distribution of active employees by location	Included within this document
Assets by fund	Included within this document
Trust Statement as of December 31, 2004	Electronic attachment
COMPANY ABC SPD and plan amendments	Electronic attachment
COMPANY ABC plan document	Electronic attachment
Copy of most recent 5500	Available upon request
Most recent ADP/ACP testing results	Passed; available upon request

Exhibits

DISTRIBUTION OF EMPLOYEES BY LOCATION

Location	No. of Employees (est.)
Boston	350
San Francisco	180
Field Employees	100
Total	630

ASSETS BY FUND (AS OF 12/31/04)

Fund Name	Asset Value	% of Total Asset Value
Equity Fund A	$10,000,000	20%
Equity Fund B	$5,000,000	10%
Equity Fund C	$3,000,000	6%
Fixed Income A	$15,000,000	31%
Money Market Fund	$8,000,000	17%
Equity Fund D	$2,000,000	4%
Fixed Income B	$5,000,000	10%
Total	$48,000,000	

LOAN INFORMATION (AS OF 12/31/04)

No. of Loans	Total Loan Amount	Average Outstanding Loan Balance
81	$562,590.17	$6,942.56

Sample Traditional Request for Proposal

NOTE: Argus Consulting Ltd does not recommend the use of this sample traditional request for proposal (RFP) for several reasons:

- Lack of focus of client-specific goals and objectives
- Inability of our clients to effectively evaluate answers to over 100 questions
- Inappropriate use of provider's time—We would rather they spend their time preparing to serve our clients' needs than respond to over 100 questions. You will get better information if they can tailor their responses to exactly what you are looking for
- Redundant—If you hire the proper consultant or do your own initial due diligence on the marketplace, you will only send RFP to qualified providers

However, you may find some questions below that in fact are helpful to you as you construct your own streamlined RFP.

Plan Administration and Daily Valuation Record Keeping, Employee Communication and Education, and Trustee/Custodial Services

A. **Background Information on Your Firm**
    1. Please provide the official name of your company, the parent company (if different), and any affiliated companies.

2. Which office location will be servicing Company ABC (including record keeping, account management, participant service center, and support)?

3. When were the parent company and your company (if different) established?

4. Please describe the financial strength of the parent company and your company (if different).

5. How long has your company been administering 401(k) and other participant-directed plans?

6. How long has your company been providing daily record keeping for such plans?

7. Please provide the following statistics on the plans that your company administers:

	All 401(k) and Similar Plans	Daily Valued Plans
Number of plans		
Smallest plan—number of participants		
Largest plan—number of participants		
Average number of participants per plan		
Smallest asset level in a plan		
Largest asset level in a plan		
Average asset level in a plan		
Number of plans with $50 million—$70 million in assets		
Number of plans in participant ranges		
0 to 100		
500 to 1,000		
1,000 to 5,000		
Over 5,000		
Plans added in past 3 years*		
Plans lost in past 3 years		

*Include plans added through vendor searches only, not through merger/acquisition of other record keepers/trustees.

8. Please describe your total quality program. Please provide your SAS #70 Report.

9. Describe your firm's philosophy toward leading-edge technology for 401(k) services.

10. Describe your firm's planned improvements for 401(k) services.

11. Please provide an organization chart, job descriptions, and training programs for all applicable positions.

12. Please provide the following information on your organization:

Item	Number of Employees	Number of Professional Employees	Average Tenure of Professional Employees	Turnover Rate of Administrative Employees
Administration and record keeping				
Employee communications				
ERISA attorneys				
Information systems support				

13. Please provide resumes of the key people in your organization in the areas of administration and record keeping, employee communications, legal, and information systems.

14. Please provide references where you provide your services to plans of similar type and size. Provide three ongoing relationships with at least 3 years' experience and any plans that have been recently converted from the current service provider.

B. Plan Design and Documentation

1. Describe your employee benefits consulting services for plan design and maximizing allowed plan contributions.

2. How do you keep the plan sponsor informed about legislative and other government requirements?

3. What plan documentation services can your company provide?

Item	Prototype Plan (Yes or No)	Customized Plan Yes or No)
Plan document		
Government-required plan amendments		
Plan sponsor–requested plan amendments		
Summary plan descriptions		

4. Do you prepare applications for determination and submit summary plan descriptions and summaries of material modifications to the IRS and Department of Labor?

5. Please describe in detail your experience with designing, implementing, and administering nonqualified plans. Include a description of the various types of nonqualified deferred compensation plans you administer.

B. Plan Administration and Daily Valuation Record Keeping

1. How will the Company ABC plan be served? Will they have a dedicated plan administrator? Do your firm representatives make regular on-site visits?

2. Please describe your record keeping hardware and software systems. What was the system's origin, when was it installed, and how is it maintained?

3. What form of database backup do you use?

4. What are your computer system development plans and how do you maintain up-to-date regulatory and technological systems?

5. What is your backup/disaster recovery plan?

6. What is your alternative site/power supply in the event of disaster?

7. What data file transmission do you require from the plan sponsor? What data and format are required?

8. What are the hours of availability of your voice response system (VRS)? Is your VRS available via a toll-free number?

9. Are customer service representatives available with your VRS? What are their hours of availability, their credentials and training programs, your audit/quality program, and the level of turnover?

10. Is there a "test" VRS account available? If so, please provide the necessary access numbers.

11. How many incoming phone lines are there in the service center's phone system?

12. Please discuss the utilization of phone lines during peak and non-peak hours.

13. Please indicate the services available on your VRS:

Item	Yes	No
Personal access codes		
Plan information and provisions		
Enrollment of employees		
Amount of current contributions		
Investment allocation of current contributions		
Change contribution levels by $		
Change contribution levels by a combination of $ and %		
Total account balance		
Account balance by source, including vesting		
Account balance by fund, including transferable amounts		
Transaction history		
Investment transfers by $		
Reallocation of investment option by %		
Reallocation of investment options by $		
On demand account statements		
Investment fund price information		
Investment fund performance information		
Status of current loans		
Loan payoff amount information		

(continues)

(continued)

Item	Yes	No
Loan modeling		
Loan transactions with plan sponsor approval		
Loan transactions without plan sponsor approval		
Hardship withdrawals with plan sponsor approval		
Hardship withdrawals without plan sponsor approval		
QDROs with plan sponsor approval		
QDROs without plan sponsor approval		
Other withdrawals with plan sponsor approval		
Other withdrawals without plan sponsor approval		
Initiate termination withdrawals		
Reallocation of investment balances		
Unit accounting		
Share accounting		

14. What fulfillment items can a participant request through the VRS? Are prospectus information, fund profile, and rate of return information available?

15. Describe your loan maintenance procedures, including monitoring, loans deemed in default and offset distributions, and processing loan payoffs.

16. What is the lag time between paying off a loan and taking a new loan out?

17. What is the frequency that you process loans, withdrawals, and distributions?

18. Can loans be requested any time during a month? How long does it take to process a loan?

19. How long, on average, does a participant have to wait before his or her call is answered?

20. Can the VRS message be customized?

21. If the VRS is down, will there be a message to that effect on the phone line?

22. When and how will Company ABC be notified about problems with the VRS?

23. Describe the trading platform and the extent of your automation (i.e., electronic trading, facsimile, phone, etc.).

24. Please indicate the services available from your Internet site:

Item	Yes	No
Personal access codes		
Plan information and provisions		
Enrollment of employees		
Amount of current contributions		
Investment allocation of current contributions		
Change contribution levels by $		
Change contribution levels by a combination of $ and %		
Total account balance		
Account balance by source, including vesting		
Account balance by fund, including transferable amounts		
Transaction history		
Investment transfers by %		
Investment transfers by $		
Reallocation of investment options by %		
Reallocation of investment options by $		
On demand account statements		
Investment fund price information		
Status of current loans		

(continues)

(continued)

Item	Yes	No
Loan payoff amount information		
Loan modeling		
Loan transactions with plan sponsor approval		
Loan transactions without plan sponsor approval		
Hardship withdrawals with plan sponsor approval		
Hardship withdrawals without plan sponsor approval		
QDROs with plan sponsor approval		
QDROs without plan sponsor approval		
Other withdrawals with plan sponsor approval		
Other withdrawals without plan sponsor approval		
Initiate termination withdrawals		
Reallocation of investment balances		
Unit accounting		
Share accounting		

25. Please indicate the services available from your record keeping system:

Item	Yes	No
Determination of eligibility		
Maintenance of participant data		
Determination of contribution levels		
Calculation of matching contributions		
Calculation of fund splits		
Loan processing with plan sponsor involvement		

Item	Yes	No
Loan processing without plan sponsor involvement		
Loan tracking and collection notices		
Loan processing with plan sponsor involvement		
Acceptance of partial loan prepayments		
Acceptance of full loan prepayments		
Hardship withdrawal processing with plan sponsor involvement		
Hardship withdrawal processing without plan sponsor involvement		
Notification to participant of reeligibility posthardship withdrawal		
QDRO form processing with plan sponsor involvement		
QDRO form processing without plan sponsor involvement		
In service withdrawal processing		
Termination of employment withdrawal processing		
Age 70½ notifications		
Death benefit processing		
Processing of chargeback of plan costs		

26. How are employees on leave handled (loans, etc.)?
27. How are employees in default on loans handled?
28. Do you provide an administrative procedures manual?
29. What training will be provided for the plan sponsor's staff on administrative procedures?
30. Can participant/plan data be transferred electronically? Diskette? Modem?
31. Do you provide the plan sponsor with online computer access to your record keeping system? Is access available at plan level, participant level, or both?
32. Company ABC currently uses Peoplesoft for payroll services. Does your firm have experience with clients using this vendor? If yes, please describe. How do you work with clients and their payroll services?

33. How do you integrate information back to the client's payroll system (i.e., new loan, loan payoff, contribution rate changes)?

34. Please list the forms that would be used in operating the Company ABC plans. Please provide sample forms.

35. Can transmissions, forms, checks, etc. be consolidated for all plans with allocations to be determined by your system through formula or supporting data?

36. What are the limits, if any, on the number of investment options, money sources, contribution changes, investment allocation changes, investment transfers, and loans?

37. What is the cutoff time for same-day processing of transactions?

38. Do you accommodate same-day trading for all funds? If not, what would be the exceptions and what would be the trading periods?

39. How does your system handle forfeitures? Can they be allocated by location?

40. What are your expected turnaround times for management reports, participant statements, withdrawals, and loans?

41. Do you include a quarterly newsletter with quarterly participant statements? If so, can the newsletters be approved by Company ABC management prior to mailing?

42. Please provide sample participant statements. Can participant statements be customized?

43. Can participant statements be generated monthly instead of quarterly?

44. Can you calculate each participant's overall rate of return and print it on the statement?

45. What are the client's responsibilities for day-to-day record keeping and what are your outsourcing capabilities?

46. How do you handle adjustments/errors?

47. Will your firm reimburse participants for mistakes that you make?

48. Please discuss your firm's nondiscrimination testing capabilities and ability to utilize all available curing options under applicable regulations when nondiscrimination problems occur.

49. Can your system handle automatic rebalancing of a participant's account to a predetermined target allocation?

50. Do you guarantee service levels for all aspects of plan administration? Please provide detailed information.

D. Trustee and Custodial Services

1. Please describe your preferred trust/custodial services arrangement along with background information on the organization providing these services.

2. Discuss the role of, and services provided by, the above trust organization in the record keeping and administration of Company ABC's plan.

3. How rapidly is trading accomplished for new contributions, transfers, and withdrawals?

4. Is your firm linked electronically to the above trust organization?

E. Investment Options

1. Do you require the client to use your proprietary funds and/or allied funds? What is the ratio of proprietary to allied funds and/or outside funds?

2. Please provide a sample lineup of investment options for the ABC plan.

3. Can you provide same-day exchange for all funds? If not, what are your limitations?

4. For each investment vehicle identified above, please provide the information requested in the following chart:

Item	
Comparative index(es) used by the manager	
Expense structure	
Inception date	
Investment vehicle objective	
Investment philosophy	
Investment/portfolio manager(s) and biographies	

5. For each investment vehicle, provide the annualized return for the 1-, 3-, 5-, and 10-year (or since inception) periods ending on each of the last three calendar quarters.

6. For each investment vehicle, provide the annualized year-to-date return.

7. For each equity investment vehicle, provide the top 10 holdings as of the last three calendar quarters.

8. For each balanced asset allocation and/or lifestyle investment option, provide the asset breakdown by cash, stocks, and bonds as of at least three calendar quarters.

9. For each international or global investment option, provide the dollar-weighted average of the investment's allocations in each country.

10. For stable value investments, describe how interest is credited, frequency of rate changes, asset type(s), credit quality, and breakdown of assets in percentage.

11. For each investment vehicle, articulate the investment strategy used by the manager to add value relative to the benchmark identified.

12. Please describe any additional information regarding the specific investment options you wish to include.

13. Please discuss your process for adding or replacing funds from your proprietary fund list, your alliance fund list, and any non-alliance funds ABC may request.

F. **Employee Communications and Investment Education (please provide samples)**

1. Company ABC has special challenges in reaching and communicating to employees/participants who may be dispersed in many locations. As a result, communications strategies and education programs are very important. Please provide a detailed discussion on how you propose to effectively communicate plan information, enrollment strategies, increasing participation strategies, education materials, etc. to the ABC workforce.

2. How do you determine employee investment education and communication objectives?

3. What preenrollment communications do you provide? Can they be customized?

4. Can you provide a customized video? If so, approximately what would it cost? What enrollment materials do you provide?

5. Who will conduct the enrollment meetings? What are their employee communications credentials? Are they full-time employee communications specialists? Are they on salary or commission?

6. What ongoing employee investment education/seminars do you provide? Do you have an ongoing series of employee investment education materials and handouts?

7. Who will conduct the ongoing employee investment education meetings? What are their employee communications credentials? Are they full-time employee communications specialists? Are they on salary or commission?

8. What materials and/or counseling are provided to participants leaving the plan?

9. Do you provide a newsletter? If so, how frequently? Do you have a separate newsletter for nonparticipants? If so, how frequently?

10. Do you provide retirement income/investment projections? If so, how often do you provide these projections and is there an additional charge for them? Are the projections provided on paper or over the Internet? Are they provided to all participants or to only those who request them?

11. Do you provide retirement planning software? If so, is there an additional charge for the software? Is the software available over the Internet?

12. Do you provide investment advice? If so, how is the advice provided? What software, if any, is used? Has the software been procured from an outside vendor or developed in-house?

13. If you provide advice, how are you managing the risk? For your company? For the plan sponsor?

G. Conversion

1. Please provide a description of your conversion process.

2. Which of your conversion teams will be provided to Company ABC? Who will be the team leader?

3. Please provide timelines (best case, worst case, and most likely case) for the conversion, including the length of the blackout period and responsibilities for each of the tasks.

4. What will be the requirements of the plan sponsor's staff?

5. How will assets be invested during the conversion process?

H. Fee Quote

1. Please provide a complete fee schedule and a fee quote specific to the plan:

	401(k) Plan	Nonqualified Plan
	Setup/Conversion Fees	
Plan document fee		
Conversion fee		
Internet setup fee		
VRS setup fee		
Loan conversion		
Enrollment materials		
Any additional conversion fees		
	Employee Communication Fees	
Meetings—first and additional		
Materials		
Coordination		
Video—first and additional		
	Annual Administrative Fees	
Annual base fee		
Annual record keeping fee		
Annual discrimination testing fee		
Annual government reporting fee, including preparation of Form 5500		
Annual loan processing fee		
Annual employer match calculation		
Eligibility determination		
Annual trustee fee		
Annual custody fee for current asset level		

	401(k) Plan	Nonqualified Plan
Postage charge to mail quarterly statements to plan participants		
Participant statements—quarterly		
Quarterly newsletter—participants		
Quarterly newsletters—nonparticipants		
Participant-level investment advisory services		
401(k)/NQDC wrap fees		
		Per Occurrence Fees
Loan setup fee		
Distribution fees		
Cost to add or change investment fund		
QDRO processing fee		
Plan mergers/conversions		
Any other fees (please list along with amounts)		

2. Are your fees guaranteed for an extended period? If so, how long?

3. According to your record keeping agreement, who pays for errors?

I. Client Contacts and Biographies

Please state the name(s) of the contact(s) who will have direct interaction with the plan sponsor's staff. Please also list any other important contacts or support people. Please provide brief biographies of all key personnel who will be working with the plan sponsor.

Sample Defined Contribution Plan Investment Policy Statement

XYZ 401(k) Retirement Plan Investment Policy

Background

The XYZ 401(k) Retirement Plan (the "Plan") is a qualified employee benefit plan established and operated pursuant to all applicable federal laws and regulations. The Plan is also an Employee Retirement Income Security Act (ERISA) Section 404(c) plan, which provides Plan participants with the ability to exercise a degree of control over the investment of their own account Plan assets. The Plan's fiduciaries are charged with the overall responsibility under ERISA to manage this Plan prudently on behalf of the participants, pursuant to the standards of the "Prudent Man Rule" as outlined under the Third Restatement of Trusts and ERISA.

The trustees of the Plan have established this Investment Policy Statement for the purpose of providing general investment guidelines to govern the management of the Plan's assets and also to communicate to the Plan's participants. This policy serves as a general framework by which the Plan's assets are to be managed, unless it is clearly prudent to follow a different strategy. It is expected that this policy statement will be on file with the trustees and is available for review by all Plan participants.

Pursuant to ERISA Section 402(c)(3), the trustees may delegate the investment management duties of all or part of the Plan to one or more professional investment managers, who, in turn, have the authority to manage the assets in accordance with the general investment guidelines contained herein.

In compliance with their fiduciary obligation with regard to the management of the Plan's assets, the Plan sponsor and trustees, with the assistance of their investment adviser, will do the following:

1. Establish and maintain investment policy objectives to govern the management of the Plan assets.

2. Act prudently in the selection of investment managers to manage the various investment options offered to participants as investment selections in the Plan.

3. Establish and implement investment performance objectives and measurement standards.

4. Establish participant control parameters and communication programs, in an effort to provide sufficient information to enable participants to make informed investment decisions.

Investment Objectives

The trustees have selected a range of investment options as described by ERISA Section 404(c) and applicable regulations. These asset categories shall be such that when taken together, participants have a reasonable opportunity to materially affect the investment returns in their accounts while considering the risk of volatility of their portfolios. The diverse investment objectives with materially different risk/return characteristics of the Plan will include at least the following:

- Cash or money market
- U.S. investment grade bond
- Common stock as represented by the Standard & Poor's 500 Stock Index
- Common stock as represented by the Russell 2000 Index or similar "small cap" index
- International stock
- Balanced or asset allocation

Initial Mutual Fund Selection Criteria

The selection of potential mutual funds as investment choices shall be as follows:

- Total annual expense ratios of less than 1.30 percent per year

- No up-front or rear-end loads
- Five-year performance history
- Five-year performance history above the median of funds in the appropriate asset category
- Quality of shareholder servicing from fund custodian

Ongoing Performance Measurement

The relative performance of the mutual fund as compared to funds in the same category will be compared over the preceding one, three, and five years. A fund choice will be considered "satisfactory" if its trailing one-, three-, and five-year performance is above the median of the benchmark category for each of these time periods. In consideration of these parameters, the trustees will give greater weight to three- and five-year performance results, and a lesser weight to the most recent one-year results. The expense ratio of the fund should stay below the maximum 1.30 percent.

A fund will be considered "unsatisfactory" if its trailing one-, three-, and five-year performance is below the median of the benchmark category for each of these time periods. In consideration of these parameters, the trustees will give greater weight to three- and five-year performance results, and a lesser weight to the most recent one-year results. If the expense ratio of the fund should rise above the maximum 1.30 percent, the fund will be considered unsatisfactory.

The trustees have the right to replace any mutual fund with an "unsatisfactory" rating with a fund carrying a "satisfactory" rating from the same asset category.

Participant Education

At Plan inception, participants will receive the current investment information for the Plan's mutual fund choices, historical return, and risk. Participants will be given a current prospectus on each mutual fund and will be given updated investment performance information on each fund choice at least once per year. Participants are also encouraged to call the investment adviser any time they have specific questions.

Adopted:

By: _____
    Trustee

Date: _____

SAMPLE DEFINED BENEFIT PLAN INVESTMENT POLICY STATEMENT

XYZ COMPANY RETIREMENT PLAN INVESTMENT POLICY STATEMENT

Background

The XYZ Company Retirement Plan (the "Plan") is a qualified employee benefit plan established and operated pursuant to all applicable federal laws and regulations. The Plan is a defined benefit pension plan with XYZ Company (the "Company") solely responsible for any required contributions.

Plan's Financial Situation

As of the most recent actuarial valuation (January 1, 1999), the Plan's financial situation is as follows:

Market value of assets	$19,000,000
Value of accrued benefits	$8,000,000
Funded status	240%
Required company contribution	$0
Annual benefit payments to retirees	$400,000
Value of benefits accruing for active participants	$400,000
Average age	
Active participants	46 years
Retirees and beneficiaries	72 years

Purpose

In general, the purpose of this Investment Policy Statement is to outline a philosophy and attitude that will guide the investment management of the Plan's assets toward the desired result. This Investment Policy Statement is set forth by the Retirement Plan Committee in order to:

1. Define and assign the responsibilities of all involved parties.
2. Establish a clear understanding for all involved parties of the investment goals and objectives for the Plan's assets.

3. Offer guidance and limitations to all investment managers regarding the investment of the Plan's assets.

4. Establish a basis for evaluating investment results.

5. Ensure the Plan's assets are managed in accordance with the Employee Retirement Income Security Act (ERISA) and all relevant regulations.

6. Establish the relevant investment horizon for which the Plan's assets will be managed.

Assignment of Responsibility

Retirement Plan Committee

The Retirement Plan Committee (RPC) is charged with the responsibility for management of the Plan's assets. The RPC shall discharge its duties in accordance with the Plan's documents and solely in the interest of the Plan with the care, skill, prudence, and diligence under the circumstances then prevailing that a prudent man acting in a like capacity and familiar with such matters would use. The RPC will adhere to the requirements of ERISA and all other applicable regulations. The specific responsibilities of the RPC, relating to the investment management of the Plan's assets, include:

1. Projecting the Plan's financial needs and ensuring that such needs are communicated to the investment manager(s) on a timely basis.

2. Defining the Plan's risk tolerance and investment time horizon, and communicating these to the appropriate parties.

3. Establishing reasonable and consistent investment objectives, policies, and guidelines that will direct the investment of the Plan's assets.

4. Selecting qualified investment professionals to the extent it deems necessary, including such investment manager(s) and investment consultant(s) as it may determine.

5. Monitoring progress to achieve the investment objectives and to adhere to policy guidelines of any investment manager(s).

6. Evaluating the performance of the investment consultant.

7. Developing and enacting proper control procedures, including asset allocation parameters and the hiring and firing of any investment professionals.

8. Establishing a proxy voting policy.

The RPC will not reserve any control over investment decisions, with the exception of specific limitations described in this Investment Policy Statement. Investment managers will be held responsible and accountable to achieve the objectives stated herein. While it is not believed that the limitations will hamper investment managers in the execution of their duties, each investment manager should request the modifications that they deem appropriate.

Investment Consultant

The investment consultant will act as a nondiscretionary adviser to the RPC. Consulting advice concerning the Plan's assets will be offered by the investment consultant and will be consistent with the investment objectives, policies, guidelines, and constraints of the Plan. To the extent determined by the Committee, specific responsibilities of the investment consultant will include:

1. Assisting in the development and periodic review of the investment policy.
2. Analyzing and recommending an appropriate asset allocation.
3. Conducting investment manager searches when requested by the RPC.
4. Assisting the RPC in the negotiation of fees with the investment manager(s).
5. Providing due diligence research on the investment manager(s).
6. Monitoring the performance of the investment manager(s) in relation to the Plan's investment objectives.
7. Communicating matters of policy, research, and investment manager performance to the RPC.
8. Reviewing the Plan's investment history, performance, and contents of the Investment Policy Statement with any newly appointed RPC members.
9. Recommending the termination and/or change of the investment manager(s).

Investment Manager

Each investment manager must acknowledge, in writing, his or her acceptance of the responsibility as a fiduciary under ERISA and other applicable regulations. Each investment manager will have full discretion to make all investment decisions for the assets placed under his or her jurisdiction, while observing and operating within the requirements of ERISA and other applicable law, and all policies, guidelines, constraints, and philosophies as outlined in this statement. Specific responsibilities of the investment manager(s) will include:

1. Discretionary investment management to buy, sell, or hold individual securities, and discretion to alter asset allocation within the guidelines in this Investment Policy Statement.

2. Reporting, on a timely basis, quarterly investment performance results.

3. Communicating any major changes in economic outlook, investment strategy, or other factors that affect the investment process or the investment management objective of the Plan.

4. Informing the RPC regarding any qualitative changes to the investment management organization(s), such as changes in portfolio management personnel, ownership structure, investment philosophy, or investment discipline.

5. Voting proxies on behalf of the Plan, and communicating such voting records to the RPC on a timely basis.

Definitions

1. *Plan* shall mean the XYZ Company Retirement Plan.

2. *ERISA* shall mean the Employee Retirement Income Security Act of 1974, any amendment thereto, and any regulations issued under the Act.

3. *Fiduciary* shall mean any individual or group of individuals as defined in ERISA, Section 3(21)(a).

4. *Securities* shall refer to the marketable investment securities that are defined as acceptable in this statement.

5. *Investment horizon* shall be the time period over which the investment objectives, as set forth in this statement, are expected to be met. The investment horizon for this plan is 10 years.

6. *Market cycle* shall refer to a minimum of three to five years.

Investment Management

The RPC is a fiduciary under ERISA, and it is responsible for directing and monitoring the investment management of the Plan's assets. As such, the RPC is authorized to delegate certain duties and responsibilities to professional experts in various fields. These include, but are not limited to:

1. *Investment consultant.* The investment consultant may assist the RPC in establishing investment policy, objectives, and guidelines; selecting investment managers; reviewing such managers over time; measuring and evaluating investment performance; and other tasks as deemed appropriate.

2. *Investment manager.* The investment manager will implement the strategy outlined in the Investment Policy Statement to meet the Plan's investment objectives. Such services also include economic analysis and deciding when to purchase, sell, or hold individual securities.

3. *Custodian.* The custodian will physically (or through agreement with a subcustodian) maintain possession of securities owned by the Plan, collect dividend and interest payments, handle Plan distributions, redeem maturing securities, and effect receipt and delivery following purchases and sales.

4. Additional specialists such as attorneys, auditors, actuaries, retirement plan consultants, and others may be employed by the RPC to assist in meeting its responsibilities and obligations to administer the Plan's assets prudently.

If such experts employed are also deemed to be fiduciaries, they must acknowledge such in writing. All expenses for such experts must be customary and reasonable, and will be borne by the Plan as deemed appropriate and necessary.

Investment Objectives

In order to meet its needs, the Plan's investment strategy is to emphasize total return, that is, the aggregate return from capital appreciation and dividend and interest incomes. The primary objective in the investment management for the Plan's assets is the emphasis on consistent growth, specifically, growth in a manner that protects the Plan's assets from excessive volatility in market value from year to year.

Current Status—Year 2000

Due to the Plan's excellent funded status (in excess of 200 percent), the RPC has determined that the Plan can tolerate more risk and volatility than a less well-funded plan. Any significant deterioration in funded status will reduce the Plan's risk tolerance. Therefore, the RPC will closely monitor the Plan's funded status with the assistance of the investment consultant and will communicate any changes in risk tolerance to the investment manager(s).

Specific Investment Goals

The primary objective for this Plan is to provide long-term capital appreciation through investment in equities and fixed-income securities.

Over the investment horizon, it is the goal of the aggregate Plan assets to meet or exceed:

- Absolute
  - Actuarial assumption for funding purposes (currently 8.0 percent)
- Relative
  - Consumer price index plus 5.0 percent
  - Weighted average of benchmark indices ("composite index", see below)
- Funded status
  - Maintain funded ratio based on accrued benefits of 175 percent

Asset Allocation Guidelines

The following asset allocation has been established for the Plan:

Asset Class	Minimum	Neutral	Maximum
Equities			
U.S. equities	30%	50%	60%
Non-U.S. equities	0	10	20
Small-cap equities	0	5	10
Total equities	30%	60%	70%
Alternative Assets	0	5	10
Fixed Income	25	35	65
Cash	5	5	45

All Equities must be drawn from recognized securities exchanges, with small-cap equities defined as companies with a market capitalization of less than $1 billion. Fixed-income securities must be weighted to reflect a portfolio average maturity of not more than 10 years, with average benchmark duration of 5 years. The credit quality must equal or exceed high investment grade quality ("BAA" or better).

Performance Objectives

The market cycle performance objective for this portfolio is to equal or outperform a blend of the Standard and Poor's 500 Stock Index (S&P 500), the Europe, Australia, Far East Index (EAFE), and the Lehman Brothers Government/Corporate Bond Index (LBGC). The static weighting for this blend will be 50 percent S&P 500, 10 percent EAFE, and 40 percent LBGC. This blend will be called the "composite index."

The volatility, as measured by the standard deviation, of the Plan's assets should be commensurate with the investment strategy employed by the investment manager.

Measurement of Performance

Performance will be measured quarterly on a total return basis and reported to the RPC.

Performance is relative to the overall objectives and capital market returns as evidenced by various market indices and other portfolios operating under similar objectives and guidelines. Consideration will be given to risk/reward relationship.

Investment Management Policy

1. *Preservation and growth of capital.* Consistent with their respective investment styles and philosophies, investment managers should make reasonable efforts to preserve and grow capital, understanding that losses may occur in individual securities.

2. *Risk aversion.* The RPC recognizes that some risk is necessary to produce long-term investment results that are sufficient to meet the Plan's objectives. However, the investment managers will be evaluated regularly to ensure that the risk assumed is commensurate with the given investment styles and objectives.

3. *Adherence to investment discipline.* Investment managers are expected to adhere to the investment management styles for which they were hired. Investment managers will be evaluated regularly for adherence to investment discipline.

Liquidity

To minimize the possibility of a loss occasioned by the sale of a security forced by the need to meet required benefit payments, the RPC will periodically provide investment manager(s) with an estimate of expected net cash flow.

Marketability of Assets

Based on the Plan's long-term investment horizon, the RPC has deter-mined that, as appropriate, up to 10 percent of the Plan's assets may be invested in illiquid, long-term investments. Illiquid, long-term investments are defined as investments that would have a noticeable impact on the market price if traded in whole or in part.

Investment Guidelines

Allowable Assets

1. Cash and Cash Equivalents
   a. Treasury bills
   b. Money market funds
   c. Short-term investment funds
   d. Commercial paper
   e. Banker's acceptances
   f. Repurchase agreements
   g. Certificates of deposit
2. Fixed-Income Securities
   a. U.S. Government and agency securities
   b. Corporate notes and bonds
   c. Mortgage-backed bonds
   d. Preferred stock
   e. Fixed-income securities of foreign governments and corporations
   f. Collateralized mortgage obligations
3. Equity Securities
   a. Common stocks
   b. Convertible notes and bonds
   c. Convertible preferred stock
   d. American depository receipts (ADRs) of non-U.S. companies
4. Mutual Funds/Common Trusts/Alternative Assets
   a. Those that invest in allowable assets
   b. Those that meet with the prior approval of the RPC

Prohibited Assets

1. Commodities
2. Future contracts (with the exception of S&P 500 futures contracts)
3. Private placements

4. Options (with the exception of S&P 500 options contracts)
5. Limited partnerships
6. Venture capital investments
7. Securities of the plan sponsor or any of its subsidiaries
8. Real estate

Selection of Investment Managers

The RPC's selection of an investment manager(s) must be based on prudent due diligence procedures. A qualifying investment manager must be a registered investment adviser under the Investment Advisers Act of 1940, a bank, or insurance company. The RPC requires that each investment manager provide, in writing, acknowledgment of fiduciary responsibility to the Plan.

Delegation of Authority

The RPC will not reserve control over investment decisions, with the exception of specific limitations described in this Investment Policy Statement. Investment managers will be held responsible and accountable to achieve the objectives herein stated. While it is not believed that the limitations will hamper investment managers, each manager should request any modifications that he or she deems appropriate.

Investment Manager Performance Review and Evaluation

Performance reports generated by the investment consultant shall be compiled at least quarterly and communicated to the RPC for review. The investment performance of the total portfolio, as well as asset components, will be measured against commonly accepted performance benchmarks. Consideration shall be given to the extent to which the investment results are consistent with the investment objectives set forth in this Investment Policy Statement. The RPC intends to evaluate investment managers over at least three years, but reserves the right to terminate a manager for any reason, including the following:

1. Investment performance that is significantly less than anticipated given the discipline employed and risk parameters established, or unacceptable justification of poor results.
2. Failure to adhere to any aspect of this Investment Policy Statement, including communication and reporting requirements.

3. Significant qualitative changes to the investment management organization.

Investment manager(s) shall be reviewed regularly regarding performance, personnel, strategy, research capabilities, organizational and business matters, and other qualitative factors that may impact their ability to achieve the desired investment results.

This Investment Policy Statement is adopted on this _____ day of _____, 2000 by the Retirement Plan Committee for the XYZ Company Retirement Plan.

401(k) Plan Investment Performance Review

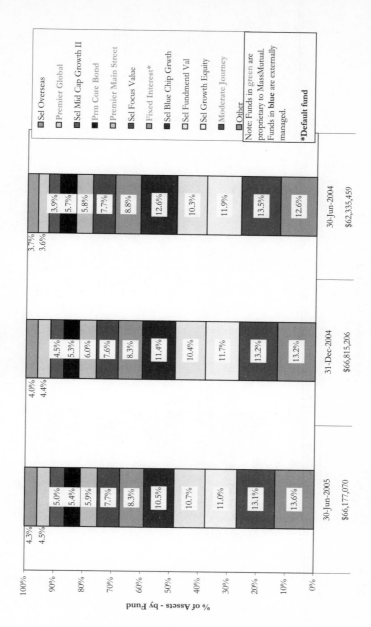

Sample
401(k) Retirement Plan
Account Balances by Fund

Legend:
- ▨ Sel Overseas
- ▫ Premier Global
- ▨ Sel Mid Cap Growth II
- ■ Prm Core Bond
- ▨ Premier Main Street
- ▨ Sel Focus Value
- ▨ Fixed Interest*
- ■ Sel Blue Chip Grwth
- ▫ Sel Fundmenl Val
- ▫ Sel Growth Equity
- ▨ Moderate Journey
- ▨ Other

Note: Funds in green are proprietary to MassMutual. Funds in **blue** are externally managed.

*Default fund

% of Assets - by Fund (vertical axis: 0% to 100%)

30-Jun-2004 — $62,335,459
Fund	%
	3.7%
	3.6%
	3.9%
	5.7%
	5.8%
	7.7%
	8.8%
	12.6%
	10.3%
	11.9%
	13.5%
	12.6%

31-Dec-2004 — $66,815,206
Fund	%
	4.0%
	4.4%
	4.5%
	5.3%
	6.0%
	7.6%
	8.3%
	11.4%
	10.4%
	11.7%
	13.2%
	13.2%

30-Jun-2005 — $66,177,070
Fund	%
	4.3%
	4.5%
	5.0%
	5.4%
	5.9%
	7.7%
	8.3%
	10.5%
	10.7%
	11.0%
	13.1%
	13.6%

Note: All totals exclude outstanding loans

Sample
401(k) Retirement Plan
Account Balances by Asset Class

% of Assets

	30-Jun-2005	31-Dec-2004
	$66,177,070	$66,815,206

Legend:
- % Other
- % Bonds
- % Non-US Stocks
- % Cash
- % US Stocks

30-Jun-2005: 0.2%, 9.0%, 10.2%, 12.5%, 68.1%

31-Dec-2004: 1.1%, 8.2%, 9.5%, 12.1%, 69.1%

Sample
401(k) Retirement Plan
Contributions by Fund

Fund	Jan-June 2005	July-Dec 2004	Jan-Jun 2004
Conservative Journey	3.5%	2.6%	2.4%
Sel Overseas	3.6%	1.1%	0.8%
Sel Sm Co Grwth	4.3%	4.9%	6.7%
Prm Small Co Opprty	4.5%	5.5%	4.7%
Sel Indexd Eqty	5.2%	4.0%	6.0%
Prm Core Bond	6.0%	5.5%	4.9%
Sel Mid Cap Growth II	6.3%	6.2%	7.5%
Premier Main Street	6.7%	6.6%	8.2%
Sel Blue Chip Grwth	6.7%	7.1%	6.9%
Sel Focus Value	6.9%	8.6%	3.5%
Aggressive Journey	7.0%	4.7%	5.4%
Premier Global	7.5%	6.2%	6.8%
Fixed Interest*	8.5%	7.4%	8.4%
Sel Fundmentl Val	10.5%	7.6%	10.2%
Moderate Journey	11.2%	10.2%	14.6%
Sel Growth Equity		11.8%	

Total Contributions ($)

Jan-June 2005: $4,276,341
July-Dec 2004: $4,212,725
Jan-Jun 2004: $3,456,181

Note: Funds in green are proprietary to MassMutual. Funds in **blue** are externally managed.

*Default fund

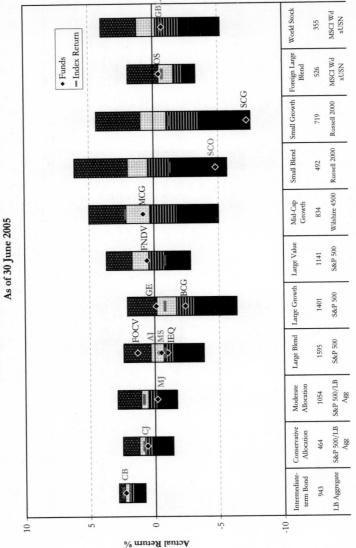

Sample
401(k) Retirement Plan
Year to Date Performance Relative to Investment Style
As of 30 June 2005

Numbers indicate # of funds within same Objective. The applicable index appears below each category
Funds in green are proprietary to MassMutual. Funds in blue are externally managed.

Sample
401(k) Retirement Plan
3 Year Performance Relative to Investment Style
As of 30 June 2005

◆ Funds
— Index Return

Annualized Return %

25
20
15
10
5
0

GB

OS

SCG

SCO

MCG

FNDV

BCG
GE

AJ
IEQ
MS

◆ FOCV

MJ

CJ

CB

	Intermediate-term Bond	Conservative Allocation	Moderate Allocation	Large Blend	Large Growth	Large Value	Mid-Cap Growth	Small Blend	Small Growth	Foreign Large Blend	World Stock
Numbers	888	286	823	1416	1307	1028	766	442	658	482	331
Index	LB Aggregate	S&P 500/LB Agg	S&P 500/LB Agg	S&P 500	S&P 500	S&P 500	Wilshire 4500	Russell 2000	Russell 2000	MSCI Wd xUSN	MSCI Wd xUSN

Numbers indicate # of funds within same Objective. The applicable index appears below each category.
Note: Funds in green are proprietary to MassMutual. Funds in blue are externally managed.

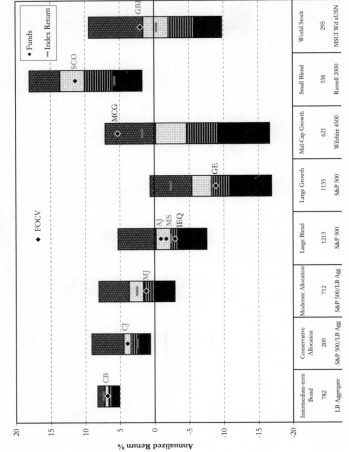

Sample
401(k) Retirement Plan
5 Year Performance Relative to Investment Style
As of 30 June 2005

Numbers indicate # of funds within same Objective. The applicable index appears below each category.
Note: Funds in green are proprietary to MassMutual. Funds in blue are externally managed.

	Intermediate-term Bond	Conservative Allocation	Moderate Allocation	Large Blend	Large Growth	Mid-Cap Growth	Small Blend	World Stock
	782	209	712	1213	1135	621	338	295
	LB Aggregate	S&P 500/LB Agg	S&P 500/LB Agg	S&P 500	S&P 500	Wilshire 4500	Russell 2000	MSCI Wd xUSN

Sample
401(k) Retirement Plan
Relative Risk and Return

The charts on the following pages provide additional information about the performance of the mutual funds offered in your retirement plan. The overall performance of any mutual fund manager is typically measured by two factors - the investment's returns and the amount of risk (measured by how volatile the returns are). Two funds may have the same investment return during the year, but the risk that each fund manager took may be completely different. One may have invested in riskier assets (i.e. high volatility), while the other took a more conservative route. Given a choice, most investors would prefer the one who took lower risk and still got the same investment return.

Also, to make a better "apples to apples" comparison, we have grouped each mutual fund with other funds who share similar investment objectives, for example, US equities, international equities, small companies, etc. This allows you to better compare fund performance among each fund's peer group.

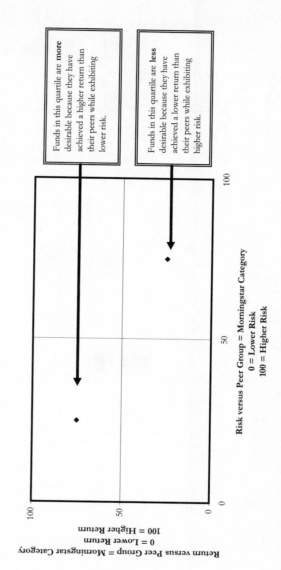

Funds in this quartile are **more** desirable because they have achieved a higher return than their peers while exhibiting lower risk.

Funds in this quartile are **less** desirable because they have achieved a lower return than their peers while exhibiting higher risk.

Risk versus Peer Group = Morningstar Category
0 = Lower Risk
100 = Higher Risk

Return versus Peer Group = Morningstar Category
0 = Lower Return
100 = Higher Return

189

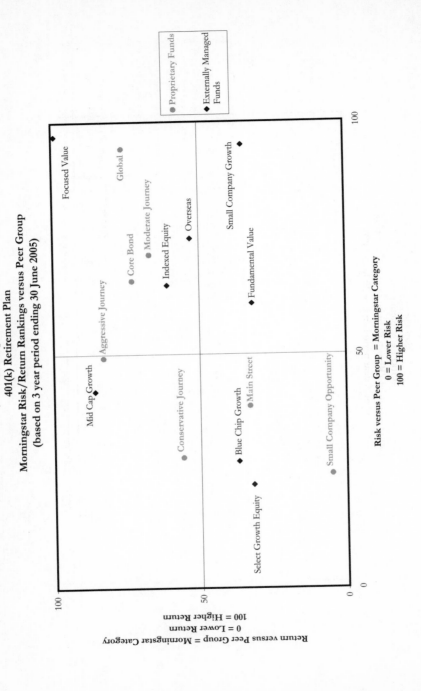

Sample
401(k) Retirement Plan
Morningstar Risk/Return Rankings versus Peer Group
(based on 3 year period ending 30 June 2005)

Focused Value

Global

Core Bond

Moderate Journey

Aggressive Journey

Indexed Equity

Overseas

Small Company Growth

Fundamental Value

Mid Cap Growth

Conservative Journey

Blue Chip Growth

Main Street

Small Company Opportunity

Select Growth Equity

Proprietary Funds

Externally Managed Funds

Risk versus Peer Group = Morningstar Category
0 = Lower Risk
100 = Higher Risk

Return versus Peer Group = Morningstar Category
0 = Lower Return
100 = Higher Return

100

50

0

100

50

0

Sample
401(k) Retirement Plan
Morningstar Risk/Return Rankings versus Peer Group
(based on 5 year period ending 30 June 2005)

Proprietary Funds

Externally Managed Funds

Focused Value

Small Company Growth

Overseas

Global

Core Bond

Moderate Journey

Indexed Equity

Aggressive Journey

Mid Cap Growth

Conservative Journey

Fundamental Value

Blue Chip Growth

Main Street

Small Company Opportunity

Growth Equity

Risk versus Peer Group = Morningstar Category
0 = Lower Risk
100 = Higher Risk

0

50

100

Return versus Peer Group = Morningstar Category
0 = Lower Return
100 = Higher Return

Sample
401(k) Retirement Plan
Nominal Risk and Return

The charts on the following pages provide further analysis of the risk/return profile of the mutual funds available in the plan. The prior charts showed risk/return on a competitive basis - compared to other funds within the same investment category. The following charts will show the nominal risk/return statistics used.

For risk, the standard deviation is shown, and for return, the average annualized return.

Risk - as measured by Standard Deviation

192

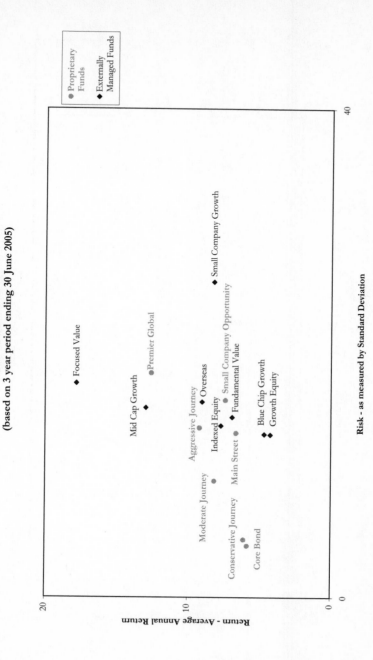

Sample
401(k) Retirement Plan
Nominal Risk and Return
(based on 3 year period ending 30 June 2005)

Return - Average Annual Return

20

10

0

Risk - as measured by Standard Deviation

40

Proprietary Funds
Externally Managed Funds

Focused Value

Mid Cap Growth

Premier Global

Aggressive Journey
Overseas

Indexed Equity
Small Company Opportunity
Fundamental Value

Moderate Journey

Main Street

Blue Chip Growth
Growth Equity

Conservative Journey

Core Bond

Small Company Growth

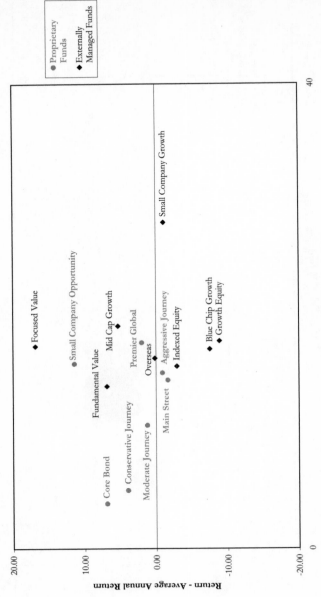

Sample
401(k) Retirement Plan
Nominal Risk and Return
(based on 5 year period ending 30 June 2005)

Proprietary Funds
Externally Managed Funds

20.00

10.00

0.00

-10.00

-20.00

Return - Average Annual Return

Focused Value

Small Company Opportunity

Fundamental Value

Mid Cap Growth

Premier Global

Overseas

Conservative Journey

Moderate Journey

Core Bond

Main Street

Aggressive Journey

Indexed Equity

Small Company Growth

Blue Chip Growth

Growth Equity

0

40

Risk - as measured by Standard Deviation

Sample
401(k) Retirement Plan
Asset Class - Five Year Risk Return Profiles
30 June 2005

Risk/Return statistics for each asset class of Brooks Automation's 401(k) Retirement Plan portfolio. Data points include all funds with risk and return statistics within one standard deviation of the mean.

Legend:
- Intermediate-term Bond
- Conservative Allocation
- Moderate Allocation
- Large Blend
- Large Growth
- Large Value
- Mid-Cap Growth
- Small Blend
- Small Growth
- Foreign Large Blend
- World Stock

Return - Average Annual Return

30 25 20 15 10 5 0 -5 -10 -15 -20

Risk - as measured by Standard Deviation

0 5 10 15 20 25 30 35 40

Labeled points: CB, CJ, MJ, FNDV, SCO, FOCV, AI, MS, OS, GBI, MCC, EO, BCG, GE, SCG

Sample
401(k) Retirement Plan
Fund Profile
As of 30 June 2005

Family	Fund Name	Floating Bar Abbreviation	Morningstar Category	Composition of Assets - By Asset Class %					Expense Ratio as of 06/30/05	Expense Ratio as of 12/31/04
				Cash	US Stock	Non-US Stock	Bonds	Other		
	Fixed Interest*[1]			100%	0%	0%	0%	0%		
Premier	Core Bond (Babson)	CB	Intermediate-term Bond	15%	0%	0%	83%	2%	0.75	0.79
	Conservative Journey	CJ	Conservative Allocation	18%	24%	8%	50%	0%	0.79	0.79
	Moderate Journey	MJ	Moderate Allocation	10%	44%	16%	29%	1%	0.93	0.93
	Aggressive Journey	AJ	Large Blend	5%	63%	20%	12%	0%	1.04	1.04
Premier	Main Street (OFI)	MS	Large Blend	1%	98%	1%	0%	0%	0.60	0.60
Select	Focused Value (Harris/C&B)	FOCV	Large Blend	8%	92%	0%	0%	0%	1.03	1.04
Select	Index Equity (Northern Trust)	IEQ	Large Blend	1%	99%	0%	0%	0%	0.45	0.45
Select	Blue Chip Growth (Fidelity)	BCG	Large Growth	1%	98%	1%	0%	0%	1.13	1.12
Select	Growth Equity (GMO)	GE	Large Growth	1%	99%	0%	0%	0%	0.99	0.92
Select	Fundamental Val (Wellington)	FNDV	Large Value	1%	97%	2%	0%	0%	0.97	0.97
Select	Mid Cap Growth II (T. Rowe Price)	MCG	Mid-Cap Growth	4%	91%	5%	0%	0%	1.09	1.09
Premier	Small Co Opportunities (Babson)	SCO	Small Blend	7%	93%	0%	0%	0%	1.13	1.14
Select	Small Co. Grwth (Mazama/Eagle)	SCG	Small Growth	1%	97%	2%	0%	0%	1.10	1.10
Select	Overseas (American Century/Harris)	OS	Foreign Large Blend	4%	96%	0%	0%	0%	1.38	1.39
Premier	Global (OFI)	GBL	World Stock	2%	38%	60%	0%	0%	0.89	0.91
	Self Directed Brokerage Account[1]			0%	100%	0%	0%	0%		

* Default fund

[1] Information not directly available. Argus estimated asset allocation.

Note: Funds in green are proprietary. Funds in blue are externally managed.

Equity Style Comparison [2]

	Value	Blend	Growth	
	1	5	5	Large
			1	Medium
	1		1	Small

[2] Of the fourteen funds with equity exposure

Sample
401(k) Retirement Plan
Sector Weighting versus Indices
30 June 2005

Sample
401(k) Retirement Plan
Correlation Matrix and Modern Portfolio Theory Statistics
30 June 2005

Correlation Matrix (36 Monthly Return)

Name	Morningstar Category	(1)	(2)	(3)	(4)	(5)	(6)	(7)	(8)	(9)	(10)	(11)	(12)	(13)	(14)	(15)
(1) Premier Small Co Opportunities (Babson)	Small Blend															
(2) Premier Global (Oppenheimer)	World Stock	0.89														
(3) Conservative Journey	Conservative Allocation	0.91	0.97													
(4) Moderate Journey	Moderate Allocation	0.80	0.84	0.86												
(5) Aggressive Journey	Large Blend	0.91	0.97	0.99	0.92											
(6) Premier Main Street (Oppenheimer)	Large Blend	0.84	0.94	0.98	0.83	0.96										
(7) Select Blue Chip Growth (Fidelity)	Large Growth	0.80	0.89	0.94	0.75	0.91	0.97									
(8) Premier Core Bond (Babson)	Intermediate-Term Bond	-0.16	-0.13	-0.13	-0.37	-0.01	-0.14	-0.20								
(9) Select Focused Value (Harris Associates/C&B)	Mid-Cap Blend	0.81	0.84	0.91	0.73	0.88	0.89	0.87	-0.15							
(10) Select Fundamental Value (Wellington)	Large Value	0.82	0.92	0.95	0.80	0.94	0.96	0.96	-0.17	0.80						
(11) Select Growth Equity (GMO)	Large Growth	0.84	0.89	0.94	0.74	0.90	0.93	0.97	-0.23	0.87	0.89					
(12) Select Indexed Equity (Northern Trust)	Large Blend	0.82	0.92	0.96	0.78	0.94	0.99	0.99	-0.19	0.89	0.89	0.96				
(13) Select Mid-Cap Growth II (T Rowe Price)	Mid-cap Growth	0.92	0.93	0.96	0.76	0.93	0.93	0.93	-0.26	0.89	0.92	0.94	0.93			
(14) Select Overseas (American Century/Harris)	Foreign Large Blend	0.87	0.96	0.97	0.84	0.97	0.95	0.89	-0.13	0.85	0.95	0.87	0.94	0.90		
(15) Select Small Co. Growth (Mazama/Eagle)	Small Growth	0.88	0.85	0.86	0.74	0.85	0.79	0.78	-0.13	0.77	0.73	0.85	0.76	0.89	0.77	

Degree of Correlation

.70 to 1.0 High
.11 to .69 Moderate
.10 to -.10 None
-.11 to -.69 Moderate Negative
-.70 to -1.0 Highly Negative

Modern Portfolio Theory Statistics (36 Monthly Return)

Name	Morningstar Category	Alpha	Beta	R-Squared	Best Fit Index	Sharpe Ratio
Premier Small Co Opportunities (Babson)	Small Blend	-3.32	0.80	0.90	Russell 2000	0.36
Premier Global (Oppenheimer)	World Stock	2.02	1.09	0.91	MSCI World	0.67
Conservative Journey	Conservative Allocation	1.62	0.46	0.78	Lipper Balanced	1.01
Moderate Journey	Moderate Allocation	0.43	1.01	0.95	Lipper Balanced	0.74
Aggressive Journey	Large Blend	-0.94	1.45	0.95	Lipper Balanced	0.6
Premier Main Street (Oppenheimer)	Large Blend	-0.97	0.89	0.97	S&P 500	0.4
Select Blue Chip Growth (Fidelity)	Large Growth	-2.04	0.95	0.99	Russell 1000 Growth	0.26
Premier Core Bond (Babson)	Intermediate-Term Bond	0.27	0.99	0.97	Lehman Bros. Aggregate	1.07
Select Focused Value (Harris Associates/C&B)	Mid-Cap Blend	1.46	1.03	0.76	Russell Mid Cap Value	0.94
Select Fundamental Value (Wellington)	Large Value	-3.83	1.00	0.96	Russell 1000 Value	0.38
Select Growth Equity (GMO)	Large Growth	-2.43	0.94	0.94	Russell 1000 Growth	0.22
Select Indexed Equity (Northern Trust)	Large Blend	-0.42	1.00	1.00	S&P 500	0.45
Select Mid-Cap Growth II (T Rowe Price)	Mid-Cap Growth	-1.00	0.95	0.97	Russell Mid Cap Growth	0.75
Select Overseas (American Century/Harris)	Foreign Large Blend	-2.97	1.04	0.97	MSCI EAFE	0.49
Select Small Co. Growth (Mazama/Eagle)	Small Growth	-4.26	1.22	0.95	Russell 2000 Growth	0.27

Sample
401(k) Retirement Plan
Fund Overlap
30 June 2005

Fund Overlap - Actual Portfolio

Top Twenty Stock Holdings Intersections	Moderate Journey	Fundamental Value (Wellington)	Blue Chip Growth (Fidelity)	Growth Equity (GMO)	Indexed Equity (Northern Trust)	Focused Value (Harris/C&B)	Oppenheimer Global (Babson)	Main Street (Oppenheimer)	Total Portfolio % of Portfolio	Total Portfolio $
1 ExxonMobil	x	x	x	x	x			x	1.70%	$1,136,204
2 Johnson & Johnson	x		x	x	x			x	1.37%	$917,186
3 Pfizer	x	x	x	x	x		x	x	1.18%	$785,658
4 Dell	x		x	x	x			x	1.04%	$691,543
5 Altria Group	x	x	x	x	x		x	x	1.00%	$666,850
6 Citigroup	x		x		x		x	x	0.98%	$655,619
7 Home Depot	x	x	x	x	x			x	0.90%	$603,788
8 J.P. Morgan Chase & Co.	x	x			x	x	x	x	0.90%	$601,826
9 Microsoft	x		x	x	x			x	0.83%	$556,885
10 General Electric			x		x			x	0.81%	$542,043
11 Bank of America	x	x	x		x			x	0.77%	$511,468
12 UnitedHealth Group	x		x	x	x			x	0.75%	$500,262
13 Intel		x	x	x	x			x	0.74%	$495,814
14 McDonald's	x	x	x	x	x	x		x	0.70%	$465,656
15 American International Group	x	x	x	x	x	x		x	0.65%	$432,274
16 Time Warner		x	x		x	x			0.62%	$415,014
17 Baxter International		x	x		x	x			0.58%	$384,602
18 Fannie Mae			x	x	x			x	0.50%	$332,713
19 IBM			x	x	x		x	x	0.46%	$307,159
20 Wyeth		x	x		x		x	x	0.43%	$284,062
Assets in Top Ten Stock Holdings									10.71%	$7,157,603
Assets in Top Twenty Stock Holdings									16.89%	$11,286,627
Total Assets										$66,815,206

Important Disclosures

The performance data given represents past performance and should not be considered indicative of future results. Current performance may be lower or higher than return data quoted herein. For more current information including month-end performance please call 877-474-5016 or visit www.massmutual.com/retire. Principal value and investment return will fluctuate, so that an investor's shares when redeemed may be worth more or less than the original investment. Investment portfolio statistics change over time. The investment is not FDIC-insured, may lose value and is not guaranteed by a bank or other financial institution.

Pre-inception Returns

The separate investment account (SIA) inception date listed is that of this SIA's share class. Other share classes of the SIA may have existed longer. Performance shown is the actual performance of the SIA since the inception date noted. Performance shown prior to the inception date given may include one or both of the following:
1. The oldest share class of the SIA or its underlying mutual fund (depending upon the investment) adjusted for fees and expenses of the newer share class up to the date of inception of the newer share class. If the adjustment would result in better performance for the newer share class than that of the oldest share class (due to lower expenses of the newer share class), then performance shown represents that of the oldest share class without any adjustment up to the date of inception of the newer share class. The fees and expenses are referenced in the report's Operations section.

While the inclusion of this pre-inception data may provide valuable insight into the probable long-term behavior of newer share classes of an investment, investors should be aware that an adjusted historical return can only provide an approximation of that behavior. For example, the fee structures between a retail share class will vary from that of an institutional share class, as retail shares tend to have higher operating expenses and sales charges. These adjusted historical returns are not actual returns. Calculation methodologies utilized by Morningstar may differ from those applied by other entities, including the investment itself.
2. A composite of all portfolios managed by the option's sub-advisor or sub-advisors with substantially similar investment objectives, policies and investment strategies and without significant client-imposed restrictions adjusted for the fees and expenses of the share class for this option. Such performance does not represent the actual historical performance of the option or predict its future performance.

Performance

Fund Return reflects performance without adjusting for sales charges or the effects of taxation, but is adjusted to reflect all actual ongoing fund expenses and assumes reinvestment of dividends and capital gains. If adjusted, sales charges would reduce the performance quoted. In addition, due to market volatility, the investment's return may vary greatly over short periods of time.

The investment's performance is compared with that of an index. The index is an unmanaged portfolio of specified securities and does not reflect any initial or ongoing expenses nor can it be invested in directly. An investment's portfolio may differ significantly from the securities in the index. Morningstar chooses the index, which may not be the same as the comparative index noted in the prospectus.

Morningstar Proprietary Statistics

Please note that some Morningstar proprietary calculations, including the Morningstar Rating, Morningstar Return, and Morningstar Risk may be calculated based on pre-inception returns. Therefore, Morningstar's three-year minimum performance history requirement for Morningstar Rating, Morningstar Return, and Morningstar Risk may be satisfied using pre-inception returns, and the Morningstar Rating,

Morningstar Return, and Morningstar Risk may be based, at least in part, on pre-inception returns. Please see the pre-inception returns disclosure (above) for more details.

Morningstar Rating™

For each investment with at least a three-year history, Morningstar calculates a Morningstar Rating™ based on a Morningstar Risk-Adjusted Return measure as of the date indicated that accounts for variation in an investment's monthly performance (including the effects of sales charges, loads, and redemption fees), placing more emphasis on downward variations and rewarding consistent performance. The top 10% of investments in each category receive 5 stars, the next 22.5% receive 4 stars, the next 35% receive 3 stars, the next 22.5% receive 2 stars and the bottom 10% receive 1 star. (Each share class is counted as a fraction of one investment within this scale and rated separately, which may cause slight variations in the distribution percentages.) The Overall Morningstar Rating for an investment is derived from a weighted average of the performance figures associated with its three-, five- and ten-year (if applicable) Morningstar Rating metrics. For more information, please see Morningstar Proprietary Statistics (above).

Morningstar Style Box™

The Morningstar Style Box reveals an investment's investment strategy. For equity investments and fixed-income investments respectively, the vertical axis shows the market capitalization of the stocks owned or the average credit quality of the bonds owned. The horizontal axis shows investment style (value, blend, or growth) or interest rate sensitivity as measured by a bond's duration (short, intermediate or long). Duration is a measure of interest-rate sensitivity-the longer an investment's duration, the more sensitive the investment is to shifts in interest rates.

Morningstar Return

This statistic is a measurement of an investment's excess return over a risk-free rate (the return of the 90-day Treasury bill), after adjusting for all applicable loads and sales charges. In each Morningstar Category, the top 10% of investments earn a High Morningstar Return, the next 22.5% Above Average, the middle 35% Average, the next 22.5% Below Average, and the bottom 10% Low. Morningstar Return is measured for up to three time periods (three-, five-, and 10-years). These separate measures are then weighted and averaged to produce an overall measure for the investment. Investments with less than three years of performance history are not rated. For more information, please see Morningstar Proprietary Statistics (above).

Morningstar Risk

This statistic evaluates the variations in an investment's monthly returns, with an emphasis on downside variations. In each Morningstar Category, the 10% of investments with the lowest measured risk are described as Low Risk, the next 22.5% Below Average, the middle 35% Average, the next 22.5% Above Average, and the top 10% High. Morningstar Risk is measured for up to three time periods (three-, five-, and 10-years). These separate measures are then weighted and averaged to produce an overall measure for the investment. Investments with less than three years of performance history are not rated. For more information, please see Morningstar Proprietary Statistics (above).

Investment Risk

Foreign Securities Investments/Emerging Market Investments: The investor should note that investments that invest in foreign securities involve special additional risks. These risks include, but are not limited to, currency risk, political risk, and risk associated with varying accounting standards. Investing in emerging markets may accentuate

these risks.

Sector Investments: Sector investments may experience greater short-term price volatility than more diversified investments, and are most suitable for use in the aggressive portion of an investment portfolio.

Non-Diversified Investments: The investor should note that investments that invest more of their assets in a single issuer involve additional risks, including share price fluctuations, because of the increased concentration of investments.

Small Cap Investments: Investments in companies with small market capitalization ("small caps") may be subject to special risks given their characteristic narrow markets, limited financial resources, and less liquid stocks, all which may cause price volatility.

Mid Cap Investments: The investor should note that investments that invest in companies with market capitalizations below $10 billion involve additional risks. The securities of these companies may be more volatile and less liquid than the securities of larger companies.

High-Yield Bond Investments: These investments are high yield bond investments subject to greater credit risks than high quality bond investments. As interest rates rise, bond prices fall. As such, this investment's share value may decline **substantially**, and it is possible to lose a significant portion of your principal when interest rates rise.

Money Market: **The investor should note an investment in a money market investment is neither insured nor guaranteed by the Federal Deposit Insurance Corporation or any other government agency. Although the investment seeks to preserve the value of your investment at $1.00 per share, it is possible to lose money by investing in the investment.**

Inflation-Protected: The investment may be appropriate for investors seeking to achieve as high a total rate of return as is considered consistent with prudent investment risk and the preservation of capital. It invests primarily in inflation-indexed bonds issued by the US and non-US governments, their agencies or government-sponsored enterprises, and corporations.

Risks of investing in the investment include credit risk, interest rate risk and foreign investment risk. Foreign investments involve risks such as currency fluctuations, market price swings, less public information and economic, social and political uncertainty. Neither the investment nor its yield is guaranteed by the US Govt. The investment prospectus includes additional detail on risk and reward.

Multi-Investment Options: It is important to note that an investment option with mutual funds in its portfolio may be subject to the expenses of those mutual funds in addition to those of the investment option itself.

Destination Retirement 2040/Ultra Aggressive Journey: The investor should note that a significant percentage of the underlying investments in these strategies have a higher than average risk exposure, such as small, midcap and international stocks. Investors should consider their risk tolerance carefully before choosing such a strategy.

Securities offered through registered representatives of MML Investors Services, Inc. 1295 State Street Springfield, MA 01111.

Premier Main Street (OFI)

Class S
as of 06-30-05

Morningstar Return	Morningstar Risk	Overall Morningstar Rating™
Average	Below Average	★★★
		Out of 1206 Large Blend funds.

Category: Large Blend
Large-blend funds have portfolios that are fairly representative of the overall stock market in size, growth rates, and price. They tend to invest across the spectrum of U.S. industries and owing to their broad exposure, the funds' returns are often similar to those of the S&P 500 Index.

Analysis Report[1] by David Kathman, CFA 02-22-05
We're not too worried about Oppenheimer Main Street's recent underperformance.

This fund just finished its second straight year of trailing both the S&P 500 (its preferred benchmark) and the large-blend category average. It wasn't too far behind in either 2003 or 2004, but that's still disappointing since the fund's goal is to modestly outperform the S&P while keeping volatility in check.

Managers Nikos Monoyios and Marc Reinganum try to achieve this goal using quantitative models that rank stocks according to valuation, momentum, and quality criteria, and which also identify style elements, such as size and credit quality, that are likely to outperform in the short run. They're always refining the models to reflect changing market conditions and new research, and they also take into account seasonal factors such as the tendency of small caps to outperform early in the year.

For about the past year, these models have been expecting large-cap and mega-cap stocks to make a comeback after several years of small-cap dominance; the fact that this didn't happen is the main reason for the fund's recent woes. Giant-cap stocks make up more than two thirds of the portfolio now, and even though the fund's weighted average market cap came down a bit late in 2004, it's still well above that of the S&P 500.

However, we're not too worried about these short-term issues, because we're confident in the team's strategy and experience. This fund has outperformed the large-blend category since the current managers took over seven years ago, and before that the team had achieved outstanding results since 1972 at Guardian Park Avenue GPAFX under original manager Chuck Albers. Although Albers retired in 2003, Monoyios worked with him for more than 20 years, and Reinganum has worked with the team for more than a decade.

Although this fund will seldom be among the category's top performers in any given year, its stability and solid record make it a fine core fund.
Analysis written from data as of 01-31-05. Data cited may differ from numbers on the page.
[1]Analysis written for the A shareclass. Share classes invest in the same portfolio, but have different expenses and return histories

Fund Details

Advisor(s):	OppenheimerFunds, Inc.
Portfolio Manager(s):	Nikolaos Monoyios.
	Marc Reinganum.
Other Fund Managed:	Oppenheimer Main Street
Expense Ratio:	—
Fund Inception Date:	12-31-04
Ticker:	MMSSX

Notes
Some of the returns and Morningstar proprietary calculations, may be based on pre-inception returns and are hypothetical. Morningstar may use the performance of the underlying investment vehicle for the prior periods, making adjustments to those returns for any difference in fee structure. The evaluation of this investment does not affect the retail mutual fund data published by Morningstar. This investment's metrics are compared against the retail mutual fund universe breakpoints to determine its hypothetical rating and category related statistics.

Performance History as of 06-30-05

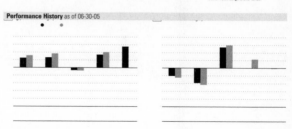

Performance Analysis as of 06-30-05

Average annual, if greater than 1 year

	1 Year	3 Year	5 Year	10 Year	Since Inception
Total Return %	6.30	6.63	-1.70	8.53	13.81
Category Avg %	6.35	7.44	-1.79	8.61	—
Standard & Poor's 500 %	6.32	8.28	-2.37	9.93	—
Russ 1000 %	7.92	9.19	-1.89	10.16	—
Growth of $10,000	10,630	12,124	9,178	22,672	—
Morningstar Rating™	—	★★★[1]	★★★[2]	★★★[3]	

[1](out of 1206 Large Blend funds) [2](out of 912 Large Blend funds) [3](out of 318 Large Blend funds)

Volatility Analysis (standard deviation relative to all funds)

Best 3-month Period	(Oct '92 - Dec '92)	27.08%
Worst 3-month Period	(Sep '00 - Nov '00)	-16.67%

In the past, this investment has shown a relatively moderate range of price fluctuations relative to other investments. This investment may experience larger or smaller price declines or price increases depending on market conditions. Some of this risk may be offset by owning other investments with different portfolio makeups or investment strategies.

Portfolio Profile as of 06-30-05

Morningstar Style Box™

	Type	% Assets
●	Cash	1.2
●	Stocks*	98.8
●	Bonds	0.0
○	Other	0.0

*Foreign Stock (% of Stocks) 0.8

Top 10 Holdings	% Assets
ExxonMobil	4.13
General Electric	3.30
Microsoft	2.48
Citigroup	2.48
Pfizer	2.23
Johnson & Johnson	2.19
Intel	2.19
Bank of America	2.12
ChevronTexaco	1.53
Dell	1.37
Total Number of Stock Holdings	495
Total Number of Bond Holdings	1
Annual Turnover Ratio %	—

Morningstar Sectors	Fund %	S&P 500 %
☍ Information	**19**	**20**
⬛ Software	4	4
⬛ Hardware	10	10
⬛ Media	2	3
⬛ Telecommunication	3	3
◐ Service	**47**	**46**
⬛ Healthcare Service	13	13
⬛ Consumer Service	8	9
⬛ Business Service	2	4
⬛ Financial Service	24	20
⬛ Manufacturing	**34**	**34**
⬛ Consumer Goods	7	9
⬛ Industrial Materials	12	12
⬛ Energy	12	9
⬛ Utilities	3	3

Replacement Ratio Study, A Measurement Tool for Retirement Planning

Preface

The Aon Consulting/
Georgia State University
2004 Retirement Income
Replacement Ratio Study

Retirement Income Needs in a Defined Contribution World

Since 1988, the Aon Consulting/Georgia State University study on benchmarking retirement income needs has been a premier source of information for retirement planning. Building on the *Interim Report of the President's Commission on Pension Policy* published in 1980, this booklet presents the results of our 2004 analysis, the sixth update to the study.

In this most recent iteration, we recognize changes that are occurring in the retirement income delivery system in the United States. With the continued movement to a defined contribution approach and reductions in medical coverage after retirement, we begin to look at replacement income in a somewhat different way.

As in prior studies, this 2004 update was completed under the direction of Dr. Bruce Palmer, Professor and Chair Emeritus of the Department of Risk Management and Insurance, Robinson College of Business, Georgia State University. Funding and technical assistance were provided by Aon Consulting. Aon Consulting's Ron DeStefano, E.A., Michael Schachet, F.S.A., and Jeff Paciero, F.S.A. worked closely with Dr. Palmer to complete the study.

Source: Aon Consulting. *Replacement Ratio Study, A Measurement Tool for Retirement Planning,* 2004. Used with permission.

Table of Contents

Replacement Ratio Study™

Source: Aon Consulting. *Replacement Ratio Study, A Measurement Tool for Retirement Planning,* 2004. Used with permission.

Introduction

Planning for retirement has never been more important or more difficult. The baby boomer generation enters its retirement years as stock market volatility makes 401(k) plan account balances less certain, employers reassess the entire structure of the private retirement system, Congress and the courts review the legality of cash balance plans, and medical inflation causes the reduction or elimination of employer-sponsored post-retirement medical plans.

The environment of the 1970s and 1980s — a time when employers felt an obligation to provide for each employee's retirement (and pay for a significant part of it) — is long gone. The 1990s were a time of change —substantial stock market gains made everyone feel confident about being able to afford a comfortable retirement. 401(k) plans became more attractive than defined benefit plans because employees got to "play the market" and everyone was a winner.

The turn of the millennium introduced a new dose of reality. Over the past four years, we have seen three poor investment years, only partly offset by returns during 2003. Employees who had enjoyed the "reward" of investing in stocks learned the hard way just what the "risk" meant.

For many employees, planning for retirement has become an urgent and immediate concern — as of January 1, 2004, the oldest baby boomers turned 58 years of age, and another boomer turns 55 every eight seconds.

Aon Consulting's sixth report on the level of income needed by an employee in retirement again answers the basic question *"How much income will I need in retirement to maintain my standard of living?"* In this iteration of the Replacement Ratio Study™, we attempt to reflect new realities resulting from the changes of the past decade by providing alternative answers to this basic question. For example, we include tables that convert the retirement income need to an equivalent lump sum. That way, employees whose primary retirement source is a 401(k) or other defined contribution plan can more easily determine if they are on track. The employee who receives a lump sum settlement of their defined benefit pension plan may also find this approach valuable.

The availability of medical benefits in retirement has a big effect on income needs. So we also include a way to adjust retirement income to reflect changes in retiree employer-provided medical benefits.

With the updated information in this report, we believe employers will be better able to provide employee education, and employees will be better armed to plan their individual retirements.

If you have any questions about how to apply this study as a planning tool (either as a plan sponsor or individual), you can contact your local Aon Consulting office. Alternatively, you may contact us by telephone at *+1.800.438.6487* or at our Web address: *www.aon.com/hcc*.

Source: Aon Consulting. *Replacement Ratio Study, A Measurement Tool for Retirement Planning*, 2004. Used with permission.

Replacement Ratio Defined

A replacement ratio is a person's gross income after retirement, divided by his or her gross income before retirement. For example, assume someone earns $60,000 per year before retirement. Further, assume he or she retires and receives $45,000 of Social Security and other retirement income. This person's replacement ratio is 75% ($45,000/$60,000).

This study analyzes the replacement ratios employees need to maintain their pre-retirement standard of living after retirement. Generally, a person needs less gross income after retiring, primarily due to five factors:

1. Income taxes go down after retirement. This is because extra deductions are available for those over age 65, and taxable income usually decreases at retirement.

2. Social Security taxes (FICA deductions from wages) end completely at retirement.

3. Social Security benefits are partially or fully tax-free. This reduces taxable income and, therefore, the amount of income needed to pay taxes.

4. Saving for retirement is no longer a goal.

5. Age- and work-related expenses generally decrease at retirement primarily because shelter and transportation expenses decrease. This factor outweighs an expected increase in health care costs.

The chart to the right shows that a 75% replacement ratio is enough to allow an employee earning $60,000 to retire at age 65 in 2004 without reducing his or her standard of living.

Because taxes, need to save, and age- and work-related expenses all decrease at retirement, this person is just as well off after retirement with a gross income of $45,299.

Appendix I describes the methodology used to determine needed replacement ratios. Appendix II shows the calculation details for our baseline cases, and Appendix III summarizes the expenditure data used for the calculations.

The primary data source for this information is the U.S. Department of Labor's Bureau of Labor Statistics' *Consumer Expenditure Survey (CES)*. This is essentially the same database used to construct the Consumer Price Index. The *CES* is done annually, and we used data from the most recent years available — 1999, 2000, and 2001. *CES* data provided information on 9,738 "working" consumer units and 5,642 "retired" consumer units. In total, this represents approximately 80% more consumer units than have been available in prior years.

Replacement Ratio Example

	Annual Income		
	Before Retirement (1)	After Retirement (2)	Replacement Ratio (2)/(1)
Gross Income	$ 60,000	$ 45,299	75%
Taxes	(11,574)	(334)	
Savings	(1,945)	0*	
Age- & Work-Related Expenditures	(34,194)	(32,678)**	
Remaining Income	12,287	12,287	

* Replacement ratios assume savings stop at the time of retirement.

** The study isolates changes in age- and work-related expenditures (see Appendix III). Expenditures not age- or work-related are assumed to be the same before and after retirement.

Source: Aon Consulting. *Replacement Ratio Study, A Measurement Tool for Retirement Planning,* 2004. Used with permission.

The table to the right shows the 2004 study baseline case results. The baseline case assumes a family situation in which there is one wage earner who retires at age 65 with a spouse age 62. Thus, the family unit is eligible for family Social Security benefits, which are 1.362 times the wage earner's benefit. The baseline case also takes into account age- and work-related expenditure changes after retirement, in addition to pre-retirement savings patterns and changes in taxes after retirement.

2004 Replacement Ratio Findings

Pre-Retirement Income ($000)	Replacement Ratios		
	Social Security (%)	Private and Employer Sources (%)	Total (%)
$20	65	24	89
30	56	28	84
40	51	29	80
50	48	29	77
60	43	32	75
70	39	37	76
80	35	42	77
90	33	45	78

The table and the graph on the following page illustrate three significant points about the replacement ratio calculations:

1. Social Security replaces a larger portion of pre-retirement income at lower wage levels. This is by design and has the effect of redistributing income from higher paid employees to lower paid.

2. Total replacement ratios are highest for the very lowest paid employees. This is because these employees save the least and pay the least in taxes (as a percentage of income) before retirement. Thus, they spend a higher percentage of their income and need higher replacement ratios to maintain that level of expenditures.

3. After reaching an income level of $60,000, total replacement ratios begin to increase slowly. This is primarily because post-retirement taxes increase as income levels increase. Post-retirement taxes increase from .7% of post-retirement income for a $60,000 person to 9.3% for a $90,000 person. To pay the additional taxes, higher paid employees need more retirement income.

Source: Aon Consulting. *Replacement Ratio Study, A Measurement Tool for Retirement Planning,* 2004. Used with permission.

One reason the highest income employees pay more tax after retirement is that as much as 85% of a married couple's Social Security benefit is taxable when retirement income (including 50% of Social Security) goes above $44,000. It is important to note the $44,000 threshold is not indexed like other tax breakpoints. As time goes on, automatic indexing of Social Security benefits will continue to increase the dollar amount of those benefits. In relative terms, more and more of a person's Social Security benefit will be taxed.

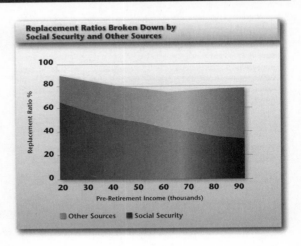

Replacement Ratios Broken Down by Social Security and Other Sources

Other Sources   ■ Social Security

Source: Aon Consulting. *Replacement Ratio Study, A Measurement Tool for Retirement Planning,* 2004. Used with permission.

The graph below compares the 2004 baseline results (blue line) with the 2001 (red line) and 1997 (yellow line) results. The needed replacement ratios increased from 1997 to 2001, and again from 2001 to 2004. The increase from 2001 to 2004 occurred primarily because people are paying less pre-retirement income tax in 2004 than they did in 2001. A $20,000 wage earner pays 28% less in taxes in 2004 than in 2001, and a $90,000 earner pays 15% less. Paying less tax increases a person's pre-retirement disposable income, which increases the amount of post-retirement income he or she needs to maintain the same level of disposable income after retirement.

It should be noted that inflation creates a slight distortion in the comparisons. For example, a $50,000 wage earner in 2004 may have been earning $46,000-$47,000 in 2001, and $41,000-$43,000 in 1997.

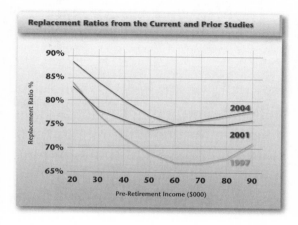

Replacement Ratios from the Current and Prior Studies

Replacement Ratios from the Current and Prior Studies

Pre-Retirement Income ($000s)	2001 Study			2004 Study		
	Social Security (%)	Private and Employer Sources (%)	Total (%)	Social Security (%)	Private and Employer Sources (%)	Total (%)
$20	61	22	83	65	24	89
30	53	25	78	56	28	84
40	49	27	76	51	29	80
50	44	30	74	48	29	77
60	39	36	75	43	32	75
70	35	40	75	39	37	76
80	31	44	75	35	42	77
90	28	48	76	33	45	78

The table above compares the 2004 and 2001 results, including the percentage of income expected to be replaced by Social Security. The table shows that even though the total amount of income needed at retirement is as much as 6% higher in 2004 than in 2001, the amount to be provided by private sources increases by no more than 3%, and it actually decreases at all income levels over $40,000. This is because Social Security is expected to replace a larger percentage of pre-retirement income in 2004 than in 2001.

6

Replacement Ratio Study™

Source: Aon Consulting. *Replacement Ratio Study, A Measurement Tool for Retirement Planning*, 2004. Used with permission.

Savings and expenditure changes can vary significantly by individual. Thus, it may be appropriate to start with a replacement ratio calculation that disregards these changes and to adjust for them individually. The graph to the right shows the baseline replacement ratios (yellow line), and the comparable replacement ratios disregarding expenditure changes (red line), and disregarding both expenditure and savings changes (blue line).

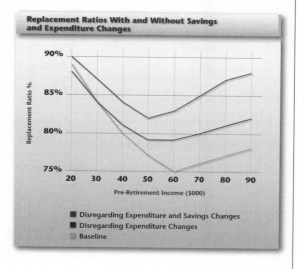

Replacement Ratios With and Without Savings and Expenditure Changes

- ■ Disregarding Expenditure and Savings Changes
- ■ Disregarding Expenditure Changes
- ■ Baseline

If a person's savings and expenditures do not change at retirement, the replacement ratios needed to maintain the person's standard of living are shown by the top blue line. To the extent the person saved before retirement and stopped saving at retirement, the replacement ratios decrease. If the person was an average saver, the replacement ratios would decrease to the middle red line. If the person saved more than average, the replacement ratios would decrease below the red line.

After adjusting for savings, the next step is to adjust for decreases in the person's age- and work-related expenditures at retirement. If these expenditures decrease by an average amount at retirement, the replacement ratios would decrease to the bottom yellow "baseline" line. If, however, age- and work-related expenditures decrease by more than average, the replacement ratios would decrease below the yellow line.

Important observations from this analysis include:

- If an individual's expenditure and savings amounts do not change at retirement, needed replacement ratios (top blue line in the graph) will range from 82%-90%, versus the baseline of 75%-89%. The largest increase is for people at the highest income levels. This is because they saved the most and are also expected to have the largest reduction in expenditures at retirement, as a percentage of income.

- Replacement ratios for lower income employees do not change much when expenditure changes and/or savings changes are disregarded. This is because most lower income employees do not save much and do not reduce their expenditures as much at retirement as those with higher incomes. In fact, the $20,000 person is actually expected to spend more after retirement than before.

Source: Aon Consulting. *Replacement Ratio Study, A Measurement Tool for Retirement Planning*, 2004. Used with permission.

The baseline family situation for this study is one wage earner retiring at age 65 with a spouse three years younger. The table below shows replacement ratio targets for this baseline case and for three other family situations. In all cases, the replacement ratios are driven by three factors:

1. Income tax tables and tax exemptions that apply in different situations.

2. The amount of Social Security taxes paid (e.g., a two-worker family may pay higher aggregate Social Security taxes at a given pre-retirement income level).

3. The amount of Social Security benefit, which influences how much of the total retirement income is subject to tax.

Single Compared to Married Baseline

At the lowest income levels, pre-retirement taxes are higher for singles than for married couples. As a result, the single worker has less to spend before retirement and, therefore, has less to replace after retirement. The replacement ratios at lower income levels are, therefore, smaller than for the married family unit (baseline or others). At higher income levels, pre-retirement taxes are also higher for singles. However, post-retirement taxes are also far greater at the higher income levels for singles. The net effect is that single people at higher income levels actually need higher replacement ratios than married couples. Also, at a given level of pre-retirement income, the effect of taxation of Social Security benefits is more pronounced for the single worker. The retirement income thresholds at which Social Security benefits become subject to income tax are lower for a single taxpayer. The threshold at which Social Security becomes taxable is $25,000 for a single taxpayer (compared to $32,000 for married taxpayers), and the threshold at which 85% becomes taxable is $34,000 for a single taxpayer (compared to $44,000 for married taxpayers).

Replacement Ratio Targets for Other Family Situations

Pre-Retirement Income ($000)	Replacement Ratio Targets			
	Baseline	Other Family Situations		
	Couple 65/62 One Working (%)	Single Age 65 (%)	Couple 65/65 One Working (%)	Couple 65/62 Both Working (%)
$20	89	82	89	89
30	84	79	84	84
40	80	76	80	80
50	77	74	77	77
60	75	74	75	76
70	76	78	75	77
80	77	81	75	77
90	78	82	76	78

Source: Aon Consulting. *Replacement Ratio Study, A Measurement Tool for Retirement Planning*, 2004. Used with permission.

One Wage Earner, Both Age 65

The table on the preceding page compares two other married situations to the baseline replacement ratios. The first is a married couple, one wage earner, both age 65. Since the age 65 spouse gets an increased standard deduction, post-retirement taxes are reduced somewhat when compared to the baseline case (where the spouse is age 62). Also, the family Social Security benefits are 1.497 times the wage earner's primary benefit (compared to 1.362 when the spouse is age 62).

At the $60,000 gross pre-retirement income level and below, retirees do not pay any significant income taxes, so there is no difference in the replacement ratios due to taxes. The combination of the increased standard deduction and the increased family Social Security benefits makes a slight difference in the replacement ratios at the $70,000 and higher income levels.

Two Wage Earners, Ages 65 and 62

Another family situation focuses on two wage earners, one age 65 and one age 62. We assumed that the primary wage earner brings in 60% of the family unit's income and the spouse brings in 40%. Results for this family situation are virtually the same as for the baseline case.

Source: Aon Consulting. *Replacement Ratio Study, A Measurement Tool for Retirement Planning*, 2004. Used with permission.

Since *Consumer Expenditure Survey* (*CES*) data are not available at income levels above $100,000, replacement ratios above that income level are not part of the Aon Consulting/Georgia State University formal study. Aon Consulting has, however, extended the replacement ratio calculations to income levels of $150,000, $200,000, and $250,000. As with prior studies, we wanted to determine whether the replacement ratios continue to trend upward above the $90,000 income level, the top level in the formal study.

The table and graph to the right show that the ratios do continue to trend upward. Although the higher pre-retirement taxes paid by higher income individuals have a decreasing effect on replacement ratios, higher post-retirement taxes have an even more powerful effect and drive the ratios upward. The net effect is that higher replacement ratios are needed as income increases.

It should be noted that the calculations for higher income employees are based on an extrapolation of the savings rate data used for the baseline study — we assumed employees at all levels over $90,000 would save 5.24% of disposable income. If savings rates turn out to be higher at these income levels than a simple extrapolation would indicate, the needed replacement ratios would be somewhat lower. Other assumptions, such as expenditure changes, were also projected beyond the $90,000 group.

It would be difficult for high-income individuals to generate sufficient retirement income solely from Social Security and an employer's qualified plans. These individuals generally need to receive a substantial portion of their retirement income from personal savings, a non-qualified arrangement, or both.

Replacement Ratios: Higher Income Levels

Pre-Retirement Income ($000)	Replacement Ratios		
	Social Security (%)	Other Sources (%)	Total (%)
$80	35	42	77
90	33	45	78
150	20	65	85
200	15	73	88
250	12	76	88

Baseline and Projected Higher Income Replacement Ratios

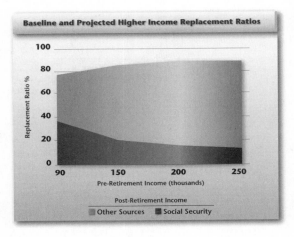

Source: Aon Consulting. *Replacement Ratio Study, A Measurement Tool for Retirement Planning*, 2004. Used with permission.

Savings rates are one of the three major components (along with taxes and expenditure changes) in the replacement ratio equation. Higher savings rates both reduce the needed replacement percentages (employees are assumed to cease their savings plans once retired) and provide the employee with the ability to develop the needed savings accounts.

For this and each prior study, we developed savings rates using recent *CES* data. Savings was defined as the sum of:

1. Net acquisition of stocks and bonds.

2. Net investment in farm or business.

3. Net change in savings and checking accounts.

4. Net change in money owed.

5. Net change in U.S. savings bond holdings.

6. Contributions to retirement plans.

This definition includes an element of investment return as well as a pure savings element. Combining this definition with the recent stock market decline results in a very low savings rate, relative to the savings rates from prior studies.

Since the stock market decline that occurred in 2000-2002 is not expected to continue indefinitely, and the economy is already in the beginning stages of a recovery, we averaged savings rates from the last three studies for purposes of this study. This technique extends the period over which savings rates are measured and better reflects future, expected savings rates. The table above details the savings rates from the last two studies and the average savings rates that were used for this study.

Savings Rates

Pre-Retirement Income ($000)	Savings Rates at Ages 50-65 as a Percentage of Gross Pre-Retirement Income (%)			
	2004	2001	1997	Average
$20	0.7	1.4	4.4	2.2
30	0.3	2.3	4.8	2.5
40	0.1	3.0	5.0	2.7
50	0.2	3.7	5.1	3.0
60	0.4	4.2	5.1	3.2
70	0.9	4.5	5.0	3.5
80	1.5	4.7	5.0	3.7
90	2.1	5.0	5.0	4.0

AON

11

Source: Aon Consulting. *Replacement Ratio Study, A Measurement Tool for Retirement Planning,* 2004. Used with permission.

Savings rates from the *Federal Reserve* in its *Flow of Funds Accounts of the United States* are shown in the chart to the right. The rapid decline in savings rates appears to have stopped in 2001. However, even the recent stock market decline and the realization that retirement looms for many in the baby boom generation has not yet encouraged significantly increased savings rates among working employees.

Higher savings rates would lead to lower required replacement ratios. This is because people who save more before retirement spend less. Thus, they are used to a lower standard of living, and they need less income after retirement to maintain that reduced standard of living.

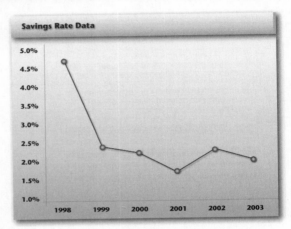

Savings Rate Data

Source: Federal Reserve statistical release *Flow of Funds Accounts of the United States, Flows and Outstandings, Third Quarter 2003*, March 4, 2004

Source: Aon Consulting. *Replacement Ratio Study, A Measurement Tool for Retirement Planning*, 2004. Used with permission.

How to Use Replacement Ratios

The numbers included in prior reports have been extensively used to determine retirement adequacy. Users include employers reviewing plan design, financial planners, and employees looking to see how prepared they are for retirement.

When applying replacement ratios, it is important to keep certain things in mind. Even though replacement ratios are precise percentages of pay, they are determined based on "average" employees. Some employees have high pre-retirement costs that end at retirement — for example, older parents who work until their children complete their college educations or someone with a high mortgage payment who moves into a much less costly living situation just prior to retirement. Employees in these situations will need less retirement income to maintain their standard of living. Others, such as employees beginning to care for an elderly parent, might find a need for a higher replacement ratio.

The answers in this study are based on many different assumptions. Two assumptions that have significant effects are savings rates and the loss of medical benefits. An employee who saves a larger percentage of income than we assume will need less replacement income. An employee who has active medical benefits but none in retirement will need a greater replacement ratio. In subsequent sections, we give the user some sense of how the resulting replacement ratios might be adjusted to fit these situations.

Outside factors also come into play. Social Security has been under review for many years, and revisions are likely at some point. Medicare benefits are also subject to change and will alter the need for retirement income to pay for medical benefits. And with the workforce aging, many older employees will find that income from work will supplement retirement plan income for many years.

Compounding this picture is the movement to defined contribution accounts in retirement. Whether arising directly from a sponsor's move to a defined contribution or cash balance plan, or because a traditional pension plan's benefits are paid as a lump sum based on a variable interest rate, the determination of *"whether I have enough money to retire"* is becoming more complicated.

When providing retirement projections, employers who are dedicated to having employees properly plan for retirement will also want to provide financial planning tools along with strong educational materials. Employers who meet this challenge creatively and proactively will gain a clear competitive advantage.

AON

Source: Aon Consulting. *Replacement Ratio Study, A Measurement Tool for Retirement Planning,* 2004. Used with permission.

Replacement Ratios as Lump Sums

Throughout this report, we define "replacement ratio" as a percentage of an employee's pay just prior to retirement. The goal of a retirement planning program is to replace income that is lost at retirement.

With the strong movement to defined contribution plans and a significant number of defined benefit plans paying out the value of all benefits in a single lump sum, it is also becoming important to define how large a lump sum is necessary to provide the targeted income levels. The answer depends on a number of factors, such as:

1. How long will a person live after retirement? Those with more retirement years need larger lump sums. People retiring at younger ages generally need more than people retiring at older ages, because they have longer remaining lifetimes. Also, females generally need more than males because they live longer. An average male retiring at age 65 lives another 17.3 years, while the average female lives another 20.7 years. Lifestyle, health, and other factors also influence one's lifespan.

2. How much will inflation increase a retiree's cost of living after retirement? The higher the rate of inflation, the larger the lump sum needed.

3. What rate of investment return will the lump sum produce? The higher the rate, the smaller the lump sum needed at retirement. Examples of how different rates of investment return affect the lump sum needed are shown in the table below. This table shows the lump sum amount needed at retirement to provide an income of $100 per month for life to an average male or female retiring at age 65. While invested, the lump sum is assumed to return 5%, 7%, or 9% per year. In all cases, inflation is assumed to increase the retiree's cost of living by 3% per year.

As you can see from the table, the lump sum needed at retirement is about 40% more if investments return only 5% rather than 9%. Also, on average, women need about 15% more than men because they live longer.

Lump Sum Needed at Retirement (Age 65) to Provide a $100 Monthly Income		
	Investment Earnings	
	5%	7%	9%
Male	$16,850	$14,167	$12,143
Female	$19,655	$16,159	$13,596

Replacement Ratio Study™

Source: Aon Consulting. *Replacement Ratio Study, A Measurement Tool for Retirement Planning,* 2004. Used with permission.

Using a 7% rate of investment return, we can convert needed replacement ratios into needed lump sum amounts, expressed as a multiple of the person's salary at retirement. (See the chart to the right). Since Social Security is not payable as a lump sum, we will do this only for the non-Social Security portion of the benefit.

Those employees with a defined benefit plan may have a portion of the need provided through that program and will need a lower lump sum.

Replacement Ratio/Lump Sum Needed from Private and Employer Sources

Pre-Retirement Income ($000)	Baseline Replacement Ratio Needed (% of final pay)	Equivalent Lump Sum Needed (as a multiple of final pay)	
		Male	Female
$20	24	2.8	3.2
30	28	3.3	3.8
40	29	3.4	3.9
50	29	3.4	3.9
60	32	3.8	4.3
70	37	4.4	5.0
80	42	5.0	5.7
90	45	5.3	6.1

AON

Source: Aon Consulting. Replacement Ratio Study, A Measurement Tool for Retirement Planning, 2004. Used with permission.

The baseline replacement ratios developed in this report indicate how much income is needed at the start of retirement to maintain a person's pre-retirement standard of living. To maintain that standard of living during retirement, we assume that all income will increase in proportion to inflation. Social Security benefits will do that automatically, as will some governmental pension plans.

However, most corporate defined benefit plans are fixed and do not increase each year, though some employers periodically grant ad hoc cost-of-living increases. If retirement income is paid as a non-increasing or fixed annuity, an income that is adequate at the beginning of retirement won't stay adequate very long. Each year, inflation eats away at the buying power of fixed income.

One way to offset this effect is to have a higher fixed income amount. A higher starting income will allow the retiree to save some income from the early retirement years for the later years. The graph below shows adjusted targets that can be used for this purpose.

The adjusted targets assume all of a retiree's income other than Social Security is paid as a non-increasing or fixed annuity. For example, if inflation is 3% and all income other than Social Security is provided in the form of a level lifetime annuity, the needed replacement income increases from 75% (the baseline at $60,000) to 84%.

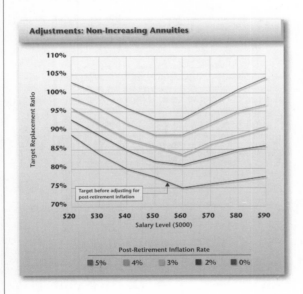

Source: Aon Consulting. *Replacement Ratio Study, A Measurement Tool for Retirement Planning,* 2004. Used with permission.

Since our 2001 study, many employers have made changes to their post-retirement medical programs. Many employees have lost their post-retirement medical benefits or have had significant costs shifted to them. The baseline replacement ratios provided in this report are based on the average benefits of a large population according to *CES* data. Some sources have suggested that retiree medical benefits are important enough to be handled separately.

To calculate the effect of retiree medical benefits on replacement ratios, we estimate the cost for an "average" Social Security supplemental benefit to be $2,750 annually. Add to that the cost of Medicare Part B premiums (just under $800 in 2004) for a total of $3,550 annually. The replacement need is based on the relationship of benefits before retirement compared to those just after retirement. Therefore:

■ If we remove the effect of any change in medical benefits from our results, we get the replacement ratios shown in the "No Change" column in the table above.

Replacement Ratios Reflecting Post-Retirement Changes in Medical Benefits

Pre-Retirement Income ($000)	Replacement Ratio		
	Baseline (% of final pay)	No Change in Medical (%)	Worst Case Medical (%)
$20	89	83	101
30	84	80	91
40	80	76	85
50	77	74	81
60	75	73	79
70	76	74	79
80	77	76	80
90	78	77	81

■ If, on the other hand, an employee had fully-paid employer health care just prior to retirement and no coverage after retirement, income would be needed to replace the total medical benefit. The column marked "Worst Case Medical" adjusts our baseline result to show the replacement ratio needed in this situation.

Obviously, the level of post-retirement medical benefits provided before and after retirement will have a significant effect on post-retirement needs. Most employees will be somewhere between the "no change" and "worst case" scenarios.

AON 17

Source: Aon Consulting. *Replacement Ratio Study, A Measurement Tool for Retirement Planning,* 2004. Used with permission.

It is axiomatic that the earlier one starts saving for retirement, the easier it is to meet a needed replacement income. With the income replacement needs presented in this report, we can estimate the level of annual saving needed to meet the income targets.

The following charts assume that benefits will be paid at age 65 and full Social Security benefits will be available. The salary shown is the current salary and assumes that salary will increase at 3% per year until retirement. Finally, we assumed a 7% rate of return on savings.

Annual Savings Estimate: Males

Goal as a Multiple of Pay at Retirement		% of Pay that Needs to Be Saved if Starting at Age:			
Salary ($000)	Multiple of Pay	25	35	45	55
$20	2.8	3.1%	5.2%	9.8%	24.2%
30	3.3	3.7	6.2	11.6	28.5
40	3.4	3.8	6.4	11.9	29.3
50	3.4	3.8	6.4	11.9	29.3
60	3.8	4.2	7.1	13.3	32.8
70	4.4	4.9	8.2	15.4	38.0
80	5.0	5.6	9.4	17.5	43.1
90	5.3	5.9	9.9	18.6	45.7

Annual Savings Estimate: Females

Goal as a Multiple of Pay at Retirement		% of Pay that Needs to Be Saved if Starting at Age:			
Salary ($000)	Multiple of Pay	25	35	45	55
$20	3.2	3.6%	6.0%	11.2%	27.6%
30	3.8	4.2	7.1	13.3	32.8
40	3.9	4.3	7.3	13.7	33.6
50	3.9	4.3	7.3	13.7	33.6
60	4.3	4.8	8.1	15.1	37.1
70	5.0	5.6	9.4	17.5	43.1
80	5.7	6.4	10.7	20.0	49.2
90	6.1	6.8	11.4	21.4	52.6

Conclusion

Compared to prior studies, this 2004 update shows an increase in the amount of income people need at retirement to maintain their pre-retirement standard of living. However, in comparison to the earlier studies, the increase is small (no more than two percentage points) for people with pre-retirement incomes of $60,000 or more, but is 3-6 percentage points greater for people with pre-retirement incomes of $20,000-$50,000. Required replacement ratios now range from 75%-89%, compared to 74%-83% in 2001.

Even though the age for full Social Security benefits has increased to 65 years and four months for people reaching age 65 in 2004, Social Security benefits for an age 65 retiree are actually greater in 2004 as a percentage of income than they were in 2001. This helps compensate for employer-sponsored plans and individual savings, which are replacing less than they have historically due to the depressed investment returns of the early 2000s.

As the baby boomer generation approaches retirement and those new to the workforce begin their lifetime journey in a defined contribution world, the need for retirement planning has never been greater. The results of this study will provide the employee and the plan sponsor with quantitative information needed to begin that planning effectively.

Source: Aon Consulting. *Replacement Ratio Study, A Measurement Tool for Retirement Planning,* 2004. Used with permission.

The data in the U.S. Department of Labor's Bureau of Labor Statistics' *Consumer Expenditure Survey (CES)* allow us to quantify key items in the replacement ratio formulas shown here.

The first formula (expenditure, tax, and savings model) takes into account changes in age- and work-related expenditures after retirement, in addition to taking into account savings patterns and changes in taxes after retirement. The second formula (tax and savings model) disregards changes in age- and work-related expenditures, and the third formula (tax only model)

disregards both savings and changes in age- and work-related expenditures. The symbols used in the formulas are defined as follows:

PrRPG: Gross pre-retirement income

PrRT: Pre-retirement taxes

PrRS: Pre-retirement savings

NCCR: Change in age- and work-related expenditures

PoRT: Post-retirement taxes

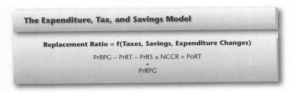

The Expenditure, Tax, and Savings Model

Replacement Ratio = f(Taxes, Savings, Expenditure Changes)

$$\frac{PrRPG - PrRT - PrRS \pm NCCR + PoRT}{PrRPG}$$

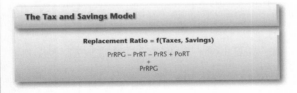

The Tax and Savings Model

Replacement Ratio = f(Taxes, Savings)

$$\frac{PrRPG - PrRT - PrRS + PoRT}{PrRPG}$$

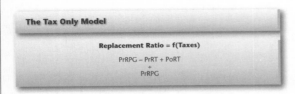

The Tax Only Model

Replacement Ratio = f(Taxes)

$$\frac{PrRPG - PrRT + PoRT}{PrRPG}$$

Source: Aon Consulting. *Replacement Ratio Study, A Measurement Tool for Retirement Planning,* 2004. Used with permission.

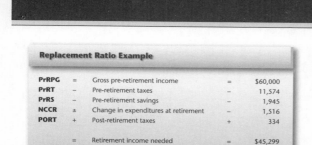

Replacement Ratio Example

PrRPG	=	Gross pre-retirement income	=	$60,000
PrRT	–	Pre-retirement taxes	–	11,574
PrRS	–	Pre-retirement savings	–	1,945
NCCR	±	Change in expenditures at retirement	–	1,516
PORT	+	Post-retirement taxes	+	334
	=	Retirement income needed	=	$45,299
PrRPG	÷	Gross pre-retirement income	÷	$60,000
		Replacement Ratio	=	75%

The development of the replacement ratios for each gross pre-retirement income level is shown in Appendix II.

Source: Aon Consulting. *Replacement Ratio Study, A Measurement Tool for Retirement Planning,* 2004. Used with permission.

	$20,000	$30,000	$40,000
1. Gross Pre-Retirement Income	$20,000	$30,000	$40,000
2. Pre-Retirement Taxes			
a. Social Security	$1,530	$2,295	$3,060
b. Federal Income	370	1,338	2,737
c. State Income	102	358	711
d. Total Pre-Retirement Taxes	$2,002	$3,991	$6,508
3. Disposable Income After Taxes			
[(1) - (2)(d)]	$17,998	$26,009	$33,492
4. Pre-Retirement Savings			
a. As a % of Disposable Income	2.417%	2.838%	3.234%
b. Amount Saved [(3) x (4)(a)]	$435	$738	$1,083
5. Spendable Income [(3) - (4)(b)]	$17,563	$25,271	$32,409
6. Increase (Decrease) in Age- and Work-Related Expenses at Retirement	$235	$59	($385)
7. Post-Retirement Taxes			
a. Federal Income	$0	$0	$0
b. State Income	0	0	0
c. Total Post-Retirement Taxes	$0	$0	$0
8. Gross Post-Retirement Income Needed			
[(5) + (6) + (7)(c)]	$17,798	$25,330	$32,024
9. Needed Replacement Ratio [(8) / (1)]	89%	84%	80%

22

Replacement Ratio Study™

Source: Aon Consulting. *Replacement Ratio Study, A Measurement Tool for Retirement Planning*, 2004. Used with permission.

$50,000	$60,000	$70,000	$80,000	$90,000
$3,825	$4,590	$5,355	$6,120	$6,755
4,175	5,608	7,040	8,784	11,172
1,054	1,376	1,678	2,035	2,515
$9,054	$11,574	$14,073	$16,939	$20,442
$40,946	$48,426	$55,927	$63,061	$69,558
3.651%	4.016%	4.329%	4.724%	5.236%
$1,495	$1,945	$2,421	$2,979	$3,642
$39,451	$46,481	$53,506	$60,082	$65,916
($961)	($1,516)	($1,975)	($2,258)	($2,272)
$0	$279	$1,264	$3,022	$5,163
0	55	278	726	1,335
$0	$334	$1,542	$3,748	$6,498
$38,490	$45,299	$53,073	$61,572	$70,142
77%	75%	76%	77%	78%

Source: Aon Consulting. *Replacement Ratio Study, A Measurement Tool for Retirement Planning,* 2004. Used with permission.

Appendix III — Analysis of Expenditure Changes

Pre-Retirement Income Level	$20,000	$30,000	$40,000
1. Reading and Education			
a. Working	$262	$365	$457
b. Retired	$217	$291	$357
c. Increase (Decrease) [(b) - (a)]	($45)	($74)	($100)
2. Health Care			
a. Working	$1,513	$1,779	$1,974
b. Retired	$2,677	$3,124	$3,409
c. Increase (Decrease) [(b) - (a)]	$1,164	$1,345	$1,435
3. Utilities			
a. Working	$2,219	$2,524	$2,733
b. Retired	$2,269	$2,575	$2,819
c. Increase (Decrease) [(b) - (a)]	$50	$51	$86
4. Household Operations			
a. Working	$204	$268	$323
b. Retired	$321	$405	$477
c. Increase (Decrease) [(b) - (a)]	$117	$137	$154
5. Shelter			
a. Working	$5,774	$6,982	$7,961
b. Retired	$4,628	$5,429	$6,103
c. Increase (Decrease) [(b) - (a)]	($1,146)	($1,553)	($1,858)
6. Entertainment			
a. Working	$1,037	$1,317	$1,548
b. Retired	$1,191	$1,507	$1,769
c. Increase (Decrease) [(b) - (a)]	$154	$190	$221
7. Total Increase (Decrease) in Age-Related Expenses	$294	$96	($62)
8. Food			
a. Working	$3,677	$4,179	$4,556
b. Retired	$3,811	$4,537	$5,005
c. Increase (Decrease) [(b) - (a)]	$134	$358	$449
9. Apparel and Services			
a. Working	$674	$847	$994
b. Retired	$607	$785	$924
c. Increase (Decrease) [(b) - (a)]	($67)	($62)	($70)
10. Transportation			
a. Working	$5,137	$6,512	$7,653
b. Retired	$5,011	$6,179	$6,951
c. Increase (Decrease) [(b) - (a)]	($126)	($333)	($702)
11. Total Increase (Decrease) in Work-Related Expenses	($59)	($37)	($323)
12. Total Increase (Decrease) in Age- and Work-Related Expenses	$235	$59	($385)

24

Replacement Ratio Study™

Source: Aon Consulting. *Replacement Ratio Study, A Measurement Tool for Retirement Planning*, 2004. Used with permission.

$50,000	$60,000	$70,000	$80,000	$90,000
$545	$634	$725	$814	$897
$418	$474	$521	$552	$567
($127)	($160)	($204)	($262)	($330)
$2,141	$2,290	$2,433	$2,554	$2,648
$3,592	$3,698	$3,751	$3,739	$3,694
$1,451	$1,408	$1,318	$1,185	$1,046
$2,905	$3,059	$3,209	$3,322	$3,398
$3,043	$3,232	$3,375	$3,420	$3,359
$138	$173	$166	$98	($39)
$379	$438	$501	$570	$642
$546	$617	$691	$768	$842
$167	$179	$190	$198	$200
$8,853	$9,683	$10,477	$11,156	$11,704
$6,781	$7,525	$8,382	$9,296	$10,212
($2,072)	($2,158)	($2,095)	($1,860)	($1,492)
$1,755	$1,945	$2,122	$2,274	$2,395
$2,003	$2,201	$2,354	$2,442	$2,465
$248	$256	$232	$168	$70
($195)	($302)	($393)	($473)	($545)
$4,891	$5,205	$5,520	$5,787	$5,998
$5,338	$5,585	$5,786	$5,902	$5,946
$447	$380	$266	$115	($52)
$1,132	$1,263	$1,391	$1,507	$1,606
$1,045	$1,159	$1,271	$1,376	$1,476
($87)	($104)	($120)	($131)	($130)
$8,696	$9,677	$10,605	$11,420	$12,092
$7,570	$8,187	$8,877	$9,651	$10,547
($1,126)	($1,490)	($1,728)	($1,769)	($1,545)
($766)	($1,214)	($1,582)	($1,785)	($1,727)
($961)	($1,516)	($1,975)	($2,258)	($2,272)

Source: Aon Consulting. *Replacement Ratio Study, A Measurement Tool for Retirement Planning*, 2004. Used with permission.

About Aon Consulting

Aon Consulting is among the world's top global human capital and management consulting firms, providing a complete array of professional services in the areas of consulting, outsourcing, and brokerage to clients of all sizes. These services help to attract and retain top talent and improve organizational performance. Solutions are provided in the following areas:

- Employee Benefits
- Compensation and Rewards
- Communication
- Human Resources Outsourcing
- Process Redesign
- Talent Selection and Development

In addition, Aon Consulting provides specialized services such as actuarial and educational consulting as well as employee commitment and employee compensation survey information for industry sectors.

Aon Consulting professionals possess extensive knowledge and experience in a variety of fields, including actuarial science, business, computer science, employee benefits, industrial psychology, organizational behavior, information systems, employment compliance, process improvement design, communication, and leadership development.

Headquartered in Chicago, Aon Consulting is the human capital and management consulting arm of Aon Corporation (NYSE:AOC), a holding company that is comprised of a family of insurance brokerage, consulting, and insurance underwriting subsidiaries. Aon serves clients through 600 offices and 54,000 employees around the world.

For more information about the services available from Aon Consulting, call *+1.800.438.6487* or visit our Web site at *www.aon.com/hcc*.

Retirement Services

Aon Consulting provides consulting services in the design, administration, funding, and communication of defined benefit or defined contribution plans, whether the plans are brand new for the company or an improvement over previous plans. To learn more about these services, visit *www.aon.com/retirement* or call *+1.800.438.6487*.

Aon Consulting

200 East Randolph Street
Chicago, Illinois 60601
+1.800.438.6487
www.aon.com

Replacement Ratio Study™

Source: Aon Consulting. *Replacement Ratio Study, A Measurement Tool for Retirement Planning,* 2004. Used with permission.

Selecting a Default Fund for a Defined Benefit Contribution Plan

Selecting a Default Fund for a Defined Contribution Plan

Research and Analysis ▸ July 2004

Executive Summary

Most plan sponsors choose a fixed-dollar fund as the default investment option for their defined contribution plan. This decision seems inconsistent with the long-term nature of retirement savings plans and with common "prudent investor" principles underlying participant education programs.

Author

Stephen P. Utkus

Default fund use. In 2003, more than 80% of Vanguard-administered plans used a money market or investment contract fund as the plan's default investment option. Since 2000 the use of a fixed-dollar fund as the default option has remained essentially unchanged. Over that same period, there has been a shift from money market to investment contract funds, most likely because of rapidly falling money market yields.

Legal framework. Under ERISA, a plan sponsor retains full fiduciary responsibility for investing plan assets for which participants have not provided investment instructions. The standard for such decisions is ERISA's "prudent investor" rule. Sponsors are expected to invest as a prudent and experienced investor would—not as an inexperienced participant might. Under ERISA, retirement plans are not required to invest in "safe" assets, and the law permits fiduciaries to invest in assets that may experience short-term losses in pursuit of long-term returns.

Investment considerations. Selecting a fixed-dollar investment fund as a default option is inconsistent with two "prudent investor" principles underlying current participant education programs: (1) the existence of a positive equity-risk premium and (2) the variation of an individual's risk-taking ability with age. These principles also underlie the construction of many committee-directed portfolios for defined benefit plans, endowments, and foundations.

Sponsor decision-making. Investment committees selecting a default fund should: (1) evaluate the objectives of their retirement savings plan; (2) determine which investment principles underlie their notion of a "prudent investor"; (3) select a fund or funds consistent with this analysis; and (4) document their decision-making process and conclusions. Sponsors seeking to reconcile the investment principles of their participant education programs with their own choice of a default fund may choose some level of equity exposure for the plan default option. Choices include: a single balanced fund, a series of balanced funds (either traditional, life-cycle, or target maturity), or possibly a managed account.

THE **Vanguard** GROUP

Scott Milne of Vanguard's Plan Consulting and ERISA Legal Department helped research legal case citations for this report. Samuel Arlen, Suzanne Cicotti, Kelly Harrison, Christine Johnson, and Martha Witt assisted with the report's editing, design, and production.

Background

In the aftermath of the 2000–2002 bear market and with the recent focus on corporate governance, employers are reviewing a wide range of corporate risk exposures, including their fiduciary duties under ERISA. Within defined contribution (DC) savings plans, employers are examining all aspects of plan administration—from complex fiduciary issues, such as the role of company stock within the plan, to more mundane questions, such as the plan's default investment option.

A default option is typically used when participants fail to make an investment choice—either for their own contributions or for employer contributions they have the right to direct. For many plans, the default fund may have been selected years ago, perhaps with little scrutiny. In the past, a typical choice was a fixed-dollar money market or stable value investment option.

Increasingly, however, sponsors are rethinking this decision, and a growing number are instead adopting balanced funds as default options.[1] Driving this trend are three factors:

• DC plans are now the dominant type of retirement plan in the United States, and employers recognize that plan participants in the default fund need to be directed to a balanced investment program to achieve long-term retirement security.

• Some employers are replacing a combined defined benefit (DB)/DC plan with an all-DC design, often by adding an employer profit-sharing contribution to an existing 401(k) plan. These employers want to ensure that DC plan

assets are invested as effectively for the long term as the DB assets would have been, and they recognize that a balanced default fund is needed to generate sufficient capital for employees' retirement needs.

• More employers are interested in automatic enrollment or in autopilot or automatic 401(k) plan designs, in which savings and investment decisions are made automatically for participants. In these designs, participants rely on their employers' default decisions, rather than making active choices of their own.

Research has shown that getting the default option "right" from the outset is critical to long-term retirement security. Once placed in default savings and investment options, participants exhibit inertia and rarely revisit the elections made for them. In other words, many participants placed in a default fund are unlikely to take active control of their accounts, and instead remain in the default. If the default fund is a conservative fixed-dollar investment, these participants are at risk of not meeting their long-term retirement savings objectives.[2]

In this report, we:

• Provide data on the current default investment options chosen by plan sponsors.

• Consider the legal and investment aspects of the default choice.

• Provide a decision-making framework for plan fiduciaries when selecting a default, as well as recommendations for policymakers.

---

1 Feinberg (2004) documents the growing interest in balanced or life-cycle funds as a DC plan's default fund.
2 Our report, *Lessons From Behavioral Finance and the Autopilot 401(k),* summarizes the relevant research on this topic (Vanguard, 2004a).

 2 The Vanguard Center for Retirement Research

Current Default Choices

Today plan sponsors most frequently select a fixed-dollar investment option as the default fund. In a December 2003 sample of nearly 1,700 DC plans administered by Vanguard, 82% of plans had selected a money market fund or investment contract fund as their default option (Figure 1). Only 14% used a balanced fund, while 3% employed an equity or company stock fund.

Compared with a similar sample in 2000, little has changed over the past three years (Figure 2). One notable difference is that reliance on money market funds has declined slightly—no doubt because of the sharp decline in money market yields during the period.

Sponsors of automatic enrollment programs take a somewhat different approach. In our 2001 survey of 15 automatic enrollment clients, 40% of plans chose a balanced or equity fund as their default option, while 60% continued to rely on a money market or investment contract fund.[3]

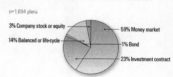

Figure 1.

Default Funds for Defined Contribution Plans 2003

n=1,694 plans

3% Company stock or equity — 59% Money market
14% Balanced or life-cycle — 1% Bond
— 23% Investment contract

Source: The Vanguard Group, 2004.

Figure 2.

Change in Default Option 2000–2003

	2003	2000	Change
n=number of plans	1,694	1,309	
Money Market	59%	65%	-6%
Investment Contract	23%	19%	4%
Bond	1%	1%	0%
Total Fixed Income	*83%*	*86%*	*-2%*
Balanced or Life-Cycle	14%	14%	0%
Company Stock or Equity	3%	1%	2%
Total Balanced or Equity	*17%*	*15%*	*2%*
Total	100%	100%	

Source: The Vanguard Group, 2004.

Today plan sponsors most frequently select a fixed–dollar option *as the default fund.*

---

3 Vanguard (2001).

Under the Employee Retirement Income Security Act of 1974 (ERISA), it is generally the plan sponsor (or the sponsor's administrative committee) who assumes full fiduciary responsibility for the investment of plan assets when a participant fails to select their individual account's investments. A plan sponsor generally cannot delegate the essential fiduciary duties of oversight and control of plan assets to participants. One exception is ERISA Section 404(c). Under 404(c), if the participant exercises affirmative control over his or her account, and the plan complies with the relevant regulations, the plan fiduciaries are able to limit (but not eliminate) their fiduciary exposure.[4]

Of course, when a participant fails to make investment choices for his or her own contributions or an employer's contributions, a default fund is automatically used and the exemption provided by Section 404(c) does not apply. A default fund also is used when the plan design specifies certain investment choices, as in the case of automatic enrollment or autopilot 401(k) plans. Under these circumstances, the participant is not making an affirmative investment decision, and so the plan fiduciaries retain their full investment oversight and control duties under ERISA.[5]

Prudent investor standard. In exercising their ERISA duties, sponsors are expected to act under the "prudent investor" standard. According to the statute, a plan fiduciary must act "with the care, skill, prudence, and diligence under the circumstances then prevailing that a prudent man acting in a like capacity and familiar with such matters would use . . ."[6]

Plan fiduciaries are supposed to act as an expert would, not as a layperson or man on the street. Hence the term "prudent investor" or "prudent expert" is sometimes used. ERISA's standard of prudence for fiduciaries "is not that of a prudent layperson but rather that of a prudent fiduciary with experience dealing with a similar enterprise."[7]

Thus fiduciaries are expected to be knowledgeable and informed about relevant investment information. They are expected to act as experienced or knowledgeable investors might, and they are called to a much higher standard of care, duty, and knowledge. "A trustee's lack of familiarity with investments is no excuse . . ."[8] According to some court opinions, if fiduciaries are unsure of what to do, they are expected to seek out professional help.[9]

No requirement to invest in conservative investments. Under ERISA, plan fiduciaries are under no obligation to invest exclusively in safe or guaranteed investments with a fixed-dollar value, such as a money market fund or investment contract fund.

4 In *Herman v. NationsBank of Georgia, N.A.*, 126 F.3d 1354, 1361 (11ᵗʰ Cir. 1997), the court noted that plan trustees cannot delegate their duties of management and control of plan assets except to: an investment manager under Section 403(a)(2) of ERISA; a participant under Section 404(c) of ERISA; or a named fiduciary not otherwise a trustee.

5 Preamble to the final regulations under section 404(c) of ERISA (29 CFR 2550.404c-1), 57 Fed. Reg. 46906 (Oct. 13, 1992).

6 ERISA §404(a)(1)(B).

7 *Reich v. Mason Tenders District Council of Greater New York*, 909 F. Supp. 882, 888 (S.D.N.Y. 1995).

8 *Katsaros v. Cody*, 744 F.2d 270, 279 (2ⁿᵈ Cir. 1984).

9 *Donovan v. Bierwirth*, 680 F.2d 263, 273-4 (2ⁿᵈ Cir. 1982).

Indeed, in drafting its regulations on prudent investments, the Department of Labor (DOL) specifically went out of its way *not* to prescribe a list of approved investments. Instead it sought to distinguish the ERISA concept of investment prudence from common law trust definitions by adopting a modern portfolio theory approach. In the DOL's view, the risk and return of an investment should be judged in relationship to the plan, its objectives, and the facts and circumstances surrounding the plan. A specific investment is not *per se* prudent or imprudent, but it must be judged from a total portfolio perspective.[10]

According to the DOL's regulations, fiduciaries should select investments "reasonably designed . . . to further the purposes of the plan, taking into consideration the risk of loss and the opportunity for gain (or other return) . . ." Specifically, the DOL notes that fiduciaries should take into account the diversification of plan assets, the plan's liquidity and current income needs, as well as "the projected rate of return on the portfolio relative to the funding objectives of the plan."[11]

Although this regulation was drafted within the context of the management of a DB trust, it is nevertheless a helpful framework for sponsors of individual-account DC plans. In the end, each DC participant's funding objective is to accumulate adequate savings for retirement, and fiduciary decisions should be made in light of this goal.

Balancing portfolio risk and return. The principle of balancing risk and return provides the basis for fiduciaries to invest in assets, such as common stocks or bonds, which may experience short-term losses but also offer the prospect for higher long-term returns. Under the statute, investment fiduciaries are justified in pursuing long-term investment strategies that may entail short-term losses, as long as they are suitable to the plan's objectives and goals.

Even if an account experiences an actual loss over time, the loss itself is not evidence that the fiduciaries failed in their duty. The decision-making process "requires prudence, not prescience [and] the ultimate outcome of an investment is not proof of imprudence."[12] Thus the fact that a fiduciary acted prudently is the standard to be applied. Moreover, the legal focus is on how fiduciaries approached the investment decision-making process prospectively—not on whether an investment experienced a loss after the fact.[13]

In the end, absent participant instructions, plan fiduciaries retain full legal responsibility for the investment of plan assets. As a result, their aim should be to invest the participant's assets in a prudent, diversified manner, for the exclusive benefit of the participant—in keeping with the core fiduciary duties of ERISA.[14]

10 29 CFR 2550.404a-1(b)(1). See also *Laborers National Pension Fund v. Northern Trust Quantitative Advisors, Inc.*, 173 F.3d 313, 317-318 (5th Cir. 1999), *cert denied sub nom., Laborers National Pension Fund v. American National Bank & Trust Co.*, 528 U.S. 967 (1999). Also Hutchinson and Ondrasik (1984), pp. 749-750.
11 29 CFR 2550.404a-1(b)(2).
12 *DeBruyne v. Equitable Life Assurance Society of the United States*, 720 F. Supp. 1342, 1349 (N.D. Ill. 1989), *aff'd* 920 F.2d 457 (7th Cir. 1990).
13 *Laborers*, 173 F.3d at 317-318. See also *Meinhardt v. Unisys Corp. (In re Unisys Savings Plan Litigation)*, 74 F.3d 420, 434-435 (3d Cir. 1996).
14 For an overview of the duties of fiduciaries with respect to plan assets, see *Laborers*, 173 F.3d at 316.

Figure 3.

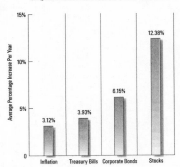

Long-Term Asset Class Returns and Risks 1926–2003

In choosing a default fund, what investment principles might fiduciaries use to satisfy ERISA's prudent investor standard? Our recommendation is to consider the principles underlying the plan's participant education program.

Two investment principles anchor most participant education programs in the United States and could be the reasoning behind a plan sponsor's choice of a default option. The first is the idea of a positive equity risk premium. Most, if not all, participant education programs include an illustration of the long-term returns on various asset classes, demonstrating that common stocks have historically provided higher returns than fixed income and cash investments (Figure 3).

Implicit in this historical data is an expectation that the positive equity premium will continue in the future, if not over the short run then for the long holding periods typical of retirement investors. Also implicit is the notion that the risks of investing in stocks are worth taking—that the premium is adequate compensation for the higher volatility of common stocks.

Of course, no investor can be certain that equities will realize higher long-term returns than bonds, or that the risk-adjusted returns of stocks will be sufficient to warrant the higher volatility that stocks entail. Historically, there have been long periods when stocks have performed poorly. The future also could be dramatically different from the past.

Standard deviation			
4.35%	3.20%	8.70%	20.39%

Sharpe Ratio			
—	—	0.25	0.41

Note: Standard deviation and the Sharpe Ratio are widely applied in modern portfolio theory. Standard deviation uses the past performance of securities to determine the range of possible future outcomes and a probability is attached to each outcome; the greater the degree of dispersion, the greater the risk. The Sharpe Ratio, developed by William F. Sharpe, is a risk-to-reward ratio that measures the risk-adjusted return of an investment. It uses standard deviation and excess return to determine the reward per unit of risk for an investment. Source: The Vanguard Group, 2004.

But, as ERISA case law underscores, plan fiduciaries are not held to a standard of certainty in the future outcomes of their investment decisions. Rather, ERISA requires that fiduciaries have a well-reasoned and thoughtful process for evaluating potential risks and returns and for pursuing an investment program that is both diversified and prudent *ex ante*, not *ex post*.

A second principle underlying most education programs is the belief that younger individuals are able to assume greater equity market risk than older individuals. One reason is that younger individuals have a longer period of work ahead of them and can recoup early investment losses with higher savings rates later in life. Another reason is that the longer an investor's holding period, the better the odds are that equity investments will provide higher returns than fixed income investments (Figure 4).

Both of these principles are widely accepted and used in investor education curriculums.[15] That said, the concept of the interrelationship between risk and age is not without debate. One criticism is that while the probability of equities earning a higher return than fixed income investments increases with longer holding periods, the cumulative wealth that investors may accumulate over time becomes more uncertain. In this sense, the suggestion that time "reduces" or "eliminates" risk is flawed. From this perspective, an investor should have a fixed percentage of equity exposure over his or her lifetime—not an age-varying one.[16]

Nonetheless, the idea that risk tolerance varies with age remains a common investment planning principle. This is especially true when based on the notion of a younger person's ability to recoup losses later in life, not on the notion that risk is lessened with time. A younger person who encounters a long period of poor stock market returns still has the ability to offset those losses with higher savings later in his or her work career.

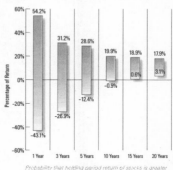

Figure 4.

Range of Holding Period Returns for U.S. Stocks 1926–2003

Probability that holding period return of stocks is greater than that from bonds

| 62% | 70% | 77% | 83% | 92% | 95% |

Source: The Vanguard Group, 2004.

15 In their well-known textbook on investments, *Essentials of Investments*, Bodie, Kane, and Marcus (2002), p. 883, discuss how an individual's risk tolerance and ability to recover from losses declines with age, suggesting a shift toward conservative assets over time. *Planning for Retirement Needs* by Tacchino and Littell (1999), pp. 440–441, which is part of the Certified Financial Planner™ (CFP) curriculum, describes the importance of time and risk in investment decision-making. Within the Chartered Financial Analyst (CFA) curriculum, Bronson, Scanlan, and Squires (forthcoming) and Maginn et. al. (forthcoming) document the importance of life stage and time horizon in an individual's ability to take risk. *Straight Talk on Investing* by Brennan (2002), p. 73, summarizes the age-based principle and its impact on equity exposure for retail mutual fund investors. Evensky's *Wealth Management* (1997) describes how time factors into the risk assessment process (pp. 86–88) as well as the pros and cons of the "time diversification" argument (pp. 201–204). He also attributes the original time diversification argument to Peter Bernstein.

16 Kritzman (1995), pp. 79–89, and Bernstein (1995), pp. 48–55, provide a good summary of the argument for and against age variations in commitment to equities. Bodie, Kane, and Marcus (2002), pp. 254–256, also provide a critique.

Figure 5.

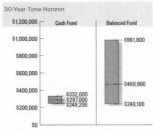

Long-Term Retirement Wealth Accumulations

For a 401(k) investor initially earning $25,000

Impact on Retirement Wealth

In the end, what financial impact would the choice of a default fund have on a participant's retirement? To answer this question, we forecast the retirement wealth of a typical 401(k) investor under two scenarios—one investing in a fixed-dollar cash investment and the other investing in a traditional balanced fund, consisting of 60% equity and 40% fixed income assets.

In these scenarios, we initially assume that the participant earns a $25,000 annual salary, with wages growing over time with inflation. Investment returns, risks, and inflation are based on historical averages from the 1960–2003 period. (See the Appendix for an explanation of our assumptions.)

The results illustrate the dramatic impact that a default fund can have on a portfolio (Figure 5). Over 30 years, our hypothetical participant accumulates wealth with a median value of $469,900 in the balanced option—compared with $287,000 in the fixed-dollar cash fund. The cash account balance represents four times the participant's salary of $59,000 after thirty years. By comparison, the balanced option median value is equal to eight times the participant's salary at retirement.

Reflecting the different volatility of a cash investment versus a balanced option, the wealth outcomes range from $249,200 to $332,000 for the cash fund (for a three-standard deviation confidence interval from 5% to 95%). By comparison, for the balanced option, wealth accumulations range from $240,100 to $981,800.

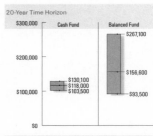

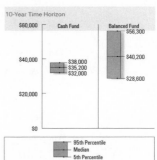

 8 The Vanguard Center for Retirement Research

Over 30 years, the expected wealth accumulation from a balanced fund exceeds that from a cash fund in an overwhelming majority of cases. For 20 and 10 years, the same principle holds, though the chance that the balanced fund will generate a higher wealth level than the cash fund falls somewhat.

Over all investment periods, there is some probability that the balanced fund will perform less well than the cash option. Committees must therefore evaluate this risk against the long-term benefit of a balanced option—namely, that over most long-term periods, participants will accumulate significantly higher retirement savings by investing in a balanced investment program rather than a fixed-dollar or cash option.

Fiduciary Decision-Making

In light of the legal and investment background, we recommend several steps for investment committees to take in selecting an appropriate default fund.

Step 1: Evaluate the plan's objective. The first question for an investment committee to consider is, "What is the principal objective of the retirement savings plan?" According to ERISA, the risk and return of investments must be evaluated in relationship to the plan's overall goals and objectives. For most, if not all, qualified DC plans, the principal objective is long-term retirement savings for plan participants.

In assessing the plan's objectives, plan fiduciaries should observe the language they have used in plan documents, the summary plan description, the plan's investment policy statement, and participant enrollment materials. The committee also might wish to note that Congress has granted tax preferences to qualified savings plans for the purpose of promoting retirement savings among American workers—a long-term, not a short-term, investment objective.

Assuming that the plan is exclusively or principally oriented toward retirement savings, the principal investment objective for such a plan will be the long-term accumulation of capital to meet individual participants' retirement funding goals. Such objectives, as we describe below, would suggest a meaningful commitment to higher-return assets such as equities. If the plan also is promoted to participants for short-term investment objectives (e.g., through the use of loans), plan fiduciaries may consider a higher proportion of conservative, short-term assets in the default option. But as we describe below, because loans are not widely used and are capped at 50% of account balances, the use of the plan as a short-term savings vehicle does not necessarily lead to an all-fixed-income default option.

Step 2: Determine "prudent investor" principles. The second question for an investment committee to consider is, "What prudent investor principles are relevant to the investment of plan assets?" As noted above, we recommend that plan sponsors use the same principles that are incorporated into participant education programs—that is, the ideas of a positive equity risk premium and the inverse relationship between age and risk-taking.

Figure 6.

Default Fund Alternatives

Rank	Options	Characteristics
Good	One balanced fund	A single fund for investors in the "accumulation" phase; rebalancing to that target allocation
Better	Various balanced funds by age group—e.g. more aggressive option if under age 50; more conservative option if age 50 or older	A more granular implementation of age-based investing; rebalancing to given allocation of each fund
Best	Target maturity funds, mapped by age, or a managed account option	Full implementation of age-based investing; daily rebalancing to target allocation, as well as gradual reduction of risk exposure over time

Note: All of the options shown are suitable choices for a default fund. These options are ranked according to the extent to which they implement the principle of age-based investing.
Source: The Vanguard Group, 2004.

A committee has an array of choices depending on how strongly it adheres to the principle of age-based investing (Figure 6). The simplest strategy would be a single balanced fund for all plan participants—under the assumption that most are in the "accumulation" phase of retirement savings, and that, once they retire, they will make more conservative allocations outside the plan.

An extension of this approach would be to select a more aggressive default option for younger participants and a less aggressive one for older participants. Arguably, all participants are still in the accumulation phase, but with more graduated risk levels by age.

One drawback to these solutions is that portfolio risk does not change as an individual ages. A possible solution would be to have a series of balanced funds based on a participant's expected time horizon until retirement, with automatic rebalancing over time—so-called target maturity lifestyle or life-cycle funds. Another possibility is the new managed account option within DC plans—in which portfolio investment decisions, both investment selection and ongoing rebalancing, are delegated to a third-party advisor.

It is true that some committees may be skeptical of these investment assumptions and will choose a conservative default fund based on concerns about the long-term outlook for equities. Yet, if they choose a fixed-dollar fund, the ramifications are much broader than simply the selection of the default fund. The belief that equities should play an important role in retirement portfolios is evident in the design of the plan's investment menu—most options within DC plans are equity funds—and in the design of participant communication materials. Committees that are uncomfortable with the long-term case for equities will need to reconsider more than just the choice of the plan's default option.

Step 3. Select funds consistent with plan objectives and "prudent investor" principles. The third step for an investment committee is to select a default option based on its findings regarding the plan's objectives and investment principles. A balanced investment strategy, consisting of both equity and fixed income securities, appears to be consistent with the long-term retirement objective for most plans, and the common investment principles underlying participant communication programs.

Step 4. Document all decisions. As with all fiduciary decisions, sponsors will want to document their reasoning in selecting a particular default fund. Committees should ensure that their decisions are not only substantively prudent—complying with the best thinking in investment and legal terms—but are also procedurally prudent, meaning that they have been actively discussed by the committee and are well-documented.

Treasury inflation-protected securities (TIPS) are another candidate for a default fund within a DC savings plan. TIPS are a government-guaranteed fixed income security providing some current income and inflation-adjusted growth of principal over time.[17]

Unlike equities, TIPS provide a near-contemporaneous hedge against inflation. Adjustments are made regularly to the value of TIPS to reflect actual inflation. By comparison, equities offer an inflation hedge subject to a considerable time lag. For example, during periods of high inflation and correspondingly high interest rates, such as the mid- to late 1970s, equities performed poorly, as high discount rates drove down the present value of stocks' future earnings, reducing stock multiples and stock prices. It was only after high inflation and high interest rates declined during the 1980s that stock multiples and prices improved dramatically when compared with inflation.

TIPS have only been issued in the United States since 1997, so there is no long-term domestic data on their price behavior in a variety of macroeconomic conditions. There are only a limited number of TIPS issues, and the market is less liquid than the regular U.S. Treasury market.

Some critics are skeptical of the case for equities and suggest that TIPS should play a dominant role in retirement plans.[18] Yet from a retirement funding perspective, the main drawback of TIPS is their risk-adjusted returns relative to equities. Equities are likely to offer higher risk-adjusted returns than TIPS in the future, especially over long periods. If this holds true, then retirement savings will grow more rapidly with some meaningful exposure to common stocks, not a portfolio predominantly or exclusively invested in TIPS.

It is worth noting that selecting a balanced investment strategy for a default fund would be consistent with common investment practices in DB plans, endowments and foundations, as well as participant decisions in DC plans.

Greenwich Associates reports that in 2003, 61% of corporate DB assets were invested in domestic and international equities, and another 9% in long-term growth assets such as real estate equity, private equity, and hedge funds. Thus, in total, 70% of corporate DB plan assets were invested in equities and other long-term growth assets. Similarly, Greenwich Associates reports that among endowments, 49% of assets were invested in domestic and international stocks, and another 22% of assets in real estate, private equity, and hedge funds—for a total of 71% in equities and other long-term growth assets.[19]

Among DC plans, the Employee Benefits Research Institute (EBRI) and the Investment Company Institute indicate that in 2002, 62% of participant assets were invested in equities, including diversified equities, company stock, and the equity component of balanced options.[20] Greenwich Associates found similar results for DC plans in 2003. And among Vanguard plans, 69% of DC assets were invested in equities at the end of 2003.[21]

17 Vanguard (2004b).
18 Bodie and Clowes (2003).
19 Greenwich Associates (2003).
20 EBRI (2003) and Holden and VanDerhei (2003).
21 Vanguard (2003).

Several concerns typically surface during an investment committee's evaluation of a default fund. We comment on a number of them below.

"Give them time to make up their minds." One conventional argument for selecting a conservative default fund is to give participants time to "make up their minds." Thus sponsors invest participant accounts in a fixed-dollar fund under the expectation that at some point in the future, participants will make their own appropriate investment choices.

The drawback with this argument is based on the emerging body of research on inertia and procrastination among participants in retirement savings plans. In a wide range of plan decisions, research has shown that many plan participants are passive decision-makers.

In such circumstances, the default fund selected by the sponsor is the participant's decision. Many participants are unlikely to revisit the option chosen for them, and so sponsors need to ensure that they make an effective investment choice from the outset. From this perspective, it is hard to argue that participants will eventually make active choices—when the accumulating evidence suggests strongly that many will not.[22]

401(k) loans. In 401(k) plans that offer loans, another argument for a conservative default fund is that a participant may use the plan for short-term savings objectives by borrowing from the plan. With a shorter time horizon for use of the plan's assets, there is a much lower chance that equities will yield higher returns than fixed-dollar investments. In such cases, a conservative default fund makes sense.

By law, however, loans are limited to half of a participant's account balance, and they are not a widely used feature in the typical plan. In 2003, 19% of participants in Vanguard-administered plans had an outstanding loan, representing 13% of the participant's account balance. Among participants with balances of less than $10,000, 15% had a loan—but those individuals had borrowed 41% of their account balance.

---

22 See our report, *Lessons From Behavioral Finance and the Autopilot 401(k)* (Vanguard, 2004a), for a summary of the research on inertia and procrastination.

 12 The Vanguard Center for Retirement Research

Thus, even among low-balance participants, the overwhelming majority had not taken loans. So the use of loans is a much less important objective than the use of a DC plan for retirement purposes. In addition, sponsors concerned about loan use will note that, from an investment perspective, a loan is a fixed income investment. If default fund users make extensive use of loans in a given plan, this might suggest a higher equity exposure for the default fund, since the loan constitutes a fixed income asset in the participant's portfolio.

Job changers. Some sponsors, particularly in high-turnover environments, observe that many participants in the default fund may be short-term employees. As a result, the plan chooses a conservative default fund because the participant may not be with the company for long and may want to use the plan assets when changing jobs.

Trustees should note, however, that throughout the legislative history on retirement plans, Congress has sought to encourage the preservation of account balances in employer retirement plans. It has done so through the 10% income tax penalty for early withdrawals, the retention rules on plan balances, and more recently through the requirement of automatic rollovers. In sum, the law is designed to encourage rollovers—not cashing out by participants.

Committees concerned about job changers need to consider this public policy objective for their plan—which suggests a focus on long-term investment of plan assets, not a conservative default fund.

Sophistication and risk tolerance of default fund participants. Many participants invested in a default fund are likely to be less knowledgeable or less sophisticated investors. After all, they have failed to make an investment decision. They also may be more risk-averse because of their lack of investment experience or education. Therefore, some sponsors suggest that the default fund should be conservative to reflect the risk tolerance of the actual default fund users.

However, this perspective fails to account for the role of the plan sponsor as an ERISA fiduciary. Under the "prudent investor" standard, investment committees are expected to make informed and knowledgeable decisions about the investment of plan assets. Relying on the lack of sophistication of the participant seems contrary to this fiduciary requirement. Investing in an appropriate long-term default fund also gives the sponsor the opportunity to educate the inexperienced participant about basic investment principles.

247

Knowing the participant's financial situation.
In some instances, sponsors choose fixed-dollar investments because they feel they are unable to assess the full financial picture of participants in the default fund. From their retail investing experience, sponsors are often familiar with the "know the customer" rules, under which a broker-dealer or investment advisor must have detailed knowledge about a customer before making investment recommendations. However, in the case of selecting a default option for a DC plan, the relevant standard for sponsors to apply is the broad "prudent investor" rule of ERISA, not the retail "know the customer" rules.

Avoiding litigation. Some attorneys counsel their clients to choose a fixed-dollar investment fund in order to minimize the risk of participant lawsuits. According to this reasoning, a participant who experiences a decline in his or her account balance is more likely to sue. Even if the participant has no basis for the lawsuit, the employer will incur legal costs.

In evaluating this issue, committees need to consider another litigation risk—the risk that participants may sue because of a failure of a plan sponsor to invest assets appropriately for the long term. If assets are not prudently invested over long periods, participant balances may fall short of what is needed to achieve adequate retirement savings. So, while there is some chance of litigation risk over "lost dollars" today, it must be balanced against the litigation risk arising from "lost dollars" tomorrow. The case for focusing on the long-term is even more compelling in light of the sponsor's ERISA duty to act as a prudent investor would.

The DOL's automatic rollover regulations.
In its regulation on the automatic rollover of small plan balances to individual retirement accounts, the DOL identified a money market fund as a default investment choice. Taking a cue from these regulations, some sponsors have suggested that a suitable default fund for a DC plan participant must also be a money market fund.

However, in drafting its automatic rollover regulations, the DOL chose a money market fund because it expected most automatic rollovers to be small balances, with no ongoing contributions. It specifically distinguished its own reasoning from the investment choices that sponsors and participants would make with regard to the DC plan itself: "The Department does not believe that an investment strategy adopted by a participant while in a DC plan or chosen by a plan fiduciary at a particular point in time continues to be appropriate . . . for an automatic rollover . . ."[23]

Put another way, the DOL believed that automatic rollovers were distinct from the investment decisions made by participants and sponsors with respect to plan assets. For this reason, the automatic rollover regulations are not relevant to the choice of a default fund for a retirement savings plan.[24]

---

23 Proposed Labor Reg. 2550.404o-2. 69 Fed. Reg. 9900, 9902 (March 2, 2004). At http://www.dol.gov/ebsa/regs/fedreg/proposed/2004004551.pdf

24 The argument in favor of a money market fund in an automatic rollover is that most participants receiving small plan balances today cash out their funds. Given that the rollover assets are short-term, a money market fund, therefore, makes sense. However, there is a strong argument that because of inertia, the automatic rollover rules will lead more participants to retain their rollover accounts for the long term—suggesting that an appropriate default option for automatic rollovers should also be a balanced fund. Today participants with a small balance receive a check, which encourages cashing out. Under the automatic rollover rules, participants will not receive a check and so are less likely to liquidate the IRA. Meanwhile, those participants who change jobs or retire and have an immediate financial need are likely to request a check from the plan, before the automatic rollover rules go into effect.

 1-4 The Vanguard Center for Retirement Research

The active use of default funds would meet the needs of participants unable or unwilling to make investment decisions. Moreover, it would be an easy way for sponsors to encourage long-term investment decision-making.

To improve the selection of default funds by plan sponsors, policymakers should take steps to encourage use of long-term investment options as a default fund. DOL regulations could offer some type of safe-harbor fiduciary relief in this area, just as 404(c) regulations offer fiduciary relief in the case of participant-directed investments.

It is important not only that employers adopt a suitable default option—*but that employers feel encouraged under the law to promote the default option to participants.* For participants who are unsure of how to make investment choices, often the simplest and lowest-cost solution is a balanced investment fund. Yet the law does not encourage employers and providers to communicate this simple fact.

In an ideal world, communication materials would actively promote the default option as an appropriate investment choice—while still describing the other investments options available to more knowledgeable investors. Sample materials might read: "Unsure of what to do? Do nothing—and the plan will make a prudent, diversified investment choice for you."

The active use of default funds would meet the needs of participants unable or unwilling to make investment decisions. Moreover, it would be an easy way for sponsors to encourage long-term investment decision-making, without, for example, the higher costs associated with a managed account option.

Conclusion

Sponsors are revisiting a range of fiduciary duties in the current environment, including the question of the appropriate default fund for a DC plan. Today more than 80% of plan sponsors choose a conservative fixed-dollar option suitable for short-term savings goals, rather than a portfolio suitable for long-term retirement investment goals.

As ERISA fiduciaries, sponsors are responsible for ensuring the appropriate investment of all plan assets when a participant fails to make a specific investment election. Any such investment decisions must conform to the "prudent investor" standard. The choice of a fixed-dollar fund seems inconsistent with the two main investment principles underlying participant education programs: the existence of a positive equity-risk premium and the inverse relationship between age and risk-taking ability.

In selecting a default fund, sponsors should evaluate the objective of their retirement savings plans as well as the investment principles they believe should govern prudent investment decisions. For those plans whose principal objective is retirement savings and whose participant communications rely on the equity risk premium and the age-based ability to assume risk, one or more balanced fund options are an appropriate default choice.

For those plans whose principal objective is retirement savings and whose participant communications rely on the equity risk premium and the age-based ability to assume risk, **one or more balanced fund options** *are an appropriate default choice.*

 16 The Vanguard Center for Retirement Research

Our retirement wealth forecast is based on investment return, volatility, and inflation averages drawn from the 1960–2003 period (see table below). These assumptions provide a very conservative basis for comparing a cash investment with a balanced fund in two ways.

First, over this period, the equity risk premium is about 6%, with stocks returning about 12% and Treasury bills near 6% calculated on an arithmetic mean basis. This premium is substantially lower than the 7% to 8% typical of longer historical periods such as 1926–present. In this way, the retirement wealth forecast understates the potential benefits of the balanced fund option.

Second, real yields on fixed income investments during 1960–present are higher than over the typical 1926–present period. For example, the real yield on long-term investment-grade bonds is close to 400 basis points, while the real yield on cash is more than 160 basis points. Both of these assumptions are more reflective of the current bond market's ability to demand significant risk premiums over inflation rather than the long-term historical data.

By comparison, if based on the common 1926–present period, our projections would show an even more favorable outcome for balanced fund investing.

Returns, volatility, and inflation 1960–2003

	Arithmetic Mean Return	Geometric Mean Return	Standard Deviation (σ)
Inflation (CPI)	4.30%	4.33%	3.11%
Treasury bills (cash)	5.92%	5.96%	2.81%
Long-term corporate bonds	8.11%	7.59%	10.65%
U.S. equities	11.79%	10.74%	16.74%
Real cash yields	1.62%	1.63%	
Real long-term bond yields	3.81%	3.26%	
Equity risk premium	5.87%	4.78%	

Note: Arithmetic mean returns are the simple average of yearly returns; they are used in the Monte Carlo simulation of projected returns. Geometric mean returns represent compound or cumulative investment results.
Source: The Vanguard Group, 2004.

References

Bernstein, Peter L., *The Portable MBA in Investment*, Peter L. Bernstein, editor, John Wiley and Sons, New York, NY, 1995.

Bodie, Zvi and Michael J. Clowes, *Worry-Free Investing*, Pearson Education, Inc., Upper Saddle River, NJ, 2003.

Bodie, Zvi, Alex Kane, and Alan J. Marcus, *Investments: Fifth Edition*, McGraw-Hill Higher Education, New York, NY, 2002.

Bronson, James W., Matthew H. Scanlan, and Jan R. Squires, "Managing Individual Investor Portfolios," in *Managing Investment Portfolios: A Dynamic Process*, 3rd Edition, CFA Institute, Charlottesville, VA, Forthcoming.

Brennan, John J. and Marta McCave, *Straight Talk on Investing*, John Wiley and Sons, Hoboken, NJ, 2002.

Employee Benefits Research Institute, "2nd Quarter Pension Investment Report," www.ebri.org., Washington, D.C., 2003.

Evensky, Harold R., *Wealth Management: The Financial Advisor's Guide to Investing and Managing Your Client's Assets*, McGraw-Hill Publishing, 1997.

Feinberg, Phyllis, "Lifestyle Strategy Grows as DC Default Option," *Pensions & Investments*, 32(5). March 8, 2004, p. 3.

Greenwich Associates, "Greenwich Associates Investment Management Research Survey," Greenwich, CT, September–October 2003.

Holden, Sarah and Jack VanDerhei, "401(k) Plan Asset Allocation, Loan Activity, and Account Balances in 2002," *EBRI Issue Brief*, **www.ebri.org**, Washington, D.C., September 2003.

Hutchinson, James D. and Paul J. Ondrasik, Jr., "Fiduciary Responsibility Under the Employee Retirement Income Security Act of 1974," in *The Handbook of Employee Benefits*, Jerry S. Rosenbloom, editor, Dow Jones-Irwin, New York, NY, 1984.

Kritzman, Mark P., *The Portable Financial Analyst*, Irwin Professional Publishing. Chicago, IL, 1995.

Maginn, John L., Donald L. Tuttle, Dennis W. McLeavey, and Jerald E. Pinto, "The Portfolio Management Process and the Investment Policy Statement," in *Managing Investment Portfolios: A Dynamic Process,* 3rd Edition. CFA Institute, Charlottesville, VA. Forthcoming.

Tacchino, Kenn Beam and David A. Littel, *Planning for Retirement Needs,* 3rd edition, The American College, Bryn Mawr, PA, 1999.

Vanguard 2001, *Automatic Enrollment: Vanguard Client Experience,* Vanguard Center for Retirement Research, Malvern, PA, **www.vanguardretirementresearch.com**

Vanguard 2003, *Participant Report Card for December 2003,* Vanguard Center for Retirement Research, Malvern, PA, **www.vanguardretirementresearch.com**

Vanguard 2004a, *Lessons From Behavioral Finance and the Autopilot 401(k),* Vanguard Center for Retirement Research, Malvern, PA, **www.vanguardretirementresearch.com**

Vanguard 2004b, *Investing in Treasury Inflation-Protected Securities,* Vanguard Investment Counseling and Research, Malvern, PA, **www.vanguard.com**

Institutional Investor Group
Vanguard Center for Retirement Research
Post Office Box 2900
Valley Forge, PA 19482-2900

E-Mail
steve_utkus@vanguard.com

On the Web
www.vanguardretirementresearch.com

The Vanguard Group, Vanguard, and the
ship logo are trademarks of The Vanguard
Group, Inc. All other marks are the exclusive
property of their respective owners.

Argus Consulting Ltd NGO Retirement Plan Survey—2005 Results

Demographics

Nine nongovernment organizations (NGOs) participated in the survey this year, down from 16 in 2002. The respondents included a wide cross-section of NGOs with various missions.

U.S. Employees

- 33 percent of the respondent's organizations have fewer than 100 U.S. employees.
- 67 percent had 150 or more U.S. employees.

International Staff

- U.S. citizens
  - 67 percent of the respondents have fewer than 50 international staff that are U.S. citizens.
- Non-U.S. citizens
  - 44 percent of the respondent's organizations have fewer than 100 non-U.S. citizens.
  - 56 percent have 150 or more.

Most organizations operate throughout the world in very similar regions.

Size of Annual Budget

The respondent's annual budget ranges from under $50 million to over $200 million.

Annual Budget	Percentage of Plans
Under $50 Million	22%
$50–$150 Million	33%
Greater than $150 Million	45%

Retirement Plans

Vehicles

Survey participants offer a variety of retirement plans to their employees. The most common retirement vehicle for both U.S. and non-U.S. employees is a 403(b) plan. Over 75 percent offer a 403(b) for their U.S. employees working in the United States, and over 50 percent offer a 403(b) for U.S. employees working internationally.

Two NGOs sponsor defined benefit plans, with one of these being a cash balance plan. For non-U.S. international employees, 55 percent offer an offshore plan. Other vehicles used include 401(k) plans and local plans.

Contribution Levels

NGOs contribute various amounts to the retirement plans. The table below summarizes the responses:

% Employer Contribution	# NGOs
3	1
4	2
5	2
6 – 10	0
10 +	2

Actual employee salary deferral rates varied from 2 percent up to 10 percent, with an average of approximately 6 percent.

Other

Many NGOs (56 percent) have contemplated making a change to their retirement program, with one-third actually making changes. The most popular reason cited for changing plan design was to reduce volatility. Two-thirds of the respondents do not have or were unsure of the existence of an investment policy. Communication, security of pension funds, and administration services were cited as major concerns looking forward.

Lessons From Behavioral Finance and the Autopilot 401(k) Plan

Lessons From Behavioral Finance and the Autopilot 401(k) Plan

THE VANGUARD CENTER FOR RETIREMENT RESEARCH   Research ▸ April 2004

Executive Summary

Research from the field of behavioral finance suggests that many defined contribution plan participants are not active, self-motivated decision-makers, as is often assumed. A new plan design strategy, called the autopilot 401(k), addresses the needs of these reluctant savers.

Authors

Stephen P. Utkus
Jean A. Young

Varied planning skills. Industry and academic research underscores the point that individuals differ significantly in their planning abilities. Some are skilled at saving and investing for the future; others are not. Some have strong convictions about their financial decisions and enjoy retirement planning; others do not.

Framing effects and the default choices. Many participants are easily swayed by the way in which savings and investment questions are presented or framed for them. Automatic enrollment is a classic example of framing. By restating the enrollment decision as a negative choice, it boosts plan participation rates. Yet participants tend to stay at the automatic enrollment defaults, which are typically too conservative to generate adequate retirement savings.

Inertia and procrastination. Many employees strive to do the right thing in their retirement decision-making. But even when they understand the need to join their employer's retirement plan and increase their savings rates, they often have difficulty following through. Commitment devices can help counteract this inertia. One example is the SMarT plan, which provides for automatic annual increases in plan savings rates.

Automatic or autopilot 401(k) plans. An autopilot 401(k) plan is designed to respond to the behavioral biases of reluctant savers by altering plan-default decisions. Unlike a traditional 401(k) plan, which relies on active decision-making, an autopilot 401(k) makes all critical choices for participants: eligible employees are automatically enrolled, participant contribution rates are automatically increased each year, and participant accounts are automatically invested in suitably diversified portfolios. At any point, however, participants can "opt out" of these default options and make their own independent choices.

THE**Vanguard**GROUP.

This report is drawn from "Lessons From Behavioral Finance for Retirement Plan Design" by Olivia S. Mitchell, professor at the Wharton School of the University of Pennsylvania and executive director of the Wharton Pension Research Council, and Stephen P. Utkus, director of the Vanguard Center for Retirement Research. "Lessons From Behavioral Finance" is currently available on the Web (see "References") and is forthcoming from Oxford University Press.

Samuel Atlee, Suzanne Cionci, John Friel, Kelly Harrison, and Martha Witte assisted with this report's editing, design, and production.

Background

Defined contribution (DC) plans are now the dominant form of retirement benefit for the U.S. private sector workforce. More than 60 million employees participated in such plans in 2003. DC plans will figure prominently in the retirement prospects of the baby boom generation, with payments from DC plans exceeding those from Social Security. Despite concerns about the declining role of defined benefit (DB) plans, workers are likely to enjoy a secure retirement through a DC plan as long as two conditions are met: their employer offers a plan and they actively contribute to it.[1]

By a number of measures, DC plans continue to be successful retirement savings vehicles. Among Vanguard® plans, the average plan participation rate was 75% in 2002. The median participant savings rate was 6%, with more than two-thirds of assets invested in equities. Despite the concerns surrounding company stock risk in the post-Enron environment, only 1 of 5 participants had company stock concentration levels that exceeded 20% of their account balances.

DC plans, however, still face several important challenges.[2] Many employees choose not to join their plans, despite the presence of employer matching contributions. Savings rates for many participants also appear to be too low. This savings challenge will be exacerbated if Social Security benefits are lower for future generations and if future retirees have to bear higher out-of-pocket medical costs.

Sponsors, providers, and policymakers need to take steps to encourage greater plan participation and to boost savings rates, while ensuring that assets remain adequately diversified. To that end, sponsors have a number of available tools: offering matching contributions; expanding employee education; and introducing advice programs that give employees explicit directions.

In this report, we outline how a new approach to plan design, known as the automatic or autopilot 401(k), can be used to improve participant savings and investment decisions, thereby enhancing retirement security. The concept has been developed based on research findings from the field of behavioral finance, which blends economics and psychology in an effort to understand the nature of individual decision-making. This research suggests that it may be possible to improve savings and investment behavior by redesigning the nature of the default decisions within a 401(k) plan.

This paper outlines the main research findings of behavioral finance in three areas—varied planning skills, the impact of framing and the default choices, and inertia and procrastination. These phenomena describe why a plan design feature like automatic enrollment helps boost participation rates in 401(k) plans, yet leaves many participants worse off by keeping them at low savings rates and in conservative investment options. The autopilot 401(k) attempts to address the drawbacks of traditional automatic enrollment.

After describing the research basis for the autopilot 401(k) plan, the paper describes the key features of the autopilot design, as well as implications for plan sponsors, providers, and policymakers.

---

1 See Poterba et. al. (2001) and Holden and VanDerhei (2002).

2 We are not addressing the challenge of increasing plan coverage. Plan coverage has remained static over the past 25 years—at about 50% of the 16-and-older private sector workforce. This figure has remained unchanged regardless of whether DB or DC plans predominated. This suggests that the question of coverage is related to issues other than the type of retirement plan that is offered.

260

The fundamental lessons of behavioral finance are simple. Individuals strive to make informed and economically rational decisions in their financial lives. They strive to do what is best for themselves and their families. However, when they try to deal with complex decisions, certain biases or heuristics (decision shortcuts) interfere. For example, a heuristic such as "staying the course" can improve financial decision-making when the stock market is falling. Equally, a heuristic such as "buy a stock based on a coworker's tip" can lead to a very poor decision.

Varied planning skills. One of the main findings emerging from economics and psychology literature is that many individuals are not the active, self-motivated decision-makers they are sometimes perceived to be. Planning skills appear to be highly varied from individual to individual.

At Vanguard, we have studied this issue in terms of the attitudes plan participants express about retirement and investment planning skills (Figure 1). About half of individuals are Planners—individuals who are disciplined at saving, enjoy retirement planning, and are willing to take equity market risks. Planners conform with many of the notions of what plan participants ought to do—yet 10% still fail to join their employer's plan.

Figure 1.

Variations in Planning Skills

All Participants

Source: The Vanguard Group, 2002.

Doers are generally disciplined savers but are disinterested in retirement planning or investment management. Avoiders are either too focused on the present or find financial matters anxiety-producing. Despite their evident lack of interest, however, a great many Doers and Avoiders still participate in their employers' plans.

These nonplanners might be described broadly as reluctant savers and investors. Evidence of them can be found in other industry research—for example, the Employee Benefits Research Institute (EBRI) reports that less than 40% of U.S. workers have calculated how much they will need to retire, 30% have not saved anything for retirement, and only 20% feel very confident about having enough money to live comfortably in retirement.[3] Academic research supports these results, indicating that savings behavior varies according to a participant's effective time horizon and that planning skills are a critical component of wealth accumulation at retirement.[4]

---

3 EBRI (2003).

4 Munnell, Sundén, and Taylor (2000); Ameriks, Caplin, and Leahy (2002); and Lusardi (forthcoming).

Figure 2.

The Growth of $1

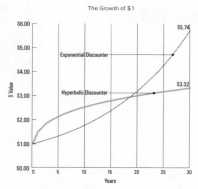

Source: The Vanguard Group, 2004.

However, psychological experiments show that some individuals may have a different perception of the time value of money. According to another calculation—known as hyperbolic discounting after its mathematical formula—a dollar invested today grows quickly in the short run, but then slower and slower over time (gray line, Figure 2). Individuals who perceive money in this way don't see as much benefit to long-term saving. In their view, the magic of compounding weakens over time.

Framing and default choices. Another bias in decision-making is a result of the fact that many individuals are easily influenced by the way a question is posed or framed. We assume that individuals are sophisticated thinkers and would not vary their responses to a question based on how it is asked. Yet in a variety of circumstances, many individuals do exactly that.

Economists and psychologists have attempted to explore these ideas in terms of how individuals perceive the fundamental time value of money. Planners are thought to save for the future because they have a strong perception of the value of future rewards. Reluctant savers, however, are thought to focus too much on the present and tend to discount the value of the future.[5]

This difference in perspective is apparent in an illustration comparing the time value of money. In the traditional calculation, a dollar invested today grows exponentially over time (red line, Figure 2). Individuals who think this way will focus on the long-term benefits of savings. Each year they wait to access their money, their savings grows faster, thanks to the principle of compounding.

Automatic enrollment is a classic example of the effects of framing in DC plans. Under automatic enrollment, employees are automatically enrolled in their plan unless they "opt out." In one study, implementing automatic enrollment boosted participation rates from 37% to 86% among new hires (Figure 3). The default decision had enormous power in shaping participant attitudes toward savings. Simply by restating the enrollment question from a positive to a negative election, it was possible to dramatically change savings behavior.[6]

5 Laibson (1997) and Laibson et al. (1998) use quasihyperbolic models of the time value of money to describe individuals who have a present-day rather than future focus.
6 The discussion in this section was drawn from Madrian and Shea (2000).

In the case of automatic enrollment, the default decision may be too powerful.

Figure 3.

Automatic Enrollment and
Participation Rates

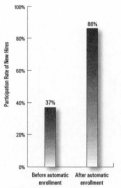

Source: Madrian and Shea, 2000, Table 5.

What this suggests is that many employees do not have particularly firm convictions about their desired savings behavior. Lacking firm beliefs about what to do, they rely on a simple heuristic and follow the default set by the plan. In a typical 401(k) plan that requires voluntary enrollment, the default decision is not saving—do nothing and no payroll contributions are made. In an automatic enrollment plan, the default decision is saving—do nothing and payroll deductions begin.

Figure 4.

Automatic Enrollment and
Deferral Rates

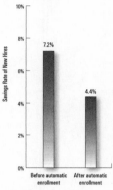

Source: Madrian and Shea, 2000, Table 6.

Unfortunately, in the case of automatic enrollment, the default decision may be too powerful. Not only do employees "decide" to stay in the plan under automatic enrollment, they also "decide" to stay at the low contribution rate and in the conservative investment choice typically selected by their employer.

In the same study, prior to the implementation of automatic enrollment, plan participants elected an average deferral rate of 7.2% (Figure 4). Yet after automatic enrollment, the average deferral rate fell to 4.4%. The reason for the decrease is that the default savings rate under automatic enrollment was 3%. As newly eligible employees entered the plan, most "chose" the 3% selected by their employer—including participants who otherwise might have voluntarily elected a higher deferral rate.

Similarly, in the same plan, the default investment option under automatic enrollment was a money market fund. Prior to the implementation of automatic enrollment, new participants directed 8% of their contributions to the money market fund (Figure 5). With the implementation of automatic enrollment, new enrollees were directing 81% of their contributions to the money market fund, evidently "choosing" the money market fund because of its role as the default option.

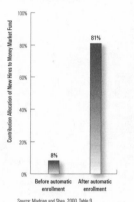

Figure 5.

Automatic Enrollment and
Use of the Default Fund

Source: Madrian and Shea, 2000, Table 9.

In the end, researchers concluded that automatic enrollment added to savings by encouraging more people to save in their plan. At the same time, it subtracted from savings by encouraging individuals to remain at too-conservative savings rates and in too-conservative investment defaults. Put another way, some people (those who would have never enrolled) saved more, while others (those who would have saved at a higher rate or invested in different options on their own) saved less. In the end, the two effects were a virtual wash, and automatic enrollment did little to enhance aggregate retirement savings.

Inertia and procrastination. One explanation for the automatic enrollment dilemma is another behavioral bias identified by researchers: inertia and procrastination. When faced with a complex or difficult decision, individuals often employ two simple heuristics—"keep things as they are" (inertia) or "put the decision off until tomorrow" (procrastination).

Inertia and procrastination are evident in surveys of plan participant behavior. In one survey, two-thirds of participants admitted that they were not saving enough for retirement. In fact, they knew they should be saving 14%, but were only saving 6%.[7] The issue wasn't awareness of the need for greater retirement savings, nor was the obvious solution more education. Instead, the problem was how to get individuals who were clearly aware of an issue to take specific action.

This example illustrates the essence of inertia and procrastination: Individuals express a desire to take a specific action, but they do not follow through. In another study, researchers asked eligible nonparticipants attending retirement

---

7 Choi et al. (2001).

Commitment devices are one way individuals attempt to deal with self-control problems.

Figure 6.
Inertia in Participant Decision-Making

Participants' Intended Versus Actual Behaviors

Action	Planned change	Actual change
Enroll in 401(k) plan	100%	14%
Increase contribution rate	28%	8%
Change fund selection	47%	15%
Change fund allocation	36%	10%

Source: Choi et al., 2001, Table 6.

plan meetings whether they planned to join the plan, and asked plan participants whether they intended to save more or change their investments. Very high percentages of individuals said they would take an action (Figure 6). But data from the recordkeeping system over the following six months revealed that a dramatically lower percentage actually took that action. As an example, 100% of nonparticipants said they would join the savings plan, yet only 14% subsequently did.[8]

As these cases illustrate, the problem isn't simply one of education. Even when individuals acknowledge or understand the need to make a behavioral change, inertia and procrastination frequently keep them from taking action.

Self-Control and Commitment Devices

Researchers sometimes describe the behavioral biases affecting savings decisions in straightforward psychological terms: Individuals lack the "willpower" to carry out their savings goals. A related term is "bounded self-control," wherein people try to save for the future but prove to be limited in their capacity or desire to execute their good intentions.[9]

Trying to save for retirement is not that different from other behavioral modification programs, such as exercising, dieting, quitting smoking, or keeping New Year's resolutions. Even when people comprehend and desire specific behavior modification, they frequently have difficulty accomplishing it.

Commitment devices are one way individuals attempt to deal with self-control problems. Individuals seek to protect themselves "from themselves" through the use of commitment devices that help foster desirable changes in behavior.[10] "Pay yourself first" is a standard commitment device used by financial planners to encourage saving; it also is the principle underlying payroll deductions in DC plans.

Save More Tomorrow. Another commitment device is the Save More Tomorrow (SMarT) program, designed by behavioral finance researchers Richard Thaler at the University of Chicago and Shlomo Benartzi at UCLA. With this program, participants sign up today to have their plan contribution rates increased automatically in the future. Once the initial commitment is made, regular increases to savings occur automatically.[11]

---

8 Choi et al. (2001).
9 Mullainathan and Thaler (2000).
10 Laibson (1997) and Laibson et al. (1998).
11 Thaler and Benartzi (forthcoming).

The SMarT plan employs inertia and procrastination to participants' benefit. Once the program is up and running, "doing nothing" means that the participant is saving more each year. The SMarT plan also makes the savings increases occur in the future. Participants find it easy to join because the plan has no immediate financial cost—the perceived pain of behavioral change, as it were, is deferred to the future.

In the initial test, the SMarT plan had a dramatic impact on savings rates over four years (Figure 7). A financial planner hired by the sample company counseled most individuals to save 5% more of their income on average. Some accepted this advice immediately. Others chose not to meet with the planner. The vast majority signed up instead for the SMarT plan with future savings increases of 3% per year.

At the time they signed up for the SMarT plan, this group was saving 3.5% on average. Four years later, after several pay increases, most of the participants who had signed up—the group that said it couldn't save 5% more—were saving 13.6%, a 10% increase. Reflecting the impact of inertia, those who increased their savings once, and those who did nothing, stayed at roughly the same level of savings over time.

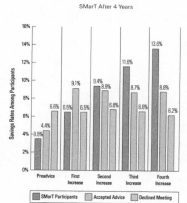

Figure 7.

SMarT After 4 Years

Source: Thaler and Benartzi (forthcoming).

The SMarT plan results illustrate yet again the power of the default option in individual decision-making. With the SMarT design, the default is to save more each year. In this case, inertia means allowing retirement savings rates to increase, rather than allowing deferral rates to remain at their current level. In this way, the SMarT plan has the potential to raise savings rates dramatically, even among those who claim that they cannot afford it.

Plan design drives participant decision-making, often in unanticipated ways.

Preferences: Hard-Wired or Situational?

In the end, behavioral finance research findings raise a provocative question: To what extent are our preferences and choices hard-wired or situational? Sponsors, providers, and policymakers often act as if participants have strongly held savings and investment beliefs, and that individuals know what they are doing and what they want. Thus, employers and providers design a neutral system for participant decision-making; participants implement their hard-wired savings and investment preferences within this neutral vessel known as the retirement plan.

 8 The Vanguard Center for Retirement Research

Another possibility is that many participants do *not* have strong convictions about their investments or savings. As a result, their decision-making is highly situational. They will change their minds depending on how a question is posed. When in doubt, they will follow the default set by the plan, the law, or the provider, rather than make an active choice. Instead of having strong convictions, they have relatively weak preferences that are easily subject to change.

Automatic enrollment illustrates this point. Change the nature of the enrollment question from a positive to a negative election, and many participants change their minds as well. The automatic savings or SMarT plan confirms this result. Participants say they cannot save 5% more after speaking with a financial planner, yet four years later they are saving 10% more because of a plan provision for automatic savings increases.

A similar lack of strong preferences applies to investment decisions. In one study, researchers gave participants a choice of three portfolios—their own and two alternatives. Each portfolio was illustrated using a well-known financial advice service. Yet given the choice between their own personally selected portfolio and two others, 8 of 10 participants chose another portfolio. Moreover, unbeknownst to them, the portfolio they chose was the portfolio held by the median participant in their plan! In other words, presented with a portfolio they had personally assembled and another representing the average investment choices of their coworkers, they preferred their coworkers' decisions to their own.[12]

These results reinforce the conclusion that many participants may not have strong convictions about the decisions they make. Yes, some participants do have strong savings and investment preferences. Yet for others, preferences are often situational and easily subject to reversal. This research challenges the notion that plan and legal frameworks are neutral vessels in which participants exercise independent decision-making skills. Rather, in a number of settings, it appears that the legal and plan frameworks are more powerful in shaping decisions than any preferences participants may have.

The Autopilot 401(k)

One implication from behavioral finance literature is that plan design drives participant decision-making, often in unanticipated ways. Plan sponsors, policymakers, and even providers have the ability to alter participant behavior by choosing different default structures. In many instances, the default is the decision.

A second implication is that the voluntary decision-making process in DC plans favors those with planning skills. Reluctant savers and investors appear to lack the requisite skills and interests. As a result, many of these individuals will make less optimal decisions compared with planners. Put simply, their chances for retirement security will be lower.

---

12 Benartzi and Thaler (2002).

Figure 8.

Autopilot 401(k)—Rethinking the Defaults

Decision	Typical Default	Autopilot Default
Participation	Join—if you like	You're enrolled
Investments	The default option is an investment contract or a money market fund	The default option is a balanced fund suited to your age
Retirement	Here's a lump sum	Here's help balancing the benefits of a lump sum with an annuity
Target Demographic	Active decision-makers or "Planners"	Reluctant savers or "Doers" and "Avoiders"

Source: The Vanguard Group, 2004.

One solution to this dilemma is to reconfigure the default decisions in a 401(k) plan around the needs of reluctant savers and investors (Figure 8). This is the key to a fully automatic or autopilot 401(k). With an autopilot design, individuals are automatically enrolled for payroll contributions, their contribution rates are automatically increased each year, and their contributions are automatically invested in a series of balanced funds appropriate to their ages.

All of these features help foster retirement security without requiring the active involvement of the individual. In this scenario, "doing nothing" and going with the default contributes to, rather than detracts from, retirement security.

Implications

The autopilot 401(k) has several implications for sponsors, providers, and policymakers.

Plan sponsors. The autopilot 401(k) is an ideal plan design strategy for employers with a large population of reluctant savers and investors. It is most suitable for employers who:

• Have low participation rates.

• Have failed nondiscrimination testing or are capping highly compensated employees because of the risk of failing.

• Feel they are on a "participation" treadmill, devoting most of their education resources simply to encouraging employees to enroll in the plan.

The autopilot 401(k) also is suitable for employers whose principal concern is long-term retirement security. For example, an employer that offers a 401(k) plan may be concerned that nonparticipants and low savers are not taking full advantage of their retirement benefits. In another example, an employer may be shifting from a DB to a 401(k)-only DC design, but is concerned that many employees will fail to participate or save at adequate rates. The autopilot 401(k) allows employers to make the shift to the more predictable funding requirements of a DC plan, while preserving elements of paternalism in their benefits design.

Employers and consultants will want to evaluate the autopilot 401(k) plan thoroughly. *Implementing an Autopilot 401(k)*, on pages 14 and 15, sets out additional detail.

Providers. Providers will have to support the various administrative aspects of the autopilot 401(k). These include automatic enrollment at the time of eligibility, automatic savings increases, and the mapping of participants to default investments by age. The automatic enrollment and savings features will require either provider or client programming, depending on which party handles these transactions in the outsourcing relationship.

For providers, the most profound impact of the autopilot 401(k) will be felt in the current model for participant education and communications. In today's approach, education is an instrument of behavioral change. Education resources are devoted to encourage participants to join a plan, increase their savings, and make optimal investment choices.

10 The Vanguard Center for Retirement Research

Research suggests that a more effective adult-learning model is to have individuals undertake the desired behavior first, before conducting extensive education.[13] In this approach, the idea is to have individuals "learn by doing" first, and then to use education to reinforce this positive behavioral change.

The autopilot 401(k) does exactly that. Plan design ensures that participants begin with "learning by doing"—saving in the plan, being invested in an appropriate default, and saving more over time. Education plays an important up-front role, notifying participants about what is happening and their rights to "opt out" or make different choices. On an ongoing basis, however, the role of education becomes less about behavioral change and more about reinforcing the desired behavior.

For example, a typical 401(k) enrollment kit today will spend considerable effort on promoting active decision-making by the employee. An autopilot enrollment kit will spend considerable time explaining why participants are already "on course" and why *they should simply do nothing*—or how they can do more. This represents a major change in the education paradigm.

Policymakers. Policymakers also play an important role in encouraging the autopilot 401(k). Just as plan sponsors help frame participant decisions, regulators help frame plan sponsor behavior. It is not entirely a coincidence that the Internal Revenue Service uses 3% as the typical employee contribution rate in its automatic enrollment regulations—and that the majority of employers adopting automatic enrollment also use a 3% contribution rate. One simple step would be for the IRS to expand its automatic

enrollment regulations to include examples using higher rates (e.g., 4% or 5%), as well as examples of automatic enrollment in an annual savings increase feature like the SMarT program.

Another step would be for policymakers to encourage the use of balanced investment portfolios as default investment options. Many employers mistakenly choose conservative fixed income funds as defaults because of confusion about their ERISA duties or concerns about litigation. Policymakers should move to counteract this trend. If employers offered balanced investment funds as default options—*and were encouraged to promote them to participants*—these options would serve as a low-cost alternative to the more expensive managed account solutions now being developed for participants.

Finally, legislators should consider developing a safe harbor for nondiscrimination testing based on the autopilot 401(k) plan. Both nondiscrimination testing and the autopilot 401(k) attempt to address the needs of the reluctant saver and investor. Whereas nondiscrimination testing acts indirectly—encouraging the employer to undertake education by penalizing the employer's highly compensated employees—an autopilot 401(k) works directly on the problem by enrolling nonsavers and increasing savings rates for low savers.

Besides eligibility and matching requirements, a safe harbor autopilot 401(k) would include minimum initial enrollment rates and specific annual savings increases. It also could include a requirement that those "opting out" of the savings plan be reenrolled after some period (e.g., every three years).

---

13 Selnow (2003).

Conclusion

Behavioral finance offers a range of insights into how individuals make financial decisions. Not all employees are the active, self-motivated decision-makers they are sometimes assumed to be. In fact, many fail to plan adequately for the future. They are unsure of their savings and investment decisions, and their preferences change based on how questions are framed and on their plan's default option. Too often, they allow inertia and procrastination to rule their financial lives.

The autopilot 401(k), an innovative plan design strategy, helps address the needs of these individuals. It can help employers address nondiscrimination testing issues, without the drawbacks of only implementing automatic enrollment. It also can help employers enhance retirement security among their workers, especially among non-participants and low savers. If widely adopted, the autopilot 401(k) has the potential to revolutionize employer-sponsored retirement plans in the United States.

References

Ameriks, John, Andrew Caplin, and John Leahy. 2002. "Wealth Accumulation and the Propensity to Plan." NBER Working Paper 8920. www.nber.org

Benartzi, Shlomo and Richard H. Thaler. 2002. "How Much Is Investor Autonomy Worth?" *Journal of Finance.* (57) 4. 1593–1616.

Choi, James, David Laibson, Brigitte Madrian, and Andrew Metrick. 2001. "Defined Contribution Pensions: Plan Rules, Participant Decisions, and the Path of Least Resistance." NBER Working Paper 8655. www.nber.org

Employee Benefit Research Institute (EBRI). 2003. *Retirement Confidence Survey: A Summary of Findings.* http://www.ebri.org/rcs/2003/03rcssof.pdf

Holden, Sarah and Jack VanDerhei. 2002. "Can 401(k) Accumulations Generate Significant Income for Future Retirees." *EBRI Issue Brief.* Employee Benefits Research Institute. Washington, D.C. No. 251, November 2002. http://www.ebri.org/pdfs/1102ib.pdf

Internal Revenue Service. 2000. "Revenue Ruling 2000-8: Cash or Deferred Arrangements." *IRS Bulletin 2000-7.* February 14, 2000. 617–620. http://www.irs.gov/businesses/lists/0,,id=98230,00.html

Laibson, David I. 1997. "Golden Eggs and Hyperbolic Discounting." *Quarterly Journal of Economics.* 112(2) May: 443–478.

Laibson, David I., Andrea Repetto, and Jeremy Tobacman. 1998. "Self-Control and Saving for Retirement." *Brookings Papers on Economic Activity* I: 91–196.

Lusardi, Annamaria. Forthcoming. "Financial Education and Saving." *Pension Design and Structure: New Lessons From Behavioral Finance*, Eds. Olivia S. Mitchell and Stephen P. Utkus. Oxford: Oxford University Press.

Madrian, Brigitte C. and Dennis F. Shea. 2000. "The Power of Suggestion: Inertia in 401(k) Participation and Savings Behavior." *Quarterly Journal of Economics*. 116(4):1149–1187.

Mitchell, Olivia S. and Stephen P. Utkus. Forthcoming. "Lessons From Behavioral Finance for Retirement Plan Design." In *Pension Design and Structure: New Lessons From Behavioral Finance*, Eds. Olivia S. Mitchell and Stephen P. Utkus. Oxford: Oxford University Press. Working paper available from the Vanguard Center for Retirement Research at **www.vanguardretirementresearch.com** or from the Wharton Pension Research Council as Working Paper 2003-6 at **http://prc.wharton.upenn.edu.**

Mullainathan, Sendhil and Richard H. Thaler. 2000. "Behavioral Economics." NBER Working Paper 7948. **www.nber.org**

Munnell, Alicia H., Annika Sundén, and Catherine Taylor. 2000. "What Determines 401(k) Participation and Contributions?" Boston College Center for Retirement Research Working Paper 2000-12. **http://www.bc.edu/centers/crr/papers/wp_2000-12.pdf**

Poterba, James M., Steven F. Venti, and David Wise. 2001. "The Transition to Personal Accounts and Increasing Retirement Wealth." NBER WP 8620. **www.nber.org**

Selnow, Gary W. 2003. "Motivating Retirement Planning: Problems and Solutions." Wharton Pension Research Council Working Paper 2003-7. **www.prc.wharton.upenn.edu**

Thaler, Richard H. and Shlomo Benartzi. Forthcoming. "Save More Tomorrow." *Journal of Political Economy*.

Vanguard 2002. *Using "Money Attitudes" to Enhance Retirement Communications*, Vanguard Center for Retirement Research at **www.vanguardretirementresearch.com.**

Vanguard. 2002. *How America Saves 2002— A Report on Vanguard Defined Contribution Plans*, Vanguard Center for Retirement Research at **www.vanguardretirementresearch.com.**

Implementing an Autopilot 401(k)

Evaluating four important aspects of the plan's design.

Costs. If the autopilot design is successful, and employees do not opt out of the program, it will mean that more participants will be taking advantage of the maximum employer matching contribution. Over time, this will raise the dollar amount the employer needs to budget for their plan contributions.

Legal framework. Employers will want to familiarize themselves with the legal framework governing the autopilot design.

The first two components of autopilot 401(k)—the automatic enrollment and automatic savings increase feature—are governed by IRS regulations on automatic enrollment, Revenue Ruling 2000-8.[14] These regulations require that employees have an "effective opportunity" not to join the plan. Specifically:

- Employees must receive prior notice of the negative enrollment feature, including procedures on how to opt out of the enrollment.

- Employees must be given a reasonable period of time to exercise their right to opt out.

When these automatic enrollment regulations were issued, the SMarT plan had not yet been invented. As a result, IRS guidance does not explicitly provide an example of a negative election for an annual increase in the deferral rate.

However, an annual change in the deferral rate is nothing more than a sequence of automatic enrollments—in this case, based on a participant's time in the plan. As such, it is governed by the same regulations as automatic enrollment. In addition, a logical extension of the regulations would be to provide not just a one-time notice about the program but an annual notice (e.g., in statements) of the annual increase program and opt-out procedures. In March 2004 the IRS issued a general information letter to this effect.

The default investment option in the autopilot 401(k) is governed by the Employee Retirement Income Security Act of 1974 (ERISA). Under ERISA, employers retain fiduciary duty for the investment of all plan assets not directed by the participants. The ERISA standard is the "prudent investor" standard. Trustees are expected to act as experienced individuals would when investing the plan's assets.

What would be an appropriate default under a "prudent investor" standard? Sponsors might rely on the investment principles touted in the participant education materials that they or their provider gives to participants. Most if not all such programs are based on two principles:

- Individuals investing for retirement should have some equity exposure given the higher long-term returns available from stocks.

- Younger individuals have a greater ability to recoup investment losses, and so have the ability to take more equity market risk than older participants.

---

14 Internal Revenue Service (2000).

  14 The Vanguard Center for Retirement Research

Autopilot 401(k) Design Considerations

Topic	Options	Observations
Covered population	All eligible employees or new hires only	Choosing newly eligibles minimizes the cost impact, but also means slower improvement in participation and savings rates. Choosing all eligibles can result in swift change, though it is costlier.
Eligibility	Implementation at current eligibility date or later	In a high-turnover environment, automatic enrollment combined with immediate eligibility will increase processing of small accounts. One option for "high turnover" populations is to maintain current eligibility for voluntary elections into the plan (e.g., immediate, one-month, etc.) with the automatic enrollment feature occurring later to control costs (e.g. after six months or a year).
Automatic enrollment initial deferral rate	4% desirable, 3% common	The take-home pay impact of the two choices at left is negligible; when in doubt, employers should opt for a higher starting rate. Also, the higher the average salary of the workforce, the higher the starting rate should be. For higher-paid workforces, 5% or more would be desirable.
Automatic savings annual deferral rate increase	2% desirable, 1% minimum	Given the negligible difference in take-home pay between these two options, employers should strive for the higher increase.
Timing of automatic savings rate increase	Single plan-wide date or date based on merit increase/anniversary	One date is simpler to administer and communicate, and many organizations have a single date when annual raises are effective. Alternatively, the annual savings rate increase could be specifically linked to the employee's merit increase schedule, though this increases administrative complexity. Some employers are reluctant to overtly link the timing of the annual savings increase to the timing of wage increases.
Automatic savings maximum cap for employee deferrals	Varies according to employer match and whether or not there is a DB plan	An employee earning $25,000 and saving only through a DC plan should have total employer and employee savings of 11–14% over a 30-year period.* Subtracting the employer contribution from this maximum will provide the cap for employee contributions.
Default investments	One or more fund options with some equity exposure	Options include: a single balanced fund; a more aggressive fund for younger individuals and a more conservative option for older individuals; or a series of lifecycle funds based on the employee's age that are rebalanced over time.
Required notices	Upon hire and annually	The autopilot 401(k) feature description, including information on how to "opt out," should be provided at plan eligibility and annually.

*See *How America Saves 2002* (page 76) for a broader discussion of savings adequacy.
Source: The Vanguard Group, 2004.

An appropriate default option, consistent with prudent investment principles, would be an investment option with some equity exposure. Choices include a single balanced fund; several balanced funds, with a more aggressive option for younger individuals and a less aggressive one for older individuals; or a series of balanced funds representing different risk/reward exposures based on the participant's age.

"Early to market." The autopilot 401(k) is a new concept and will be most attractive to those employers interested in experimenting with an innovative approach.

Specific design decisions. Finally, employers will want to consider the merits of different design elements and rollout strategies. These include whether to target new or existing eligible employees (or both) and how to design the annual savings and default investment options (see *Autopilot 401(k) Design Considerations*, above).

Institutional Investor Group
Vanguard Center for Retirement Research
Post Office Box 2900
Valley Forge, PA 19482-2900

E-Mail
steve_utkus@vanguard.com

On the Web
www.vanguardretirementresearch.com

The Vanguard Group, Vanguard, and the
ship logo are trademarks of The Vanguard
Group, Inc. All other marks are the exclusive
property of their respective owners.

For more information about Vanguard funds, visit www.vanguard.com, or call 800-523-1036, to obtain a prospectus.
Investment objectives, risks, charges, expenses, and other important information about a fund are contained in the prospectus;
read it carefully before investing.

INDEX